SOUL IN PRINT

IAN McCARTNEY

NEW HAVEN PUBLISHING

Published 2021
First Edition
New Haven Publishing
www.newhavenpublishingltd.com
newhavenpublishing@gmail.com

All Rights Reserved
The rights of Iain McCartney, as the author of this work, have been asserted in accordance with the Copyrights, Designs and Patents Act 1988.
No part of this book may be re-printed or reproduced or utilized in any form or by any electronic, mechanical or other means, now unknown or hereafter invented, including photocopying, and recording, or in any information storage or retrieval system, without the written permission of the Author and Publisher.

Cover design ©Pete Cunliffe

newhaven
publishing

Copyright © 2021 Iain McCartney
All rights reserved
ISBN: 978-1-912587-50-6

INDEX

THE SIXTIES

THE SEVENTIES

THE EIGHTIES

JOCK'S VIEW OF SOUL – EARLY 1980
THE SOUND OF SOUL - 1981
MIDNITE EXPRESS – APRIL 1981
OUT ON THE FLOOR – JUNE1981
A COLLECTORS GUIDE TO DETROIT
SOUL SIDE RENDEZVOUS – 1982
THE FACE – No.29 – SEPTEMBER 1982
NORTH OF WATFORD – DECEMBER 1982
THE DRIFTER – MARCH/APRIL 1983
PHILATELY – OCTOBER 1983
SOUL-SCOOT/SOULSIDE – LATE 1983
SHADES OF SOUL – JANUARY 1984
THE OTIS FILE/SWEET SOUL MUSIC – MAY 1984
SOUL SURVIVOR – 1984
SAILORS DELIGHT –1982(?)
GROOVE WEEKLY – 1980(?)
SOUL BLOWIN – 1982(?)
BOSS – MARCH 1986
VOICES FROM THE SHADOWS – SUMMER 1986
MOVIN' UPTOWN – SUMMER 1986
THE OWLS EFFORT – EARLY 1987
DETROIT CITY LIMITS – NOVEMBER 1987
GROOVIN A LA GO-GO – DECEMBER 1987
SOUL FILE – JULY 1988
SOULFUL KINDA MUSIC – MARCH 1989
BEATIN' RHYTHM – JULY 1989

THE NINETIES

MOTOWN INTERNATIONAL COLLECTORS CLUB – 1990
MOTORCITY BEAT - 1990
THE GOSPEL ACCORDING TO DAVE GODIN – 1990
COME AND GET THESE MEMORIES - 1990
MODERNITY – JULY 1991
BUZZ – 1991
NORTHERN NITELIFE – JUNE 1991
VINTAGE SOUL – SUMMER 1992
SOUL CD - 1992
SOUL & BLUES ON CD – 1992
SOUL UP NORTH - 1993
SOUL UNDERGROUND – SUMMER 1993
VIBE - 1993
TRACKS TO YOUR MIND – 1994
MANIFESTO – SEPTEMBER 1994
R SOUL – 1995
WHISPERS GETTIN' LOUDER – JANUARY 1995
LOVE MUSIC REVIEW – DECEMBER 1995
SOUL TIMES – DECEMBER 1995
IN THE BASEMENT - FEBRUARY 1996
LADIES OF SOUL – JULY 1996
SOUL GALORE – OCTOBER 1996
SOUL VIEW – DECEMBER 1996
SOUL RENAISSANCE - APRIL 1997

4

THE NEW MILLENNIUM

P.S. AND THERE'S MORE...

FOREWORD

BY SHARON DAVIS

As you may know, I'm no stranger to fan clubs or fanzines, and appreciate only too well that they resulted from the selfless dedication of enthusiastic diehards to a particular American artist or group and, more often than not, were a huge drain on personal finances. However, having said that, these clubs and amateur publications were extremely rewarding because they were responsible for spreading the printed word and, later on, musical note. So, if I may, here's a bitesize version of my minor involvement in this wonderful world of soul publications - produced by fans for fans.

Briefly then, when Dave Godin closed The Tamla Motown Appreciation Society, fan clubs opened up across the UK for Motown's individual acts, and I was honoured to steer one for The Four Tops from my family home in East Sussex. Prior to this, I'd dabbled in Dusty Springfield's London-based fan club by overseeing members in the South of England and this kinda stood me in good stead to take on The Four Tops. Motown in Detroit spasmodically posted photos and information to me which I could then sell to club members to help boost the 5/- annual membership fee. The stencil duplicated newsletters I cobbled together were, by today's standards, archaic on so many levels, and my attempts to liven up the text with hand drawn pictures were amateurish to say the least. To reduce my printing costs, I used my employer's cumbersome printing machine after hours when everyone had left for the day. How I got away with it for so long I'll never know: the very cheek of me! But somehow, I did.

When Motown decided it wanted one fan club to represent all their artists in the UK, Motown Ad Astra was born during 1969. Part of that new operation was the fanzine *TCB – Takin' Care Of Business*, which, as it turned out, outlived the actual fan club. Once again, these pages of wisdom - and childlike drawings of course - were printed on a temperamental Roneo machine which regularly managed to shoot out blank pages as the large drum spun round leaking ink as it did so. I'm told the fanzine is now considered by some to be an in-demand item. Who would have thought! Anyway, due to lack of finances – meaning my wages didn't support me let alone cover printing and postage costs – *TCB* folded. Happily though, that wasn't the end of my Motown journey as I joined *Blues & Soul* – John Abbey's ground breaking publication - to pen a Motown page from the early seventies; a position I thoroughly enjoyed for nearly two decades. Oh lor, I'm afraid this bitesize version grew legs as I wrote it.

Anyway, returning to the matter in hand. I think it is true to say the history of soul music in the UK was one of struggle, disappointment and prejudice. Yet there was always hope for a brighter future. Music emanating from America, generally referred to as R&B, attracted a devoted and loyal cult following here until the time arrived, several years on, when R&B evolved into a type of commercial soul for mainstream record buyers.

It's this early history of R&B and Motown music that needs to be protected for future generations and, of course, to remind us what wonderful formative years they were. Alongside the music, fans relied on specialist publications and the remarkable number of fanzines that were produced. And it is these historical printed footprints that need to be protected as they form a vital and irreplaceable reference to the early days of soul/R&B and gave column inches to American artists who otherwise may never have seen their name in print in a British publication.

So, thank you Iain McCartney for taking on the challenge to protect our heritage. I know it's been a mammoth task – much bigger than you first anticipated – but I reckon you've cracked it.

Sharon Davis
January 2021

INTRODUCTION

Soul music remains the biggest 'underground' music scene in the world, with each weekend (pre-Covid19) seeing countless soul nights and weekenders fill the diaries. Records, on often obscure labels, change hands regularly for four figure sums, while many artists come to Britain, countless years after they first stepped into a recording studio, to sing tracks that they had to re-learn the words to as it had been so long since they last sang them to an appreciative audience.

The dictionary definition of a 'fan' is "devoted admirer; an enthusiast", but many take that devotion and enthusiasm that one step further. Not content to collect the records and memorabilia of the music they love, attending soul nights, all-nighters and weekenders the length and breadth of the country, they seek out details of an artist's career, compile discographies of the labels on which they recorded and then take the time to put their admiration for every genre of soul music into a printed format, be it a basically produced fanzine, laboriously typed and stapled together, or if finances allow a glossy, full colour, more professionally produced magazine, or a book.

Over the years there have been countless publications devoted to 'Soul Music' and in the following pages all those publications, excluding books, are pulled together - or perhaps that should read: as many as could be found - to produce both an insight into the world of soul music in print, and what could also possibly be classed as a collectors' guide to fanzines and magazines from what is undoubtedly the longest lasting music genre in the world of popular music.

Some of those publications failed to last beyond one issue, others slightly longer. Stretching from the early/mid-sixties to the present day many of those publications are as eagerly sought after by collectors as the records, with numerous titles also considered 'rare'. But although they do not command the same monetary value as the records amongst collectors, many will fetch considerably more than the music publications found on magazine shelves today.

This is certainly not a discography style book, as it would be simply impractical to list the contents of every individual publication, and had I done so it would have stretched into several volumes, with the likes of *Blues & Soul*, *Echoes*, *Manifesto*, *Soulful Kinda Music* and *Soul Up North* requiring one volume each.

What I have done is look at each publication individually, giving the basic details, sometimes an interview with an editor, and a mention of particular issues that contain an article or whatever of interest to the soul scene in general; all done in an effort to keep the book as interesting and appealing as possible. A book that can be perused at leisure – a coffee table volume.

Over the years those fanzines, magazines, call them what you wish, changed as printing changed, never mind the music, with some managing to last beyond that one solitary issue due to the grit and determination of the editors; and with the odd exception they are all worthy of a place within the history of soul music.

Putting this book together will most probably take longer than it should, as new acquisitions are picked up and what should be a simple look through the pages of previously bought titles becomes a complete re-read. It is also something that I never imagined I would do, as my personal collection of soul reading material failed to stretch beyond a few dozen issues of *Blues & Soul* from the late sixties and early seventies, as the music took second place to following a certain football team around the country. Then a chance meeting with someone I knew only really to say hello to opened up a bright new world and an introduction to the likes of *In The Basement* and *Manifesto*. Before long eBay was scoured for more, and there were bargains to be had, and slowly the pile began to increase and what I had missed in those bygone years began to appear and rekindle the love affair.

A list was made of the titles I knew about and had found, but it was soon an ever-increasing one, with previously unknown publications coming to light. I am also certain that there are many still hidden away that I have yet to discover. I must also add that countless books on the music were also added to the overflowing shelves, creating a considerable library of soul music material.

Hopefully when you turn the pages of this book it will bring back memories of those bygone days when you perhaps bought copies of certain publications at the various venues you attended, or via subscription. It might also make you scour the bottom of cupboards, or visit your lofts, to find those publications of old (if you do find any, I'm always interested), allowing you to put the kettle on and enjoy a nostalgic journey back in time.

THE SIXTIES

For those who had latched onto the rhythm and blues music scene in the late fifties and early sixties, following the gradual decline of rock and roll as Little Richard turned to preaching, the death of Buddy Holly, alongside Ritchie Valens and Big Bopper in a plane crash, Jerry Lee Lewis marrying his thirteen-year-old cousin and Elvis Presley having been drafted into the army, they were caught in something of a void. Or to be more precise, stranded on an island with a huge un-opened vault of tunes, but with little in the way of information as to what gems lay inside. Reading material on rhythm and blues was few and far between.

Jazz lovers had been well catered for since the mid-forties when Sinclair Traill had launched *Pick-Up*, transforming it into *Jazz Journal* a couple of years later, with the magazine continuing in print until December 2019 when the decision was made to move it in its entirety online. *Jazz News*, *Jazz Monthly* and *Jazz Beat* were another three publications that would whet the appetite of those connoisseurs of the time. But jazz was of little or no interest to those who had latched upon the phenomenon that was rhythm and blues, although if you perused the last of that trio

of above publications you could come across the likes of an 'R&B Extra' feature in 1963, with record reviews by Guy Stevens, where you could find anything from Slim Harpo, Rufus Thomas and Jimmy Reed sitting alongside The Olympics and a 'Various

Artists' Motown compilation. Of the latter, Stevens rates it as "*nothing short of superb*" and "*exceptional value for money*", although he is quick to point out that "*the Tamla sound has so far failed to catch on in this country, which to me is inexplicable, especially with the current interest in R&B type music*". Stevens could also be found penning profiles of artists who could crossover from jazz/blues into what would eventually become soul.

The landscape continued to change in 1963 with the introduction of not one, but two publications with 'Blues' in their title. One was *Blues Unlimited*, founded by Simon Napier and Mike Leadbitter as "The Journal of the Blues Appreciation Society'; according to its own Wikipedia page it was "*a typed mimeographed pamphlet which rapidly grew into an A4 size magazine which continued for 149 issues.*" It was only the sudden death of co-editor Mike Leadbitter that saw the long-running publication finally grind to a halt.

This publication, however, drifted more towards the original 'blues' of the American deep south, and like the afore-mentioned jazz publications only held a minimal interest for those who preferred a bit of rhythm with their blues.

The second of those two 1963 publications was certainly more to the liking of the nation's R&B lovers and it was to become the launching-pad for publications devoted to the music that in due course would become known as 'northern soul'. This was the finely named **RHYTHM AND BLUES GAZETTE.**

Chuck Berry had the honour of appearing on the cover of the first issue of this new and groundbreaking publication, which sprung to life following a letter to the editor of *Record Mirror*. It read: "*the time has come to launch a magazine devoted entirely to this type of music, strangely neglected by many branches of the music industry in Britain.*"

Issue No.1, a 16.5 x 23cm publication, consisted of a dozen pages, printed on quality paper, but at times the font size could be considered on the small side.

An article on The Coasters, another on cover star Chuck Berry and one attempting to preach to the unconverted as to 'What Is Rhythm and Blues?' If they didn't already know about the music then why were they reading this publication in the first place?

Reader letters, British and American record reviews, a mention of the 'Rhythm and Blues Record Club' (running from the same address in Petersfield, Hants as the magazine) and a 'Rhythm and Blues Top 30' reprinted from *Billboard* take up the remainder of the publication. The latter, when glanced over today, and perhaps even back then, would leave the reader somewhat bemused with the likes of 'Can't Get Over Losing You' by Andy Williams at No.7 and the truly mind boggling 'Puff the Magic Dragon' by Peter, Paul and Mary at No.14.

Amongst the contributors could be found respected names such as Mick Vernon and Pete Wingfield, names we will find to be involved in other publications as we travel through the sometimes weird but always wonderful world of soul music publications.

R&B Gazette was to span some five issues, with the last appearing in January 1964.

If you digested everything you could find on this side of the Atlantic and it failed to satisfy your appetite then you could always have cast an eye Stateside, where **RHYTHM & BLUES** might have grabbed your attention.

With a sub-title of 'Covering the Blues and Jazz Scene' and published in Derby, Connecticut, it first appeared in 1960, although the first issue I have seen came from April 1964 and is far removed from anything blues, jazz or R&B related you would have found in the UK.

Although it contains some three dozen pages, the only readable content, of this issue anyway, covers articles on Sonny Stitt, Dee Dee Sharp, The Isley Brothers, Sleepy John Estes and an interesting piece entitled 'Cash In Your Blues – Part Two', which deals with selling records. What would probably be regular features – 'Dig Me - A Look at the Jazz Scene', 'Rhythm and Blues Roundup' and 'R&B Record Review' make up the bulk of the reading. The latter mentions live albums such as the *James Brown Show*, *The Miracles On Stage* and *Marvin Gaye On Stage*. The James Brown offering was considered the *"most exciting of the lot"*, Marvin *"handled himself well"*, while *"Smokey Robinson's lead voice is uninspired"*.

If you fancied a sing-a-long then you would find the lyrics to forty-one tunes of the day, which included the likes of 'What's Easy For Two Is Hard For One', 'You're No Good', 'When The Lovelight Starts Shining Thru 'His Eyes', 'You Lost The Sweetest Boy' and 'You Gotta Dance To Keep From Crying'.

This magazine, however, is advert strewn with everything from wigs to corsets, 'Be a Pop Singer' to 'Poems Wanted' and 'Make Money Meeting Beautiful Girls'. Sadly, the address and phone number for the last mentioned is now non-existent!

Mick Vernon had cut his teeth with the previous publication, *Rhythm & Blues Gazette*, but branched out on his own with **R&B MONTHLY** in 1965 stating: *"The aim of this magazine is to bring to the many Rhythm and Blues enthusiasts in the country, the true picture – to the best of our ability – of both the American and the British Blues scene"*. It was also cheaper, priced at one shilling, compared with the two shillings and six pence cover price of *Rhythm & Blues Gazette*. The page count was the same, so it was certainly value for money, whilst also being slightly larger in size, measuring 20.5 x 25.5cm.

Assisted by Neil Slaven, Mike put together a good mix of artist biographies, discographies and record reviews, issuing the magazine/fanzine, call it what you like, on a monthly basis, while the 'adverts' section offered everything from records to addresses for artist fan clubs and details of how to obtain the likes of *Blues Unlimited* or a forty-page booklet on Lightnin' Hopkins. Perhaps the big plus for the dedicated readers was the listing of recent American R&B releases, giving record number and both the A and B side. It was large in format, but space certainly wasn't wasted.

As well as Mick and Neil, other contributors soon found their way on board, people like Kurt Mohr and Roy Simonds, while issue number twenty-one carried 'An Appreciation of Eric Clapton' by John Mayall.

Originally side stapled, it stepped up a notch when it moved from the teens to the twenties as it was then printed on glossy paper with centre staples, whilst also increasing in size to sixteen pages, but with the January/February 1966 issue (No.24) stretching to a highly creditable twenty-six.

JIMMY McCRACKLIN

Unfortunately, that twenty-fourth issue was to be the last, with Mick writing in his Editorial, under the heading of 'So Long Baby, Goodbye': *"We are indeed very sorry to see the end of the magazine, but pressure of outside work has made it nigh impossible to keep things ticking over properly. Letters are piling up and there is no time to answer them. The two booklets which should have been ready by now are I'm afraid, far from being completed. Work will be continued on these two projects during the next few weeks and the booklets will be despatched just as soon as they are ready."*

Mick continued: *"We have had talks with the management of 'Jazz Beat', the journal of the National Jazz Federation. And we hope, that as from March, two or three pages of this journal will be taken up by news, articles, reviews etc. from the pens of Neil Slaven and ours truly. Both Neil and I will continue to write for other magazines, i.e. 'Blues Unlimited, 'Blues World', 'Soul' etc. In this way, we hope to keep in the field of Blues journalism."*

Gone, but not forgotten, *R&B Monthly* had certainly set the benchmark in the field of such publications.

Roger Eagle was a DJ at the Twisted Wheel in Manchester's Brazennose Street, a venue that was primarily a coffee bar-cum-night club, owned by the Adabi brothers Jack, Philip and Ivor. Eagle was enthusiastic, to say the least, as regards R&B, but would supplement his sets with any form of 'black music' that he could lay his hands on.

His enthusiasm knew no bounds and, in the summer of 1964, he managed to persuade the Adabis to fund a magazine he had put together entitled **R'NB SCENE**, later to be re-titled **R&B SCENE**, proclaiming itself 'Britain's Leading Rhythm & Blues Magazine'; and it was no idle boast.

VOL. 1. No. 6.   APRIL 1965

1/6

BRITAIN'S LEADING
Rhythm & Blues
MAGAZINE

CHUCK BERRY
JAMES BROWN
LAZY LESTER
HOMESICK JAMES
WILLIE MABON
SCREAMIN' JAY HAWKINS

— PLUS —
Record Reviews
Rhythm & Blues Quiz
Readers Letters
The Horror Scene
Say Man

SCREAMIN' JAY HAWKINS meets Brian Smith. The reason why we put a photo of our photographer on the cover may never be fully explained, but we do know the reason for the tremendous success of Jay's tour. SEE INSIDE

In the book *Sit Down! Listen To This – The Roger Eagle Story*, written by Bill Sykes, two of Roger's friends, Brian Smith and Neil Carter, who were also contributors to the magazine, had this to say.

Neil: "I *worked on the R&B Scene magazine. I was sort of the assistant editor if you like, so I helped Roger put it together. I helped with interviewing people, writing articles and such like.*"

Brian: "H*e talked the Adabi's into doing R&B Scene and they published the first one, but he [Roger] was just taking it round in Neil Carter's car boot, selling them a dozen at a time to record shops – that*

was it. It lost several hundred pounds on that one issue, and this is in 1964. The Adabi's panicked and he bought it off them, or rather his mum did. I think he took it on to about seven issues, and then his mum paid off the £1,000 accumulated debts, mostly print bills. I've still got the copper printing blocks for the photos [Brian was also the photographer at the Wheel.] *I think his poor old mum bailed him out on more than one occasion. She did with the magazine more than once.*"

It is difficult to imagine how such a publication would not have made money given the popularity of the Twisted Wheel, even in those early pre-Whitworth Street days, as a friend who went said it was always busy, and also due to the emerging interest at the time of R&B; but perhaps it was simply before its time. Certainly today, in regards to the magazine, copies can change hands for more than most of its stablemates and I imagine that the unsold copies that reputedly held up the bed of Roger Eagle in his Wilbraham Road home would, in today's market, go close to achieving a figure that would have paid off his debts back in the day. An advert in the magazine back then proclaimed 10/6d for six issues. How much would those half dozen copies sell for today?

R&B Scene was certainly a step up from the early editions of *R&B Monthly* and *Rhythm and Blues Gazette* and was the first to come out of the northwest, as the previous publications had all been 'southern' produced.

The Twisted Wheel
presents
LATE NIGHT RHYTHM & BLUES
Every Saturday from 12 midnight

Brazennose Street, Manchester
(off Albert Square)
FORTHCOMING ATTRACTIONS

6th June .... The Cheynes
13th June .... John Lee Hooker with John Mayall Blues Breakers
20th June .... Jimmy Powell and the Five Dimensions
27th June .... The Graham Bond Organisation
ADVANCE TICKETS NOW AVAILABLE

ADVERTISEMENT

The Twisted Wheel
presents
RHYTHM & BLUES

FOR DETAILS OF FORTHCOMING ATTRACTIONS SEE THE DANCING COLUMN IN THE MANCHESTER EVENING NEWS

OPEN NIGHTLY
7.30 p.m. to 11 p.m.
SATURDAY
7 p.m. to 11 p.m.
and
12 midnight to 6.30 a.m.

Brazennose Street, Manchester
(off Albert Square)

WE PROUDLY PRESENT
DANCING IN BLACKPOOL'S
MOST UNIQUE ATMOSPHERE
AT THE
TWISTED WHEEL
Coronation Street, Blackpool

11

Professionally printed on glossy paper throughout, it saw Mike Leadbitter named as 'contributing editor', with Brian Smith's photography giving it that cutting edge, and as *Northern Noise* would be for the Wigan Casino in the distant future, it was unashamedly the advertising arm of the Twisted Wheel, with full page adverts for the club adorning the back page, announcing its forthcoming attractions.

The initial issue carried features on the likes of Sonny Boy Williamson, Bobby Bland and James Brown, along with a piece on the 'Northern Club Scene', but alongside those American artists in this and future issues, you could also find articles on British artists, such as Georgie Fame in issue one and Spencer Davis in issue two; which wasn't too unexpected, as a look through the early years 'gigography' of the Twisted Wheel is like a who's who of British R&B acts, including everyone from the two previously named artists to the likes of Graham Bond, John Mayall, Long John Baldry and Zoot Money.

Volume 1 No.5 actually carries a 'Rhythm & Blues In Britain' feature, with one of those included being Rod Stuart [sic].

But it wasn't all music, as amongst those articles, discographies, letters and record reviews they also for some unknown reason included an article on horror films, about as far removed from rhythm and blues as you could possibly get.

There was, however, one particular oddity in the fact that on occasion, as in issue number six, an article would start on one page and then be continued several pages further on. For example, an article entitled 'The British Scene' began on page four, but was continued on eleven. 'Chuck Berry in Person' began on five, but was continued on nine. 'Willie Mabon, Homesick James' started on seven, but finished on eighteen! Why, I do not know.

Had this magazine been properly run, perhaps more as a business venture, and by people who were more experienced in such a field, then there is no telling how long it might have lasted, but with the ongoing financial problems and the Wheel's eventual move from Brazennose Street to Whitworth Street, it disappeared from view. But like the club itself, it left a lasting legacy.

In my original draft for this book *Soul Beat* had been slipped in amongst the late sixties publications, as only one solitary issue had come my way at the time of writing and in the top right-hand corner it has the legend 'Vol.2 No.1'. However, as luck would have it, a huge gap plus a few more lines in the book were filled as I was able to obtain earlier copies of this particular publication.

There was to be little in the way of success, fame and fortune to be gained from producing a soul music fanzine, certainly way back in the early sixties, but such matters would have been far from the teenage mind of Pete Wingfield when he started SOUL BEAT in 1964. Later years would see the Liphook born journalist become a highly respected musician, producer and songwriter, who was also to gain chart success with the record 'Eighteen With A Bullet'.

But it was Wingfield's interest in R&B that was to see him put pen to paper and produce one of the earliest fanzines in its roughest forms, as he felt that the continuing upsurge within the British Isles for this type of music warranted a publication given over to that genre of music.

"May I point out that the journal is not aimed at out and specialist addicts. It will on no account contain full discographies, recording dates etc, of underrated blues greats – these are of only limited interest to the hard core of fanatics" began Pete in his initial editorial, continuing: *"Of course, it is inevitable that this issue is not exactly a masterpiece of literature, but you will, I am sure, appreciate the enormous difficulties to be faced when producing something of this kind. However, I trust that you will find it a little to your liking and interest in the following pages."*

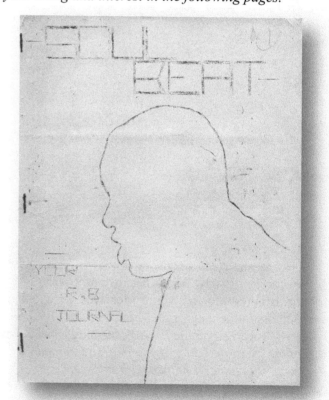

Wingfield was at Wellington College at the time and would produce copies of *Soul Beat* on the school Roneo duplicator. He was later to admit that sales were minimal, but that he had only started the fanzine in order to get free records.

The publication was as raw as some of the music the editor, and I imagine the readership, enjoyed, but it served a purpose, stoking the UK R&B fire and keeping that flame burning, whilst filling something of a void in reading matter concerning this particular form of music.

'The Sound of Booker T and the MG's'; 'The U.S. Disc Scene'; 'News and Comment'; 'Slayer Slabs'; 'The Isley Brothers – Most Frantic Group On Record' and 'Disc Reviews' filled the dozen pages, plus a form, in the middle of the back page for some reason, to send off, together with one shilling, if you wanted a copy of the next issue. It was bad enough having to contend with rusty staples fifty-six years on, never mind a page with a hole in the middle! There is also a handwritten note at the foot of the last page saying – *"apologies for the low technical standard – rest assured it will be much higher in the future."*

Issue two did appear – twelve pages again, but with the inner and outer covers blank, and it could be considered something of an improvement on issue one, although a couple of pages are given over to 'Slayer Slabs', which was in effect readers' favourite tracks. Interesting to note that out of the seven who listed their 'top ten' only one listed what could be classed as 'soul' rather than 'R&B', listing the likes of The Impressions 'It's Alright' (at number one), The Marvelettes 'Please Mr Postman' and Maurice Williams and the Zodiacs' 'Stay'. Pete Wingfield produced four issues of *Soul Beat*, all undated, although issue four does mention that it is the first

issue of 1965. It was also to be the last under Pete's editorship as he said: *"Number five will I hope be superb, as I won't be the editor.... In order to concentrate on important exams in the summer, I have decided to place the esteemed task for a while in the very capable hands of Lenny Gill, a rare species of walking musical encyclopaedia; you can therefore look forward to a brief period of something approaching sanity."* Initially I had wondered if perhaps Wingfield had stopped due to having been caught churning out his fanzine on the school copier! What happened to Lenny Gill, who had been a contributor to *Soul Beat*, is unknown, or it certainly is to me, as issue number five never appeared; but *Soul Beat* did resurface, although more confusion reigned as when it did re-appear it was under the editorship of Mick Brown, with his first issue numbered Volume 1 Number 1.

Before we begin a look at what *Soul Beat* had to offer under the new editor I am going to diversify somewhat. I know the book hasn't moved too far forward in regards to publications or editors, but bear with me.

As I plodded through the publications at hand, and as you will find out in the pages that follow, I managed to trace a number of those who burnt the midnight oil as they fought sleep, financial destruction and whatever else to put those often-treasured publications together. Anyway, one of the last that I spoke to was, for no particular reason, Mick Brown. Prior to our conversation, I only knew that he had been involved with *Soul Beat* and as a contributor to *Soul Music*.

What I didn't know was that of all the esteemed editors who are scattered throughout this book Mick is the one who went on to bigger and better things during his career as a journalist. But first, his involvement with *Soul Beat*.

"*Yes, and it all began as a teenager, around the age of fifteen,*" said Mick. "*Journalism was always what I wanted to do, so I suppose editing 'Soul Beat' was a good launching pad.*"

So how did taking over the reins of *Soul Beat* from Pete come about, I wondered? "*It was just a case of Pete saying that he was going to give it up and he was looking for someone to take it on and I was asked if I fancied doing it*" came the reply. "*A typewriter was secured and my parents provided the other resources and off it went. I would write to the American record labels such as Duke and Peacock and I found that they basically had no idea as to the popularity of their records and R&B music in Britain. They would then send over boxes of records and press releases, which was great.*" A bit like Christmas every day? "*Yes, yes I suppose it was.*" It must have been quite exciting as a teenager to be involved in something that was, in reality, more than simply running an R&B fanzine? "*It was I suppose, as with R&B, it was something like being involved in a secret society. With getting press releases etc, you were always just that one step in front of everyone else. At times I couldn't believe what I was involved in.*"

What about print runs and distribution? "*Probably fifty issues, or something like that. There was a record shop in West Croydon – 'Diamond Records' that would have them on the counter. I actually worked there as a Saturday boy, circa 1966/67. In any event, on Saturdays the shop would be filled with mods, checking out the Tamla/Atlantic/Sue records that had been played by Jeff Dexter at the Orchid Ballroom in Purley, and whoever was manning the decks at the Top Rank Suite in Croydon. The place was like a party on Saturday afternoons.*

"*There was another shop in Central London, Lisle Street in Chinatown, Soho called 'Transat Imports', under a Chinese Restaurant that had them. This place had boxes upon boxes of records. It was a great feeling knowing that people were actually buying the magazine.*" So, for those who have never seen a copy, what was *Soul Beat* actually like as a publication? "*Well, here it is. The first edition of the new Soul Beat. The idea of this magazine is simply to continue where Pete Wingfield's original Soul Beat left off, doing a very small part in promoting Soul Music in this country.*

"*You will find all the usual Soul Beat features in the magazine plus some new articles of which I hope you approve*" were the opening few lines of Mick's editorial and this issue of *Soul Beat* measured 18 x 24cm and consisted of twenty pages, including the covers; but for some peculiar reason, the numbering doesn't begin until page four, even although there is content on what would have been page three. The inside front, and two back pages, are blank!

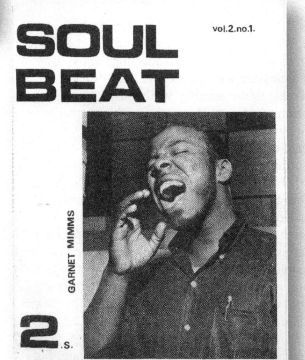

The publication is undated, but the listed Top Twenty Records in the US come from October 30th to November 27th, so let's assume that it made an appearance in late 1965. This is perhaps substantiated, as issue two mentions that it was delayed due to the Christmas rush.

It was, as Mick mentioned, more or less a continuation from where Pete left off, although for some unknown reason it was decided to include a page on gospel music.

Why did he include gospel, I wondered? *"I loved gospel music and the record companies would send over gospel records, so they were included within the pages,"* replied Mick.

Although *Soul Beat* and the like could be called 'primitive', these were groundbreaking publications, paving the way for other, more forward-thinking editors who had the ways and means to produce more professional-looking publications. Those early editors were the pioneers, venturing out into the great unknown and sowing the seeds from which latter-day publications would flourish.

Soul Beat quickly became *The New Soul Beat*, the first issue under the new name being No.5, expanding to a twenty-two-page publication, but due to the lack of dates, either on the cover, or within the pages, it is extremely difficult to trace what sort of journey this publication took. But once again, I am going to take something of a calculated guess.

I have up to Vol.1 No.6 and the records reviewed came out in 1966, so I think it is safe to say that volume one covered that year. But prior to obtaining those early issues I had added a completely different looking *Soul Beat* to the collection. As mentioned previously, this particular issue was undated, but had Vol.2 No.1 on the cover, alongside a photo of Garnett Mimms, who Mick had interviewed in a London hotel. It was a more professional-looking publication, including good quality photographs, and was still edited by Mick Brown. In his editorial, he mentions *"being two months late again, but our New Year Resolution is to get the magazine out monthly from now on"*, so let's assume that volume two and the new look began at the start of 1967.

When I mentioned the 'new look' format to Mick he said that that issue was possibly the last one, but he then had a change of mind and suggested that there was indeed one more, with a great photo of Linda Carr on the front. *Soul Beat* was over; but why, if he was enjoying it? *"It was simply because my musical tastes began to broaden into the likes of Hendrix and it was time to move on."*

Move on Mick Brown certainly did, going from the world of bedroom publishing and a teenager with a couple of A level passes to a respected journalist with the likes of the *Guardian*, the *Sunday Times* and the *Telegraph*, interviewing people such as James Brown, Marvin Gaye, Bobby Womack, Phil Spector, Aretha Franklin and Berry Gordy.

1965 was to spawn only one publication and it was back down south, to Bexleyheath in Kent this time, to the home of a man who was to become as much a legend on the northern soul scene as many of the acts that he championed – Dave Godin.

Godin was passionate about a number of causes, but black American music was his forte, with the sound first brought to his sixteen-year-old ears when Ruth Brown's 'Mama He Treats Your Daughter Mean' drifted through the speakers of the juke-box in a local ice-cream parlour.

As he gazed transfixed at the revolving record, as if hypnotised, the builder who had selected the disc told him what it was and that the music was called rhythm and blues, whilst giving him a handful of sixpences and pointing out a few more records that he might like to hear. The small silver coins were fed into the juke-box, Godin was hooked, and the rest, as they say, is history.

Caught under the R&B spell he most certainly was, eagerly seeking out records of this genre, but he was quick to appreciate the sounds coming out of Detroit, kickstarting the Tamla Motown Appreciation Society, which not only led to Berry Gordy sending a number of his leading acts across the Atlantic, but saw Dave Godin launch the HITSVILLE USA newsletter/magazine.

Hitsville USA was not Godin's initial venture into the world of publications, as he had started a fan club for Motown's Mary Wells, producing five issues of the *Mary Wells and Motown News* between December 1963 and June 1964. Content was arguably more about Motown as a whole than the talented Miss Wells, but who cared?

For example, issue No.5 included a symposium on why Motown records did not sell in the UK, while an article in issue two (March 1964) had drifted well away from the music as it focused on muscular dystrophy, a disease that Mary at one time thought she had.

Looking through those publications from the late sixties, they are obviously dated, but they are often made even more so by some of the actual content. Take the last issue of the Mary Wells fan club newsletter for example, Vol.1 No.5.

In his editorial, where Dave welcomed 'Dear Swinger and Friend', a welcome he used in all his publications and something that takes on an entirely different meaning today, he mentions that he was *"recently asked by a journalist if the members of The Tamla-Motown Appreciation Society were mostly 'mods or rockers'"*. He had replied *"we are neither, but were all 'swingers and friends'. That what we term*

Rhythm & Blues, and what most people term Rock & Roll is usually connected in the public mind with delinquency and trouble making, is a sad but true fact."

He went on to mention trouble being caused at concerts between rival factions adding *"one of the most controversial groups here that has provoked these kind of disturbances is The Rolling Stones, who have been a source of controversy amongst the R&B fraternity since they first appeared."* He added that it was difficult to stay away from Stones concerts when the likes of Bo Diddley were on the bill, and it was looking like Mary Wells was also going to be appearing on the same bill as the group at some point.

His dislike for the Stones clearly shone through despite his having known them prior to becoming famous.

It could be reasoned that the publication came to an end due to the ongoing dispute between Mary and Motown over her contract with the company.

That particular publication certainly laid the groundwork for *Hitsville USA*, which was not only unique in the fact that it was more or less just dedicated to one record label, but also in its size and format. It measured a strange 13 x 20.5cm, printed on quality paper, with a numerical system that continued from one issue to another (i.e. Issue No.1 finished on page twenty, with No.2 starting on page twenty-one). It also left no 'wasted' space within its pages as text and photographs were tight together.

For some reason, *Hitsville* wasn't strictly 100% Motown, as Godin's love for all black music saw a regular feature being entitled 'People We Like', which was to include the likes of Barbara Lynn, Irma Thomas, Ike and Tina Turner, Esther Phillips and Nina Simone. Issue one also carried a Sam Cooke 'In Memoriam' tribute. But such inclusions took nothing away from this excellent publication, with all the Motown acts featured at some point or other within the dozen issues, with many exclusive and never previously seen photographs.

I did say that there were a dozen of these publications, but in a way, there were actually thirteen, as there was a special, un-numbered issue in September 1965 which was dedicated to Tamla Motown Appreciation Society member Mike Page who had died the previous month. That final issue also included an index as to content featured in Nos.1-12.

Hitsville is certainly one of the outstanding publications of the time and it is little wonder that copies seldom appear anywhere for sale, as they are firmly entrenched in the collections of the Motown and northern soul diehards. If and when copies become available, they can change hands for much more than other fanzines/magazines.

Tony Cummings is another name that will be familiar to many on the northern soul scene. A prolific writer whose name can be found in numerous publications, he will also be remembered for his own publication **SOUL**, which was first available in January 1966.

Yet another 'southern' based magazine, out of Plymouth this time, it was a rotary–duplicated publication, using typed stencils, changing to litho-printed for issues three and four, as the pages increased from thirty-six to forty.

Assisted by Derek Brandon, with contributors such as the Parisian, Swiss born Kurt Mohr, Roger St Pierre, John Abbey and Bill Miller, you knew you were going to get a magazine of quality. Despite the content being classed as similar to most, it was also varied, featuring names such as T-Bone Walker, The Impressions, Screamin' Jay Hawkins, Fontella Bass, Paul Butterfield Blues Band, Sam and Dave and Tammi Montgomery. Reviews of shows by a number of touring artists were also well covered, with 'exclusive' interviews often carried out, which helped enhance *Soul* even more.

Although it lasted only four issues, it certainly wasn't to do with the quality of the publication, nor the writing within, and in all honesty it didn't really disappear at all as it was simply transformed into *Soul Music Monthly* the following year.

Keeping in mind that those early to mid- sixties years were still very much the formative years of soul music publications, with the music still not having shrugged off the rhythm and blues mantle, how did Tony Cummings suddenly become embraced with the music and go on to edit his own magazine?

"By 1963 I'd moved from being a typical teenager enjoying the pop music I heard (I bought the Beatles 'Love Me Do' the week it came out) to being a soul and blues fan. The word 'fan' doesn't really do it justice. I'd become completely immersed in soul and blues," he began. "I should explain that I wasn't solely locked into the modern soul music, I was equally passionate about early R&B, Roy Brown, Louis Jordan, doowop, etc and the blues of Howlin' Wolf and Slim Harpo and even had a passing acquaintance with gospel - Mahalia Jackson and The Dixie Hummingbirds, and also jazz, though the latter was largely picking up a bit of my dad's enthusiasm.

"Soul/R&B records weren't just the means to make the tedium of life bearable. Listening to those records made me feel more alive than anything I'd ever encountered before. Interests and hobbies that I'd had now took a back seat in my life. My enthusiastic support of Plymouth Argyle FC was waning. Even my interest in girls, though retaining some of the usual nagging ache of teenage years, weakened. Now nothing absorbed me like this thrilling, life-affirming African American art form. It seemed to do something

deep within me. No wonder it was called soul music.

"I craved more of these amazing records and more and more information about these records and the people who made them. Norman Jopling's 'Great Unknowns' pieces in 'Record Mirror' had given me a starting point for these mysterious creative shamen like The Isley Brothers, John Lee Hooker and dozens more. And Norman's articles and reviews had me scampering down to Moons, the electrical supplier in Plymouth's town centre that had the best record department, to order up 'Tango' by The Isley Brothers on United Artists or 'Boom Boom' by John Lee Hooker on Stateside. But that was only the start of this Great Adventure that now enveloped me.

"To get more and more music I'd started using my dad's tape recorder, which he had set up in the cellar of our home and where he'd once recorded a demo for an amateur folk group. With this 'pro quality' Bang & Olufsen machine he was making tapes of the big band jazz music he liked for his friends at the Freemasons. I put a classified ad in 'Record Mirror' and was soon swapping tapes of the records I had with a chap in Derby called Rod Patton who had a big collection not only of the Motown and Otis Redding records I'd missed but even old urban blues records and ancient doowop releases.

"I joined the Tamla Motown Appreciation Society. I'd read every word of Mike Vernon's 'R&B Monthly' and even felt the thrill of having my name printed in his mag for additions I contributed to their Little Richard session discography and I'd been thrilled to read in 'Soul Beat' that my beloved Isley Brothers had an amazing record 'Testify Pts 1 & 2' out in the US on their own T-Neck label.

"But my craving for more music and more information about the music could not be satisfied. I wrote to my small band of pen friend brothers, Rod Patton, Bill Millar (who was the first person I'd known who'd interviewed an R&B singer) and Rick Winkley (who had a seeming encyclopaedic knowledge of Gary US Bonds and Carole King – then considered by most a

SOUL
THE MAGAZINE FOR THE R. & B. COLLECTOR.
Price 2/6   No. 3   April 1966
Sam & Dave
Editor: Tony Cummings, 102, Beaumont Road, St. Judes, Plymouth, Devon.
Assistant Editor: Derek Brandon.

one-hit- wonder) and asked them for anything they felt able to put in my own magazine, to be called 'Soul'.

"I had no money to buy a proper duplicating machine but I was able to buy a crude contraption designed for schools and clubs where small numbers of duplicated sheets could be printed by typing out a stencil, putting it on a wooden frame, applying a generous dollop of printing ink and then running a roller by hand over the frame once it had a bit of paper on top. It was a crude, messy and time-consuming process, but with a cover I'd had printed bearing the word 'Soul' in large letters it constituted a magazine.

"When I bought that crude duplicator, I had very little that some might have thought I could possibly fill a magazine with. I had no direct access to any soul or blues artists. I had no direct contact with record companies. I had never even been to any soul or blues concerts. All I had was this compulsion fuelled by a pile of records, a larger pile of reel-to-reel tapes, a stack of cuttings mainly from 'Record Mirror', a pile of magazines – 'R&B Monthly', 'Blues Unlimited', 'Hitsville USA', 'Soulbeat' and some fan club mags, and letters from my fellow soul music obsessives. I'd never met those pen friends face-to- face but we seemed of one mind, religious zealots wanting to declare to the world that the best popular music that had ever been made was being created by black Americans and that the whole world needed to hear The Falcons 'I Found A Love' or The Marvelettes 'Please Mr Postman' and hundreds more and that the creatives who made this music deserved reverence. These singers and groups deserved to have their lives properly documented. And it seemed that even in the USA there were precious few fans or journalists who appreciated the significance of the latest creative explosion in America's ghettos. "I knew, through conversations I'd had with my jazz fan father, that books had eventually been written about the significance of Louis Armstrong's Hot Five. And I knew from my trips to Plymouth Library that decades on from recording their music, the lives of early blues singers had been celebrated by authors like Paul Oliver and Sam Charters. But what about Mary Wells or Chuck Jackson, let along Hattie Littles or Billy Soul? There was a wealth, a vast ocean of extraordinary music being created and my friends and I, despite our non-existent journalistic experience, despite our frugal resources, despite knowing nothing about how to get our efforts to a readership beyond classified adverts in 'Record Mirror' were willing to give it a shot. And so 'Soul' started."

So the seeds were sown and Tony Cummings had his feet planted in the world of soul music publications; and he continues his fact-finding venture, akin to some explorer venturing into the unknown.

"After two issues I was having regular correspondence with a young soul fan from Southampton called Derek Brandon. We got on like a house on fire and in our school holidays we'd arranged with our parents to have me go and stay with him for a few days and then for him to come to stay with me. In Southampton we trawled every second-hand shop and even found a showroom selling juke boxes which had piles of old American records. I was able to gleefully buy such rarities as The Cruisers on V-Tone Records. Back in Plymouth we made our plans for a new, improved magazine, with offset litho printing, and 'Soul' issue No.3 was duly published in April 1966 with a picture of Sam and Dave on the cover and an interview Derek had been able to do with Fontella Bass even though at the age of fifteen Derek wasn't legally old enough to be in the club where the 'Rescue Me' soul star was playing.

"By the fourth issue of 'Soul', Bill Millar was really coming into his own. He weighed in with what was the definitive interview with Screamin' Jay Hawkins while Swiss discographer extraordinaire Kurt Mohr's sent in a Lee Dorsey discography, with additions from Britain's R&B experts Trevor Churchill and Peter Gibbon. The cover sported Lee Dorsey.

"But with no shop distribution save for some copies in Plymouth's jazz and blues specialist shop Pete Russell's Hot Record Store and London's more famous one Doug Dobell's printing bills weren't being offset by sales of the mag. Depressed, I suddenly decided to relocate to Derby where Rod Patton lived. He was writing regularly to me, telling me of the soul acts he was seeing quite regularly in the Derby clubs. Rod had a job, was nicknamed 'Rod The Mod' and was something of a face. I knew nothing about mod culture but I was keen to get to those clubs and got Rod to ask his mum and dad whether I could come up and live with them until I could get a job. My brief sojourn in Derby wasn't a success. I loved seeing The Vibrations singing 'Hang On Sloopy' in clubland. And I got through a job interview to become a bus conductor. But my girlfriend refused to relocate from Plymouth to Derby and after a couple of weeks I was ready to return to Plymouth. When I got back everything was different."

"Dear Swinger & Friend. As you can see, the magazine has undergone yet another 'facelift'. This has been entirely due to the increased circulation which has been brought about by readers introducing the magazine to their friends, and because of the general trend of more people to buy the records that are dealt with in our pages. To help this snowballing trend to gain more momentum, you will see that the price for British readers has been reduced." So opened Dave Godin's editorial in the initial issue of **RHYTHM & SOUL USA**.

The magazine hadn't actually undergone any "facelift" as it had never actually been out previously, but what had happened was that *Hitsville USA* was no more, gone into the world of collectibles, and here in its place was something completely different and equally groundbreaking.

Measuring slightly bigger, and I do mean slightly (14 x 21.5cm), this publication was to embrace all forms of what was now generalised as 'soul music'. Motown was still there, with reviews of *The Supremes A Go-Go* and The Four Tops *On Top* albums – the latter considered as not being their best, which was very true, but the singles and the other album reviews were more or less a who's who of soul and indeed R&B. Reviewed singles were the likes of Shirley Lawson 'The Star'; Homer Banks 'A Lot Of Love', Donald Height 'Talk of the Grapevine' and Darrell Banks 'Open The Door To Your Heart' – "*a resounding and quite splendid success*". There were albums by Bobby Bland, Nina Simone, Gloria Jones and more.

Twenty pages in all, with features on Aretha Franklin (by another name that would become familiar to the readers of soul music journals – David Nathan), Solomon Burke and Darrell Banks, all with accompanying photographs. The image of Miss Franklin is not one I have seen previously and, to be honest, looks nothing like her.

Like *Hitsville* this publication is printed on quality paper and excellently produced with no wasted space. Adverts are at a minimum – a few 'classifieds' alongside one for Oxfam, one for the New York Apollo and another which read: "*Soon, everyone will be talking about Soul City. Watch for the opening date of Britain's first 100% R&B and Soul music record Shop – Soul City*".

For some strange reason the second issue of *Rhythm & Soul USA* was also given the number 1. There was no explanation for this, and neither was there an explanation for the six pence price increase after having said in issue one that the price had been reduced! The page numbering was also different to that of *Hitsville* as it kept to each issue seeing the pages numbered from 1-20, instead of the continuity of its predecessor.

The April issue carried features on Wilson Pickett, Irma Thomas, Billy Stewart, while May (No.3) had Bessie Banks, Dee Dee Warwick and Sam and Dave, with the following issue seeing James Brown, Bettye LaVette, Martha Reeves and Gloria Gaynor as the featured artists.

It was only to run for four issues and Godin was later to say: "*Although Motown had given me a degree of financial support, I was on my own with this venture and, not being rich, it only ran to four issues.*"

With the northern soul scene very much about rare records that change hands for tidy sums, there are also rare publications and while copies of *Rhythm & Soul USA* are not as rare as *Hitsville*, they are certainly up there in the 'top five'.

Although 'soul' was now part of the music vocabulary, 'blues' had certainly not been erased, as May 1966 saw the birth of a publication which, like Dave Godin's twins, would take on a name change further down the line. It would eventually see Mr Godin rule the roost within its pages, go from strength to strength, and still be found on the magazine shelves today.

HOME OF THE BLUES was the brain child of John E. Abbey and surfaced at the same time as Godin's penultimate issue of *Hitsville USA*. Published monthly, side stapled, priced at two shillings and measuring 20.5 x 25.5cm, the cover of issue No.1 was printed on glossy paper with the fonts in black, but changed to red for issue two and then back again to black up to issue seven.

In his first editorial, John E. Abbey was to write: *"This is Home Of The Blues – the magazine intended for the connoisseur of American Blues music.*

"We shall endeavour to cover all sides of R&B from Major Lance to Howlin' Wolf – from Detroit to Memphis. "One of our correspondents will cover at least one date on each and every tour in Britain made by an American Blues, Soul or Rock artist.

"Our monthly regular articles include reviews of all releases in this country by Blues artists.

"Another regular will be a genuine American Top 50 Blues records – this list will be completely up-to-date and will be obtained actually from inside America.

"We need one thing from you – your support! If you have any comment whatsoever on this magazine (but please remember it's our first attempt!) please drop a line to the Editor. Every comment will be of future use and will help to improve our magazine.

"We hope we shall be responsible for a great deal of interesting reading on the American scene for you."

Perhaps unaware as to how the public would take to this new publication, it was, on the whole, quite basic, even compared to *Rhythm and Blues Gazette* from three years previously. Content, although varied, was somewhat bland, and had the font size been smaller, then there could have been more content or fewer pages. Most of the general articles, other than concert reviews, appeared to come from the pen of the editor himself.

Putting time, effort and more so money into your own publication was a brave step for anyone to take, so why did John decide to kickstart *Home of the Blues*, I wondered, and did he see it as something of a short or long-term project? *"I had been submitting interviews for other magazines,"* came the reply, *"and I thought I could do this for myself and do more. As regards to a time frame, I am honestly not sure that I really thought*

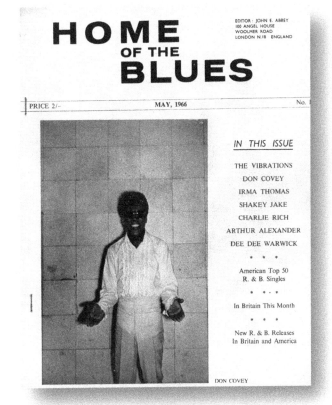

about it at the time!"

There was little in the way of costs involved in producing that first issue as, like many other publications that followed, it was produced on 'borrowed' equipment. John at the time was working in a travel agency and his boss was happy for him to use the office equipment, as long as nothing interfered with his normal working hours. As if!

Issue No.1 carried articles on The Vibrations, Don Covay, Irma Thomas, Dee Dee Warwick, Arthur Alexander, Charlie Rich and Shakey Jake, with the Top 50 American singles, plus new releases from both sides of the Atlantic, thrown in for good measure.

The number of pages in those early editions varied between twenty and thirty, but then, in March 1967 (issue No. 8), it suddenly burst into life, taking on a more professional look and published by Contempo Publications. It also adopted a new size format - 18 x 24.5cm - and was printed on glossy paper throughout. Only the font size didn't change, which was unfortunate. Adverts for record companies such as EMI, Ember, President and Sue suddenly became a regular feature as did those for the Flamingo Club at 33-37 Wardour Street, London and Soul City at 21 Deptford High Street. The latter took up a whole page when half of one would have been quite sufficient, but you get what you pay for.

Photographic content also became something of a strong point.

It had certainly gained in popularity during that first year in the public domain and was now a must-

HOME
OF THE
BLUES

EDITOR : JOHN E. ABBEY
100 ANGEL HOUSE
WOOLMER ROAD
LONDON N.18 ENGLAND

PRICE 2/–	NOVEMBER, 1966	No. 6

THE CORSAIRS

IN THIS ISSUE

PERCY SLEDGE	* * *	BOBBY HEBB	* * *	ROBERT PARKER
THE CORSAIRS	* * *	THE 5 STAIRSTEPS	* * *	LINDA CARR
BOBBY POWELL	* * *	OTIS REDDING	* * *	THE TONICS
5th AMERICAN FOLK BLUES FESTIVAL			* * *	Usual Articles

read, but did its standing amongst the R&B and soul crowd come as something as a surprise to its forward-thinking editor? "*Timing is everything! It (Home of the Blues) coincided with the advent of the more popular soul music – Stax, Motown and later Philadelphia International,*" came John's reply.

home of the **BLUES**

No. 11   July 1967   Two Shillings

But all good things come to an end and issue No.11 in July 1967 marked the end of *Home of the Blues*. There was no warning in the editorial, no hint that this was the last issue of a magazine that had grown in stature amongst the soul fraternity, nothing, and just when Dave Godin had begun to send forth his thoughts to the multitude. 'Swingers and Friends' had now become 'Fans and Followers'.

Perhaps even Abbey himself at that point did not know what the future held, as on page seventeen there is mention as to what the next issue had in store – Aretha Franklin, The Isley Brothers, B.B. King, Little Milton, Chuck Jackson, the Dave Godin Column, the return of the Ska Column, plus a new regular surprise inclusion. All would be confined to the filing cabinet for a later day, if they ever appeared at all.

So *Home of the Blues* bit the dust, but John E. Abbey had only just begun his assault on the soul music publication world. He had done enough to test

the water, to give those who enjoyed the music a whiff of a regular quality publication. Within three months he would be back, once again moving forward, with a brand-new publication.

Prior to the appearance of *Blues and Soul* another magazine was to surface - SOUL MUSIC MONTHLY, which made its debut in January 1967, professing itself to be "*The World's Leading Rhythm and Blues Magazine*". Eat your heart out *Blues and Soul*.

Tony Cummings had given the soul fans *Soul* the previous year and here he was back with more of the same. "*With this editorial I'm welcoming back all our old readers of SOUL and saying hello for the first time to many new readers. Negro R&B music is so incredibly popular today that a regular R&B journal is essential for anyone interested at all in this music form, and this is that journal. I hope that in the following pages, you'll find something of interest, whatever your particular preference as the range of music we'll be covering under the general framework of R&B is wide indeed. Something for everybody in fact!*
"*A special word of welcome to Bill Millar, who'll be joining Derek [Brandon] and myself on the editorial staff, though he's already become a favourite with his quite excellent articles.*

"*So, all you new readers, write and tell me if you like the magazine and what YOU would like to see featured in future copies of the world's leading rhythm and blues magazine, SOUL MUSIC MONTHLY.*"

So, was it simply a publicity stunt to pull in new readers or was *Soul Music Monthly* indeed the leading magazine for this type of music in the world?

It had certainly picked up the baton that Dave Godin's *Rhythm & Soul USA* had dropped. Small, compact, measuring 16 x 20cm, it had a card cover with an artist photograph on both the back and front. It carried a price tag of two shillings and sixpence, or if you lived in the States 35c.

Consisting of two dozen neatly typed pages, well laid out with page space maximised, you got a bit of everything due to its interesting and varied content. Issue No.1 featured Alvin Robinson, Carl Holmes, The Drifters, Jimmy Soul, Bobby Lewis, The Capitols and Clarence Henry, alongside single, L.P. and E.P. and concert reviews. Issue No.2 (Feb. 1967) included The Coasters, Solomon Burke, The Miracles and Edwin Starr, while two months later you could read about Maxine Brown, Jnr. Walker and The Spellbinders. There was also the odd discography thrown in for good measure to keep the anoraks happy.

In that fourth issue (April 1967), the final one I believe, there is a most interesting letter from Mr J. S.

Kruger who was the owner of the Flamingo club in London, who was writing in reply to Bill Millar's comment in the second issue – "*the fact that the 'Flamingo' is seldom booking American acts is rather disquieting.*"

Mr Kruger replied: "*The Flamingo, London, was the first club of any prominence in the United Kingdom to take the gambit and go whole-heartedly for a full-time R&B policy and slowly but surely the decision paid off. However, of necessity this change of policy from pure Jazz to R&B meant a change of atmosphere and the club drew on all lovers of R&B and naturally a high percentage of our Jamaican, West African and American negro friends had started visiting the club.*

"*We reached an impasse last summer when our coloured R&B fans began to outnumber our white R&B fans and despite thinking that music, and more especially R&B music, was above personal prejudices, we were indirectly given an ultimatum by our regular caucasian members to modify our policy or they would quit regular attendances to the club.*

"*We refused to be intimidated and in consequence lost a hard core of some 200 odd regulars every weekend. So much for the background. We booked Ike and Tina Turner to the club - response was pathetic - 'we've seen them before' said the R&B fans. We booked Inez and Charlie Foxx and only 175 ardent R&B fans thought them interesting enough to warrant a visit. We had the Soul Sisters with a negative reaction, but still trying to please we booked James and Bobby Purify (subsequently cancelled through lack of support). If it is disquieting to you that we don't book American R&B stars what do you think it is to us? How can we operate an American name policy without the support of all the R&B enthusiasts, regardless of colour?*

"*I put it to you that too many people are R&B fans in name only because it is perhaps the 'in' cult of the moment and their snobbishness about mixing with other fans shows the depth of their insincerity.*"

Strong stuff!

But getting back to the publication in general, to be honest, looking through back issues today, I think Cummings was justified in his boast, and having spoken to Tony earlier in regards to his initial publication, *Soul*, what did he have to say about his latest venture? "*My parents had moved to a smaller house and there was hardly room for me to run the magazine from the tiny room adjoining the kitchen. I decided, however, to make a fresh magazine start. I changed its name to 'Soul Music Monthly', which was an optimistic moniker considering I was hardly meeting the printing costs, and tried to make a living, vainly trying to give a few pounds to my mum for my upkeep and buying insurance stamps. I was handling all the commissioning, writing and editing copy, addressing envelopes and everything I could to keep Soul Music Monthly's head above water.*

"*Soul Music Monthly No.1 had Bill Millar interviewing Roy C and Bobby Lewis, Derek Brandon had got to talk to Alvin Robinson (whose signed photo we used on the cover caused a smile as it was credited 'To Derek and staff'); good ol' Kurt Mohr had come through with a discography and interview with obscure twist practitioners Carl Holmes & The Commanders; and Mike Vernon had interviewed Clarence 'Frogman' Henry.*

"*Soul Music Monthly No.2, with Otis Redding on the cover, had Derek Brandon reviewing The Dixie Cups Southampton gig, Bill Millar interviewing Robert Parker and, much to my delight, Kurt Mohr's Isley Brothers discography. But all this precious information wasn't getting to too many people. I needed more help and I needed to relocate to London.*

"*But this relocation to London was a little more thought out. My plan was to go and stay with Bill Millar, quickly find a job and a bedsit, get my girlfriend to live with me and gather my trusty band of soul brethren – Dave McAleer, who was running the*

SOUL MUSIC MONTHLY
THE WORLD'S LEADING RHYTHM AND BLUES MAGAZINE

ALVIN ROBINSON
INSIDE THIS ISSUE: CARL HOLMES, DRIFTERS, ALVIN ROBINSON, JIMMY SOUL, BOBBY LEWIS, CAPITOLS AND CLARENCE HENRY.

NO. 1 JANUARY, 1967   2/6° (U.S.A. 35¢)

'Fame/Goldwax Appreciation Society', Jon Philibert, who had a publication 'The Organisation' specialising in jazz and R&B organists, and Mick Brown, who had taken over the editorship of 'Soulbeat' – and start a new, bigger, better magazine.

"My first days in London proved almost as disastrous as my first days in Derby. It had started well. I'd gone with Bill Millar and some of his friends to see the big Stax concert with Otis Redding, Sam and Dave and Arthur Conley. But on the tube home I got parted from Bill and friends and ended up having to walk from London's West End to Bill's home in Streatham, South London. Things got worse for me when Bill's wife took an instant dislike to me and I was asked to leave after a couple of days. I had nowhere to go. I ended up sleeping in the park before the cold, the hunger and the quacking of the ducks keeping me awake when trying to sleep on a bench in St James' Park, forced me to seek help. In desperation I made a reverse charge call to my brother who lived in Ipswich. Arriving there, he and his wife put me up and even gave me some money to get back to London to continue my master plan to become a soul music magazine publisher. "Over the next couple of months, I got a job in the music industry... kind of. Jon Philibert and Dave McAleer had been working together in the copyright department of the huge music publishers Chappell Music and though Dave had left to take up a new job at Pye Records, Jon was able to put a word in someone's ear and though I knew absolutely nothing about the arcane

rules of the 1956 Copyright Act and could only type with one finger (two if you counted one on the space bar) I got a job at Chappell.

"That and with my girlfriend installed in a bedsit I was soon having weekend meetings with Dave, Jon and Mick where we made plans for the launch of 'Soul Music'. This was to be A4 (A3 size simply didn't do it), would have adverts, would be properly printed and get distribution in newsagents and record shops.

"Mick Brown had some kind of connection with magazine distributors so we pushed on and planned and wrote the actual contents. It indeed had the best stuff so far. Bill Millar was continuing to interview R&B artists. Kurt Mohr was continuing to send detailed session discographies and we had high hopes that this would be the magazine we were adamant the still growing soul scene needed. But our woeful lack of experience ensured we stumbled at issue one.

"Soul Music failed to get any distribution. We failed to get the glossy printing we'd hoped for. And we failed to get any paid advertising and ended up putting in a couple of fake ads – even though the idea of Parlo Records taking out a page ad in a UK magazine for an Aaron Neville single was extreme wishful thinking even for soul music idealists.

"The one and only issue of Soul Music was another licence to lose money. But still I was driven on. My music fanatic friends, now including new ones Clive Richardson, who had run the Don Covey fan club, and Charlie Gillett, who was the only person I'd ever heard

of who'd managed to get a degree with a treatise on the evolution of rock 'n' roll, R&B and soul, and I would meet in the Cummings bedsit. I reasoned that if I could do away with the print bills and do away with the need for any shop distribution, a magazine crammed with information could be put together which would meet the needs of the soul cognoscenti, our subscribers list. The print bills were largely overcome by using, entirely without their permission, Chappell's photocopier (for the cover) and sometimes their duplicating paper.

"By now my trusty team were supplying enough material to plan a weekly magazine and though I had to soon modify that idea the next couple of years saw a stream of 'Shout' magazines emerge thanks to the unwitting help of the Chappell's photocopier and my regular visits to Jon Philibert's home so I could use his father's duplicating machine. Clive Richardson bravely took 'Shout' to its next season of fax 'n' info excellence and the path that I took was to lead me to a career in music copyright, then a career in journalism, then spectacularly unsuccessful spells in song writing, record production, reggae company A&R man, soft drugs dealer and finally a long career in gospel music/Christian music journalism.

"As you will no doubt have gathered from that last clause, I long since dropped my soul music religion so I suppose you could say I have failed to keep the faith. But now I look back upon my years as part of the soul music underground I find I have nothing but respect for Dave McAleer, Clive Richardson, Bill Millar, Jon Philibert, Charlie Gillett, Mick Vernon, Derek Brandon and all those others who served soul/R&B so well in those formative years."

a brief chat. *"Yes, there were four issues printed. It was a one-man job and the copies were 'run-off' at Jon Philibert's house."*

Unlike its counterparts, and those that would follow in the months and years ahead, this was an A5 publication, but printed landscape rather than portrait. As I only have issue two, I am not sure if it is standard format, but for the first eighteen of the thirty-two pages, there is text only on one side, for some unknown reason.

Although the subject matter centres around the Fame/Goldwax label, like other similar publications soul music in general is also covered. It has something of a primitive look about it, but it was 1967, and although the covers left a little to be desired, the content was commendable and the print on the pages clear and readable.

But why did Dave decide to centre his magazine/newsletter around the Fame and Goldwax labels, I wondered, and why go with a rather unconventional landscape size publication? *"I chose Fame and Goldwax as they were the main labels at the time with the Muscle Shoals Southern Soul sound that I loved,"* Dave replied. *"Although they were not part of the same company, the owners, Rick Hall and Quinton Claunch, were long-time friends and Goldwax often used Fame's Muscle Shoals studio to get that special sound. I liked almost everything that the labels released and saw them, and also the Muscle Shoals Sound, as the next big thing in soul."*

"As for the size, I honestly can't recall why the mag was landscape – maybe it was simply because you could get two pages from one A4 sheet of paper instead of one – and any saving was good in those days."

With the popularity of R&B increasing with each passing month, the enthusiasm fired up by the music lingered long after the needle slipped across the run-out groove, prompting many to form 'fan clubs' or 'appreciation societies' for not just artists but for the labels that they recorded on. One such appreciation society was centred around the Fame/Goldwax label and was run by Dave McAleer, who produced the **FAME-GOLDWAX SOUL SURVEY** newsletter/ magazine. I have only seen three issues of this publication, and the only copy I have is issue number two, which appeared in 1967. There were, however, four issues published, as Dave confirmed during

Trying to throw some further light on the, let's say rather strange, size format, it is worth noting that Dave mentions that he printed the magazine off at Jon Philibert's house, and that Jon used the same size format for his own publication *The Organization*.

Speaking with Dave, I also wondered what made him cease producing it after only four issues, was it a time thing or what? "*I stopped the mag when I joined the team who formed 'Soul Music' magazine - Tony Cummings, Jon Philibert, Mick Brown and regular contributors Charlie Gillett, Clive Richardson and Bill Millar.*

"*There was no real time difference between the end of 'Soul Survey' and the launch of 'Soul Music'.*

"*After thirty-three editions of 'Soul Music', the name was changed to 'Shout' and Clive ran it and it had over 100 issues. I personally was not closely involved in the mag for long, as I was trying to get my music business career started and it was taking up most of my time. As you may know, after a long record business career, mainly in the black music/soul/northern soul/disco/rap and hip-hop areas, I did go back to writing and have had a couple of dozen music books published and have written hundreds of sleeve notes.*"

Dave was also to add: "*The majority of soul fanzines were run by real fans, after all it was not a profitable exercise, and were brimming with interesting facts about acts the majority of the public were unaware of and uninterested in. The people behind them knew there was only a very small market for their wares – they were simply specialist mags targeted solely at specialist music fans.*"

Another 'fan club' issue from 1967 was produced by Clive Richardson and saluted the man whose hit single 'See-Saw' filled countless dance floors – Mr Don Covay. Clive recalled having received newsletters from other fan clubs that he had joined, but was particularly impressed by the one covering the Fame/Goldwax label and another entitled *The Organization*. So much so that he decided to produce one in honour of DON COVAY.

Venturing into the printed word for the first time, Clive put together a six- page (seven if you include the cover) quarto size newsletter that covered news on Don Covay, a mention of new and future releases on both the Ember and Island record labels, a couple of pages of reviews of recent soul singles, a track-by-track review of the *See-Saw* album and a review of some of Don Covay's previous recordings.

A second issue, with a copy of a signed publicity photo of the man himself, obtained by Clive during his recent UK tour, featured on the cover, came out in April 1967. Like many of the publications dedicated to a solitary label or artist, Clive didn't simply devote every square inch to Don Covay, as this second issue also contained a review of the recent Stax tour that he attended.

Mentioning that the show had inadvertently been re-named 'The Otis Redding Show', Clive, although not critical of the performance of the top of the bill act, was to say that it should have been called 'The Sam and Dave Show' due to the duo's "*fantastic, professional, polished, fast and soulful*" performance. One thing that Clive was critical about was the appearance of Sharon Tandy, who he felt was an "*unwanted inclusion*".

Unfortunately, the club and the newsletter were to be somewhat short-lived, with Clive to write: "*Despite Covay's prolific activities as songwriter and recording artist in the U.S.A., Polydor had little news or information on his recent work, or couldn't be bothered to keep me informed which comprised in the fan club magazine comprising some guesswork.*"
I also imagine this was behind the club's eventual disappearance.

Just going back a few lines, Clive mentions THE ORGANIZATION. This was a fan club run by Jon Philibert, who had also contributed to *Soul Beat*. Thankfully I managed to catch up with Jon and he was able to throw some light on this 'club 'and its newsletters. "*I was in my late teens or maybe early twenties when I started a club/fanzine (although as you probably know, they weren't called fanzines in those days) called 'The Organisation' which after a while was renamed 'The Organization' (with a Z like Liza Minnelli!) presumably on the grounds that it sounded more American and/or more trendy!*" began Jon. "*I was a massive soul fan in those days but also enjoyed soul-jazz, in particular funky organists like John Patton, Don Patterson, Billy Larkin, Larry Young, Jimmy Smith etc and decided I might be able to produce a magazine. I couldn't help but include R&B and soul music in the mix too. I think I must have got my subscribers from advertising in the small ads in Record Mirror which was the most soul music-friendly of all the music periodicals of the day.*

"*I had the facility of producing the magazine, as my father ran a business at home and he had one of those old- fashioned ink duplicators, which he needed for his business. I used it to create the magazine. I think there were four or maybe five editions. I only have two, though maybe Mac [Dave McAleer] has some.*

"*First one would 'cut' a stencil on the typewriter and then wrap the stencil around the drum and turn the handle and produce the pages. Ink went everywhere and it was great fun though my mother was not amused! I think I must have used this duplicator process to produce Mac's magazine and maybe Mick Brown's 'Soul Beat' and I'm pretty sure that the*

magazine for the James Brown fan club called the James Brown Admiration Society (not 'appreciation') was produced by the duplicator too. That club was run by Alan Curtis, and he also contributed something on James Brown to the French magazine 'Soul Bag'.

"*As regards 'The Organization', I must say, that whenever people ask me about it, I tend to be rather evasive as it was a weird hotchpotch of stuff and I'm frankly embarrassed by it now. I was only young then but apart from the record reviews – which were just about OK – there was a lot of silly, puerile and immature schoolboy stuff and irritating in-jokes in it. I fancied myself as some kind of humorist at the time and I wrote a feature that took a Batman story from DC Comics and rewrote it with gags. What on earth that was doing in a music magazine is anyone's guess. I wasn't even on drugs!*

"*When I dug out the two editions I have I was quite surprised that there was less about soul music and more about jazz than I remember.*

"*In the magazine there was a feature I remember doing called something like 'Ten Questions with...' I did Booker T – it was all done by letter in those days - and also, in the same interview/Q&A format, with Dave Godin, although in person with Dave. I made the pilgrimage to his home in Bexleyheath, almost a soul music rite of passage in those days, but I was so unprepared that I didn't even have questions ready. Dave took pity on this poor youth and not only answered the questions but wrote them too!*"

What we really have to remember is that way back in those mid-to-late sixties days, there was no internet, and no widespread coverage through publications, so I wondered if Jon ever realised that he and his friends were at the forefront of something that would eventually become a worldwide phenomenon? "*In answer to your question about whether we thought we were part of something that was of, shall we say, historical importance, I would say no. We were just an ultra-tight community and a lot of us knew the same people inside our little clique.*

"*The likes of Mick Jagger and Paul McCartney would say how much they were in to soul in the early days but none of them were ever part of our circle or subscribed to our magazines, although, to my delight, Jimi Hendrix was once spotted in the west end of London with a copy of Soul Music – the first edition – tucked under his arm!*"

"Incredible to think this was all done before email. We just met at live gigs, record fairs and specialist shops and there was a lot of letter writing between ourselves and to the music papers of the day. Of course, the music became part of the mainstream as the sixties progressed and we watched the rise of Motown, Stax etc in the UK charts and on TV. But in the very early sixties it was just us few with no idea of how the music would grow outside of its core American black audience."

Whilst in conversation with Jon he went on to add: *"There was a Scepter/Wand Appreciation Society run by Gloria Marcantonio, now no longer with us. I Googled it and only one result seemed to come up when I Googled her name and it was in reference to journalist David Nathan writing about Dave Godin. I believe there was also a Timi Yuro fan club and presumably there were magazines for her. I thought she was about the best white singer in the whole of soul music, although I wouldn't have admitted it at the time as, like so many of us diehards at the time, it was only black artists that we entertained. Mind you, apart from Yuro there were precious few other white artists that got anywhere remotely close to the black artists' sound and feel – and experiences – although a few individual records like 'I Found A Love' by Jo Ann and Troy, 'Take Me For A Little While' by Evie Sands come to mind as being really good. I seem to be wandering from the point now – it happens at my age!*

"In my soul days I contributed to Shout and Soul Music and maybe others but I can't recall now. For one magazine I remember interviewing Arthur Conley who gigged at a pub near to me and in the interview, I used a cassette recorder which was something quite new at the time and to have actual quotes from the artist in the subsequent article was something I hadn't found in soul/R&B magazine articles before. I may be wrong historically on that and stand to be corrected but that is my memory of it."

NB. The illustration is the actual cover of issue five of the *The Organization* newsletter and it was printed, like the Fame/Goldwax publication, in landscape format rather than portrait.

Before drifting away from Jon Philibert and his *Organization* it is interesting to note that he was to go on to bigger and better things, moving into country music and writing for *Country Music People* magazine as well as writing sleeve notes etc, before quitting in 2012 to concentrate on song writing. Jon added: *"Despite being a limey and based in the UK I have managed to get cuts consistently over the years by American country singers, and I wrote a song called 'I've Been Rained On Too' which was a top ten country hit for Tom Jones."*

Continuing on the 'fan club' theme the Martha and the Vandellas 'club' was run from Edinburgh by Mick Critchley and Ray Cutkelvin and they certainly did issue a publication, which was entitled **R&B HEATWAVE**, which, according to a letter that was sent out with a sample copy to an interested 'fan', was issued on a monthly basis.

Again, I only have the one issue, which comes from 1967, consisting of sixteen pages, and once again, it is not entirely about the subject matter – Miss Reeves. In fact, only a very brief interview between Martha and Rosalind (Ashford) and a mention of the hobbies that the trio enjoyed, all of which takes up two and a bit pages, is on the girls. The remainder is made up of record reviews (not all Motown), a feature on Chris Clark, a member's viewpoint and various snippets of info.

However, I managed to speak to Mike Critchley, who updated me as follows:" *My association with Motown and Fan Clubs started when Dave Godin decided to give up on the 'Tamla Motown Appreciation Society'. He said that he felt Motown was getting less soulful and wanted to move his energies towards 'Deep Soul'. Raymond Cutkelvin and I took over the mantle and we re-named the club 'The Motown Fan Club'. We were based in Edinburgh at the time.*

"In our first contact with Motown (Esther Gordy), we were told that Motown would like to have different fan clubs for different acts. So, the Tamla Motown Fan Club was very short-lived and I think we only did a couple of newsletters.

"In the newsletter and in the musical press (Disc, Melody Maker, Record Mirror) we placed adverts asking if anyone was interested in running Fan Clubs for the top Motown acts. Esther informed us that we could have whichever artists we wanted, plus the remaining acts that had no fan club. We assigned different acts to various people. I can't remember everyone... Lynne Pemberton - The Temptations - Roger Green & Frank Copperstone - Gladys Knight & The Pips. Sharon Davis - Marvin Gaye [Sharon actually ran The Four Tops Fan Club]. Phil Symes - Jimmy Ruffin. Can't remember who originally did The Supremes.

"We ran The Martha & The Vandellas Fan Club and issued many newsletters and small booklets called 'Heatwave'; we covered many of the lesser-known acts too. This was in the sixties, during which time we moved first to Manchester and then London.

"When Florence Ballard left The Supremes, I started 'The Florence Ballard Appreciation Society', which I did under the name Noel Davis, as I didn't want Motown to be aware of this... I used my parents' address to conceal myself further.

"During the seventies I moved out to other things and moved abroad, all papers I had went bye-bye. I never gave it a thought... I then lived in South America and New York before returning to the UK in 1979."

Like the Fame/Goldwax publication, *R&B Heatwave* is somewhat primitive, more so the cover, but we have to remember that this was way back in the pre-computer days. I think that there may have been three issues of the actual magazine.

If one guy was going out of his way to make an impression on the soul music scene through the written word then it was Tony Cummings. Already more than familiar through *Soul* and *Soul Music Monthly*, he was back with a vengeance in July 1967 with yet another publication – SOUL MUSIC.

In his introduction to the latest hot off the press publication, Tony wrote: *"To all those wonderful people who have given their support to 'Soul' and 'Soul Music Monthly', I would like to say thank you and I hope that this mag. will repay you for the diligence and patience*

which the British soul fan has shown in his wait for a UNITED soul magazine; by soul people for soul people. All R&B fans can now enjoy each month, the final word in soul journalism. Keep reading and stay soulful."*

Published out of London, the editorial board also included Mick Brown, Sir Jonathan Philibert and Dave McAleer. Whilst speaking to Jon regarding the *Organization* I had to ask where the knighthood had come from. *"Oh, the Sir Jon bit was all part of the general silliness and immaturity I mentioned earlier. Another embarrassment!"* came the reply.

Soul Music kicked off as a 21 x 25.5cm, centre- stapled, litho-printed publication and remained as such through its entirety. It lacked the class and quality of *Soul* and *Soul Music Monthly* and had reverted to side stapling and reduced the regularity by which it was published, but on the plus side, offered more pages.

Issue one was a massive thirty-six- page issue, not including the cover, and, as could have been expected, was certainly value for money, with the pages jammed with record and gig reviews and articles on a number of artists. Featured gigs covered were Sam and Bill and Garnet Mimms, while featured artists were the aforementioned Sam and Bill and Garnet Mimms, The Ad-Libs, Bill Pinkney, The Piney Woods Sound, Gladys Knight, The Glories (including a full-page photo) and The Cardinals. There were also two and a half pages listing recent US releases plus a couple of full-page adverts for new releases from Aaron Neville and James Carr.

There was also the first part of a Drifters discography and a notable inclusion of a contribution by Charlie Gillett entitled 'Sound Of The City' which would eventually materialise into a book a few years later.

If there had to be a complaint as regards *Soul Music*, it would be that the articles were too brief.

In his book *Soul Citizen* Clive Richardson wrote: *"With a cover price of 2s 6d the idea of 'Soul Music' was not to compete with 'Blues & Soul' as such, but to provide a more erudite, scholarly and detailed alternative, the contents being derived from the co-operative of committed soul fans. Unfortunately, however, as is often the case, there was a disparity between economics and ideology, and in the short-term economics won.*

There were also, it seems, some credibility gaps in

our sales expectations, in that the subscription list for the new magazine was thought to need a print-run of 2,000 copies, but it was actually far less than that. Despite a promotion campaign, which included ads in 'Billboard', the magazine didn't sell enough copies to cover the printing costs, and under other circumstances that would have been that.

"Tony Cummings was (and is) a man of immense principle and the next step in his crusade was a phone-call to me, in which he asked if I would be interested in becoming more actively involved in the fanzine world. I was positive, so we got together and worked out a plan to continue publishing 'Soul Music', even if it meant taking a massive reality check and a couple of steps back."

Jon Philibert was to add: *"As you know, there was a kind of merger when various magazines came together, Dave McAleer's 'Fame/ Goldwax' magazine, Tony Cummings magazine and Mick Brown's 'Soul Beat' morphed in to a magazine called 'Soul Music'. This time the duplicator was replaced with the brand-new Letraset process. The first edition was massively over produced and for years I had hundreds of copies in my loft before they were finally consigned to the recycling! As has been stated, 'Soul Music' transitioned, as they say these days, into 'Shout' and back to the duplicator.*

Excitingly, the seminal soul/R&B book Charlie Gillett's 'Sound Of The City' was serialised in the magazine long before it appeared in print and I seem to remember the stencils were given to us independently by Charlie – the typeface was different to the rest of the magazine as I recall now!" Continuing, Jon went on to say: *"One day Mick Brown and I had the idea of a Soul Music poll. Best male/female singers, best record, best group etc and Dave Godin very kindly boosted the poll by including it as a free sheet in one of the editions of his 'Hitsville' magazine. I think there was a follow up sheet discussing the results, spelling mistakes and all – mine, not Mick's! – and again bashed out on the duplicator! There was a special record made by Motown artists thanking members of the Tamla Motown Appreciation Society with the singers talking over their hit records thanking members of the club for their support. The Temptations actually made reference*

to the poll during their segment."

But despite the initial fanfare and the quality of the publication, it would be some six months (January 1968) before issue two of *Soul Music* would appear, having reverted to typing copy onto wax stencils and using a duplicating machine, but it would soon appear on a more regular basis, almost weekly, but by then, due to the expectancy having been higher than what had actually materialised in the way of sales, there were dramatic changes. The cover price was also halved to one shilling and three pence.

Roy Stanton told the story in issue 100 of *Shout* in December 1974 – *"Issue number one of 'Soul Music' was great and we eagerly awaited issue two. We waited until February 1968 and got a duplicated mag. Priced at 1/3d - still fantastic, but what happened? The editorial board, so disillusioned that their 2000 plus print-run had sold 200 copies, had given up – all, that is except an amiable loonie called Tony Cummings, who soldiered on."*

Had he not brought Clive Richardson on board, then Tony Cummings, left on his own, might well have struggled and the magazine might have bitten the dust. In the meantime, the other three co-editors, who had decided to jump ship, looked at publishing their own fanzine *Soul Express*, but this failed to materialise and the three dissenters were soon to return to the fold.

The difference between issue one and what followed was akin to comparing night and day. Where that first issue had well produced photos – Gladys Knight and the Pips, James Carr and Aaron Neville, The Glories, Garnet Mimms and Bill Pinkney, those that followed had nothing more than a poorly produced image on the cover. Gone also were the large black solid font headings.

It had also by now taken on the sub-title of 'The World's Only Weekly Rhythm and Blues Magazine', later to be replaced with 'A comprehensive journal covering the vast field of Negro rhythm and blues music'. Content was obviously greatly reduced, and print was often faint, with label listing, discographies and reviews taking up the majority of the pages, but it was the leader in its field and a publication that was eagerly looked forward to each week by its readers.

If there was a groundbreaking issue, then it was

number eight - week ending 9th March 1968 - which contained a thoroughly thought provoking article from Dave Godin entitled 'R&B and The Long Hot Summer'. The master scribe was, at this time, a contributor to *Blues and Soul*, but its editor, John E. Abbey, had refused to publish this particular contribution, a two-thousand-word piece in which Godin was to question whether or not the people who bought the records of the black American artists gave any thought or consideration to the prejudices endured by those same individuals in their homeland. Clive Richardson was to write that Abbey was to decline the article on the basis that "*it might cause offence to readers of the large circulation journal. Tony* [Cummings], *however, saw it as a reasonable item of free speech with which to balance the soul music staple diet of rather dry discographies and in-depth interviews.*"

But getting it out in time often conjured up the odd problem and from time to time there would be a 'double issue' and eventually in changed from weekly to monthly.

Now it was simply a case of onwards and upwards and the format basically remained the same until issue No.33, when it was announced that it would be reverting to fortnightly. Then came the news that it was to change yet again, not in publication dates, but in title. *Soul Music* was no more, as from then on it would be known as *Shout*.

Having seen Motown enjoy untold publicity through the sterling efforts from lovers of the brand of music produced by the Detroit label, it was not really too much of a surprise when the 'Atlantic and Stax Appreciation Society' appeared on the scene. Run by Janet Martin and Judy Webb from an office in London, it subsequently saw the arrival of SOUL MESSENGER, which was to begin life as nothing more than a simple photocopied sheet. The 'Society' was also to issue A4 and postcard sized photographs of the acts on the Atlantic and Stax labels, but unfortunately mine have long since gone. Where?

I have no idea. Only the membership card remains.

Although the first issue of the magazine-style *Soul Messenger* is dated August 1967, it didn't in fact come out until September, and although it is the first in the magazine format, it is in fact numbered '2'.

With card outer covers, it is just slightly smaller than A4 in size (measuring 20.5 x 25.5cm), that initial issue containing twenty-three inner pages, one page having been left blank by mistake. *Soul Messenger* was certainly to do justice to the Atlantic and Stax cause and there was certainly no bias shown within the pages of that initial issue, as the likes of The Vanilla Fudge and Sharon Tandy could be found alongside Booker T, The Bar-Kays and Otis Redding.

It is interesting to note that DJ Johnnie Walker was the club's 'honorary president' and he penned a two-and-a-half-page article under the heading 'ISEETHELIGHT'. Johnnie was certainly a DJ I listened to, and in his article he talks of how he was drawn into soul music through hearing 'Respect' in a Birmingham discotheque, reading about the Otis Redding version of 'My Girl' in a Tony Hall *Record Mirror* article on the *Otis Blue* album and playing tunes like 'In The Midnight Hour', 'That Driving Beat', 'See-Saw' and 'Something About You' in the early days as a ballroom DJ. He is also quick to point out the difference between a Motown record and one out of Atlantic/Stax, speaking of "*the complete and utter togetherness that makes the record and makes soul the one thing that completes my existence.*" Reading back over the article today you can tell that the guy did actually have a genuine feeling and love for the music.

At the top of that first page there is also a list of honorary members. Some, like Willy Walker, Keith Hampshire and Mike Lennox, mean nothing (sorry!), while there are others such as Tony Blackburn, Eric Burdon, Geno Washington, Mike Raven, Emperor Rosko, Vicky Wickham and also The Bee Gees. Familiar names all. There was also a selection of small photographs showing some of the Stax/Atlantic artists arriving in London for their tour, plus another of The

Bar-Kays, with one of the two girls responsible for it all, busy in their office.

One Stop Records, of 40 South Molton Street, London, commanded the back page, as they did in every issue.

Issue No.3 (October 1967) had expanded to thirty-two pages, and honorary members had also been expanded with Donnie Elbert, Jimmy James and - perhaps even more surprising than The Bee Gees - John Peel, while the 'club' was now run solely by Janet due to Judy's personal commitments.

The publication went from strength to strength with a varied number of pages, but always very readable. Issue No.4 was back down to twenty-six pages, but contained what must be the earliest written UK history of Atlantic records, written by M. Neil Carter and Rick Green, under the title of 'Shake, Rattle and Soul'. Johnnie Walker was by now something of a regular contributor.

Issue No. 6 saw a slight change in font style and size (most likely due to Janet's explanation in issue seven that she had dropped her usual typewriter on the floor) with photographs now inside both front and back cover, while issue No.7 (April 1969) plodded along as normal, with no indication that the end was in sight. Had it anything to do with Tom Jones now also being an ' honorary president'? Anyway, after seven issues that was it. The Atlantic/Stax Appreciation Society was no more, which was a pity really as the publication certainly added something to the world of music reading and soul music in particular at that

time. Especially to a soul-starved youngster in soul back waters of south-west Scotland.

Those seven publications only seem to surface very occasionally today, while it is also worth noting that the Society also issued a *Complete Listing of Atlantic Group Records from 1956 – 1967*.

It was way back in December 1969 that BLUES AND SOUL first came to my attention, and by pure accident I must add. Unlike today, with shelf upon shelf of magazines in the likes of W H Smith's, where you can spend a considerable amount of time browsing through those that appeal to your particular taste, the late sixties, in a small Scottish town at least, saw the magazines of the day spread out across the newsagent's counter, and if you had no cause for venturing into the shop in the first place, you had no idea what was there. Throw into the mix that all the other people I had been at school with were into a different type of music altogether, then I was never going to be in the know when it came to a definitive music publication such as *Blues and Soul*.

But anyway, that afternoon towards the end of the swinging sixties I ventured into one of the three local newsagents to see a girl who had been in my class at school, but what caught my eye was a colour shot of The Temptations on what was the cover of *Blues and Soul* No.24, which was lying on the shop counter alongside countless other magazines. Noting the price, out came the required two shillings and six pence (or did I pay twelve and a half new pence?), a thanks very much and off I went. My thoughts upon entering the shop had completely disappeared from the mind! A regular order was duly placed at the newsagents where my parents got their daily papers and it was to appear through the letter box on a regular basis for the next three years or so.

Three months had passed since the last *Home of the Blues* had appeared, but suddenly John E. Abbey was back and the iconic publication that was *Blues and Soul* was born, with the first issue appearing in the newsagents in October 1967, a publication that was soon to become the staple diet of soul music lovers the length and breadth of the country. Even today, those who were around at the time continue to comment on the publication, whilst often paying £20 or more for certain sought-after back issues.

But what about the demise of *Home of the Blues* and new next of kin? John Abbey: "*Home of the Blues was the title of a Johnny Cash song and initially we included a little Country music within its pages. I am a big Country fan still! However, as Soul became the driving force of Black American music it seemed right to make the change. Both commercially, but also to reflect what the magazine was covering/offering."*

"Firstly, welcome to the first issue of 'Blues and Soul Monthly Music Review'. Many of you will know us from the days of 'Home Of The Blues', the predecessor (and guinea-pig) to the magazine you are now reading," began the editorial of that very first issue of *Blues and Soul*. It continued: *"Home Of The Blues spent 18 months building from nothing to become the most successful R&B/Soul magazine in Europe. Mostly on a subscription or small distribution basis, it reached an enviable status within those 18 months. Now, its successor is able to start off as a ready-made success.*

"Gone are the days when R&B music was just for a handful of purists. Nowadays, it is readily accepted by the average record buyer. We sincerely hope that this publication will help promote the sales of records that come under the heading – BLUES & SOUL.

"For the benefit of new readers, several of the articles and much of the format has been handed down by 'Home Of The Blues'. Why change a winning team?"

Perhaps that initial issue was, as the name suggests, more 'blues' orientated but, although the title remained, and as one decade blended into another, with the music moving from the often raw early R&B to the southern Stax/Atlantic sound and the black/pop youth club dance floor filling Motown beat, so did the magazine. Was this something that surprised John Abbey? *"As before, we merely reflected the growth of interest in the music, but I do think 'Blues and Soul' did a good job of covering everything and the journalists with the magazine both loved and understood the music, so not really surprised, we could feel it."*

The title *Blues & Soul Monthly Music Review* lasted until January 1970 when it went fortnightly, a move that simply proved just how well received the publication was by the British public.

Articles, record reviews (many readers bought blind just on the reviewer's comments, I certainly did), chart listings and records for sale were the basic content, soon to be joined by adverts for various soul nights around the country. But for the soul boys and girls of the seventies, Dave Godin's regular article was the first port of call, with the highly respected soul guru's every word eagerly devoured.

Godin had of course put pen to paper in *Home of the Blues*, but here, within the pages of *Blues and Soul*, he found a new and ever-growing audience, and his presence within its pages could be considered a masterstroke and would surely, through time, have added to the magazine's circulation figures. *"Dave had been a good friend for some time,"* said John, *"so it*

was a natural decision. But certainly, Dave was a huge addition, but not sure it added sales, but definitely brought credibility to 'Blues and Soul' and satisfied a certain element of 'Blues and Soul' readers."

He had first appeared in issue number eight (May 1968) and weaved a continuous thread until issue No.90 (August 11-24 1972). Digesting every word of his always interesting articles, it would come as a shock to his loyal readers when they reached the third last paragraph of that August 1972 article.

Having mentioned a few more of his 'secret sounds', he dropped his bombshell. *"Why then am I bowing out of the Soul scene? Well, I have many reasons. Mainly I think I am getting a little stale, and when you consider that next year, I'll have been a Soul collector for twenty years (which is longer than many of you have been alive) you'll appreciate that I'm getting to be less starry and dewey eyed than I perhaps should be. I know I have many friends (both known and unknown) whom I have made through this column, and whom it will now seem like I am abandoning, but I need to return to the simple joys of being a fan because this business of being an 'authority' can be awfully tiresome."* He finished: *"So, for a while then I'm putting away my typewriter and putting on my dancing shoes and getting back in the Soul flow, and the grass roots. But until next we meet – keep the faith! Right on now, brothers and sisters."*

It was in issue No.36, covering June 19 – July 1st 1970, that Godin, quite unintentionally, changed the world of soul music. Up until this iconic issue of what was now the undeniable top publication (in the UK at least) for this genre, the music had been 'Blues', 'R&B' and 'Soul' inter-mixed however you pleased. But on page sixteen, the headline above Godin's piece proclaimed: 'The Up-North Soul Groove Part One'. The accompanying article read: *"One of the biggest troubles of living in London is that it does tend to create an insularity that makes its inhabitants think the country begins and ends with the GLC perimeter."* He continued: *"Places like the Blackpool Mecca and The Wheel at Manchester have provided the very best in Soul dancing music, and in the process have created regional hits which slowly have floated down to London and become in-demand oldies. So, as an exercise to see how hip your record collection is, let's just run through a few of these regional breakouts and see if you have missed out on any winners."*

In this, and the following issue, Godin went on to list some two dozen tracks, including tunes like The Fascinations 'Girls Are Out to Get You', Barbara Randolph 'I Got A Feeling', The Elgins 'Heaven Must Have Sent You' and Mary Wells 'What's Easy For Two

Is So Hard For One'. Those two dozen in-demanders made my own meagre record collection definitely "unhip". But within a matter of weeks, that two dozen, and others, were all there, and I was getting up to speed, with many being still played today when out DJing.

John E. Abbey had also been instrumental in starting the Action, Mojo and Contempo record labels, but soon after closing the latter of the trio down, he was to leave the now firmly established *Blues and Soul* and head Stateside. Was he disappointed to let his 'baby' go, or did he feel he had taken it as far as he could? *"I regret the circumstances that it happened, but I always feel there's no future living in the past and sometimes things happen for a reason so..."* But were there ever any thoughts towards starting another magazine? *"No! Timing would have NOT been good. Life in general had progressed beyond that."*

So, John E. Abbey took off for a new life across the Atlantic, taking with him countless memories; but what stood out? *"Probably meeting so many wonderful people and opening doors for my own career. Many of the artists became friends, some very close friends and many who I subsequently got to work with. I have many wonderful and even amusing (hilarious?) memories, I wouldn't change it for the world."*

If it hadn't been for *Home Of The Blues* and *Blues and Soul* I personally don't think there would have been so many other publications surfacing over the years, so John's contribution to the world of soul in print is, in my opinion, massive, and something that he should be given great credit for.

1970 saw *Blues and Soul* issue *The Motown Story*, a one-off thirty-six page special devoted to the Detroit music machine. *"It is, indeed, a great honour and a privilege for us at 'Blues & Soul' to be asked to compile a European and British version of The Motown Story. More so, because Motown is synonymous with what 'Blues & Soul' is all about and during the life span of our regular publication we have been fortunate enough to witness Motown's startling rise to fame, to the extent that it is now the best-selling company in America for sales of singles. It goes without saying that the Motown Sound is by far the most successful Soul sound of all time."*

The publication contained little in the way of text; two pages on the Motown Story, one on the Diana Ross and the Supremes Story, while the others, not just the big-hitters like The Four Tops, Marvin Gaye, The Temptations and Martha and the Vandellas, but also Chuck Jackson, Brenda Holloway, Tammi Terrell and The Fantastic Four, were given nothing more than a brief pen-picture alongside a colour or black and white photograph. There was also a complete UK discography. A collectable item to this day.

It is also two of Godin's countless articles that make a couple of those seventies *Blues and Soul* issues much sought after: issue No.50 from January 1971, which covered his first visit to Manchester's Twisted Wheel club, and issue No.67, from September that same year, which saw the London based scribe visit the Highland Room at the Blackpool Mecca.

He was to return to writing for the magazine in issue No. 157 (April 1975), having written a 'preface' in No. 156, whilst having appeared in *Black Music* and other publications during the period of his absence. But by the time *Blues and Soul* hit the 250 mark, he was once again missing from the list of contributors. Although arguably the most respected, Godin was not the only journalist of note to pen articles for the magazine, with the likes of Sharon Davis and David Nathan also making a valued contribution.

Another new contributor, Frank Elson, was to make his debut in issue No.102 with his 'Check Out The North' and can still be found within the magazine's pages today, sometimes controversial, always saying what he thought and often going in with all guns blazing as he did in issue No.151 (January 7-20 1975), tearing into *Black Music* columnist Tony Cummings in regards to his article on the northern soul scene, the first such article published in that magazine.

Elson would also traipse up and down the country visiting countless soul clubs and venues, many of which conjure up countless memories if you look through the back issues of the magazine today. He was also quick to support the Torch in its fight against closure and following its demise he was to write: *"So, all those pillheads can cut another notch on their guns. To a trophy with the words 'Twisted Wheel' they can add one with 'Torch'. They can start looking around for another club to defile and ruin. They make me sick."*

But not only do Elson's articles take you on a rollercoaster ride back in time, the adverts within *Blues and Soul* itself do likewise. The Catacombs, Cleethorpes, Va-Va's, The Pendulum, Blackpool Mecca, The North Wales Soul Club, Todmorden Soul Club, The Ritz, then in issue No.118 (September 14-27 1973) you will find on page five the first advert for a certain 'Wigan Casino Soul Club' who were proudly presenting their first ever all-nighter on September 22nd - 2am to 8am, admission 75p. Whilst mentioning the Casino, issue No. 261 (September 26 – October 9) was to see a special nine-page 'B&S Salutes Wigan Casino' feature to celebrate the club's fifth anniversary.

Initially published on a monthly basis and under the heading *Blues & Soul Music Review incorporating Reggae*, *Blues and Soul* changed to fortnightly and issue No.30 saw 'Reggae' dropped from the title. It went glossy in September/October 1970 with issue No.43 and was now printed in the northern soul outpost of Carlisle, and the title was soon changed again to *Blues & Soul International Music Review*. No.157 had seen an increase in pages to forty-eight, with a price increase to 30p. Twenty-two issues further on (February 10th 1976) saw it go weekly, with the price cut to 20p for the thirty-two- page publication. Then, as the music began to change, the title went with the flow and became *Blues and Soul and Disco Music Review*. Not only that, issue No.237 also brought the first 'B&S Page 3 Girl' *"highlighting the Foxy Ladies from the UK disco's"*. This lasted about as long as some of the records played on the scene and was gone by issue No.250. I wonder if the former saw a drop in sales and the latter an increase?

Summer 1979 (issue 284) saw Bob Killbourn take over the editorial duties from Jeff Tarry, at a time that saw many of the 'old-school' soul crowd get married, take on mortgages etc. and depart, momentarily, from the scene. This prompted the magazine to look at capturing a new readership and with the changing face of 'black music' the magazine content soon diversified towards hip-hop (disco had already claimed its share), then onwards to the likes of jazz, jazz-fusion, house and whatever else.

A look, however, at the 30th Anniversary edition (No.727 - November 12th-25th 1996) shows just how far things had moved, with the regular features being the likes of 'Sound Advice' - the new American releases; 'Apple Jam' - Jeff Lorez's New York Breakdown; 'Oblivion Express' - Jazz and ambient encounters with DJ Debra and 'Two Turntables and a Diktaphone' - The beatz, the rhymes, the dope and Mat-C's world of hip-hop. It is obvious why the old-school soulies looked elsewhere for their reading material.

Credit must be given to those who worked on the magazine for keeping it going while other titles fell by the wayside, although when the landmark issue 1000 appeared - July 18th 2007 - Bob Kilbourn wrote in the editorial: *"This may have been the last paper version of the magazine, but we are pleased to announce that the cream of the B&S writers are still with us to bring you interviews with all your favourite artists, from your old-style Motown to the fresh faced. You'll soon see there's only one bookmark you'll ever need..."*

So, it was gone, leaving the fanzines to fill the void, as many preferred to hold printed paper in their hands rather than read something online. It is worth noting, however, that those online editions continued to run in the numerical order of the printed version.

Following its extended sabbatical, it returned in August 2010 (issue No.1034) with a special vintage edition, followed almost a year later with a re-launch in July 2011 (issue No.1046) with a bi-monthly publication running hand in hand with the continuing online presence. But it is a far cry from the publication of old and with only the contributions of Richard Searling and Frank Elson being of interest to many who graced the northern scene and I imagine that sales today are a mere shadow of what they were back in the magazine's hey-day.

Back issues of *Blues and Soul* are readily available throughout the internet, even those very early issues, but prices vary from seller to seller, with some priced so high that they remain unsold for months on end. Whilst writing this book, I picked up a copy of No.12 for £1. There will be hundreds, perhaps thousands of copies in lofts and cupboards up and down the country just waiting to be re- read and for the memories to come flooding back.

N.B. You might wonder why there are no cover illustrations of any back issues of *Blues and Soul*, when every other publication within these pages sees such images used. The answer is simple. The current owners refused permission for any of their cover images to be used and asked for £200 if any were to be used, or legal action would be swiftly taken. That is despite numerous *Blues and Soul* covers having been used in countless magazines, books, websites etc. over the years. So, with that threat of legal action, none are shown, and in any case the ones that I would have used will be owned by many of you and have certainly been seen before, countless times.

By the late sixties, the regular British music publications had also tuned into the increasingly popularity of black American music, with the likes of the *New Musical Express* carrying front page adverts for the Motown tour and the latest releases by Martha and the Vandellas and Major Lance.

RECORD MIRROR had no qualms about putting Betty Everett on its front page, while even the likes of *Beat Instrumental* was not averse to featuring 'Soul' and

'R&B'. Its May 1966 issue contained a 'Special R&B Report'. August that same year featured a piece on Otis Redding, with March 1968 throwing in a two-page Motown Special. Articles on the likes of The Isley Brothers, Booker T and Geno Washington could also be found amongst its pages.

No-one could say that the soul enthusiast was being ignored.

But those general music publications - well, the *Record Mirror* really, with Tony Cummings penning his thoughts on the 'black music' side of things - caused something of a rift between the north and the south. Following Dave Godin's visit to the Blackpool Mecca and his article in *Blues and Soul*, Cummings wrote in its September 11th 1971 issue, under the title of 'Black Hits, No Soul', about the "*monotonously, insidiously ordinary*" tunes and that soul fans in the north were "*an unsophisticated audience*". He would go on to rubbish tracks like Leon Haywood 'Baby Reconsider', Joy Lovejoy 'In Orbit', Barbara Randolph 'I Got A Feeling' and The Invitations 'What's Wrong With Me Baby' - all big tunes at the time (and arguably still today).

The Cummings article was ripped to shreds by Dave Godin in his *Blues and Soul* column in issue No.68 (September 24th – October 7th 1971). In it, Godin wrote that the article was "*somewhat ambiguously written, [it] amounted to an attack on the Northern scene in general, condemning it for shallowness and lack of true Soul depth! In short, the article was a scurrilous blasphemy, and its tone of dogmatic pedantry and doctrinaire authoritarianism was truly in keeping with the times in which we live.*"

A few lines down he went on to mention that he knew that many readers were incensed by what Cummings had written and that he also thought it was way off beam and that he had heard that when Cummings was told that he intended to reply, he told his informant that he had already written his reply to whatever was said!

'Soul Civil War' was the response of the *Record Mirror*!

But if *Record Mirror* caused something of a rift in the scene via Tony Cummings, then it was to regain

much of its credibility and keep its readership through its promotion of soul music, with another of those who penned articles and carried out interviews for the publication securing his own place in the world of soul in print. He was Norman Jopling.

Credited on the 'Rocks Back Pages' website as "*instigating a pioneering coverage of the hitherto-neglected area of American rhythm and blues and the flag waver for the UK R&B boom*", I managed to catch up with Norman as I was working through the final stages of this book and asked him about his career.

"*The best birthday present I ever had was in 1961 when I turned seventeen and got a job that same week as office boy at Record & Show Mirror in London's Shaftesbury Avenue. Two weeks later the owners dropped the '& Show' bit and all the show-biz schmoozing, as well as sacking revered editor Isadore Green. The fascinating-yet-horribly-dated 'R&SM' was replaced by 'New Record Mirror', leaner and cleaner, with new editor Jimmy Watson – but inheriting a pitiful circulation of around 18,000: Issy's 1959 metamorphosis of the original 'Record Mirror' into 'Record & Show Mirror' had proved a sales disaster. "'New Record Mirror' was the only independent amongst the four national weekly pop papers (a journalistic genre now sadly extinct); the others – 'New Musical Express', 'Melody Maker' and 'Disc' - were all affiliated with major newspaper publishers. Unable to compete with their teams of staff writers, Watson first upped the ante with a supercharged chart coverage – UK and USA Top 50, plus LP and EP charts. The circulation began to climb. Three months into the job, NRM's only staff writer Ian Dove, and freelance Peter Jones began to encourage me to write – and I took to it like the proverbial duckling does to water. Soon I was churning out concert reviews, record reviews, dinky little articles, chart commentaries. No interviews though – I had to wait a year before I was let off the leash to meet the stars.*

" '*New Record Mirror' featured, among the requisite pop, various specialist music columns including Benny Green on modern jazz, James Asman on country and western and traditional jazz, and a rhythm 'n' blues column from Ian Dove. This latter fascinated me mightily. Like many another rock 'n' roll devotee disappointed by its recent slow demise (not helped by the death, disgrace, imprisonment, conscription, etc, of several of its major practitioners), it was beginning to dawn on me that rhythm 'n' blues – essentially black American pop music*

was in fact the wellspring of rock 'n' roll and that there was a vast untapped reservoir of it lurking in many an undiscovered corner. It was, after all, for racial reasons in the USA essentially an underground phenomenon. Excavating it from that underground was fast becoming a crusade for many a British fan, musician, or writer, and I determined to do my bit by plugging it with as much enthusiasm as I could muster and presenting it to NRM's increasing band of enthusiastic readers. I'd already profiled lots of black US hitmakers who'd had UK success, including The Drifters, The Shirelles, Ben E. King, Sam Cooke and Little Richard, but I still needed a reason to write about the artists who hadn't yet had a hit in the UK.

"Thinking about it years later, I have no clear idea of why the staff of NRM let me have my head when it came to writing. I had no training at all. I can only assume they considered me to be some sort of

'primitive' whose scribbles would be good for the paper because my tastes effectively coincided with that of legions of other teenagers. Luckily for me, this proved to be the case. I'd already instigated a column called 'Fallen Idols' which enabled me to write

about my erstwhile rock 'n' roll heroes, and my next brainwave, early in 1963, was a column called 'Great Unknowns'. By now I was no longer the office boy, and had been let loose interviewing – my first two victims being Little Richard and Ketty Lester – and when I interviewed Paul McCartney in 1962, what we talked about most was our mutual love of Arthur Alexander, James Ray, The Shirelles et al.

"This 'Great Unknowns' concept enabled me to write about the (then) more esoteric black artists, particularly the wonderful Tamla-Motown stable. I

kicked off with The Miracles, following over the next few months with Roy Hamilton, Mary Wells, Jimmy Reed, The Majors, Arthur Alexander, The Marvelettes, John Lee Hooker and dozens more. But it wasn't easy finding facts about these artists. I'd pore over 'Cash Box', 'Variety' and 'Billboard', crib snippets from EP and LP sleeves, study the exhaustive sales catalogues from quirky one-stop US record stores with names like Stan's or Ernie's, and generally dig up info from hither and thither – anything to cobble a column together.

"By mid - '63 our circulation had shot up to 64,000, and the UK R&B boom was exploding, local beat groups cranking out Diddley, Berry, Jimmy Reed covers in the clubs, rapidly displacing trad jazz as the new hip thing. At NRM we couldn't keep up with the demand: I recruited experts like Guy Stevens, Dave Godin and Alan Stinton to supply more (and usually more expert) coverage. It was thrilling. Over the following years I would come across loads of people – and actually still do – who were inspired by NRM's R&B coverage, many inspired enough to start their own publications, or find work in the music press and the music business.

"In the USA, the actual term 'Rhythm & Blues' was simply an umbrella for any music selling in black markets, coined by music journalist and A&R genius Jerry Wexler, to replace the obnoxious 'race music' tag. But in Britain, R&B had become a rallying cry, a religion, the high priests and priestesses being black and American. The white British groups who tagged themselves R&B and were having huge domestic success may have been scorned by the purists, but nevertheless their love of black music was the engine that powered the UK beat boom that developed from Merseybeat in 1963 and the following year conquered the world.

"At that time 'soul' wasn't much used as a noun – that took another couple more years to kick in (although 'soulful' was a frequently-used adjective). The richly- rewarding sounds of what became known as 'soul music' were a continuation and development of black American rhythm 'n' blues, the discovery of which by mainstream white music fans in Britain and then America finally propelled this marvellous and life-enhancing art form out of the ghetto and on to the world stage."

Norman Jopling's contribution to the somewhat fledgling soul music scene was also seconded by fellow scribe Tony Cummings who was to say that he had a *"huge influence on all soul magazines"*.

With the odd publication (there were actually quite a few more if I am honest) being found and bought during the course of writing this book, there was always the need of a re-write with regards to some of those I had already featured, with the next publication being one of those, as I only had one issue and it wasn't No.1.

The appearance of *Hitsville* may well have kickstarted the idea to create something similar for Chess records, as it might also have done for Atlantic/Stax, hence the appearance of CHESS FULL OF GOODIES issued by the Chess/Checker Appreciation Society in conjunction with Pye Records and edited by a guy named 'John'. There was no indication whatsoever as to when his first publication appeared.

Measuring 12.5 x 20.5cm and consisting of a mere sixteen pages, well, fifteen to be more correct as the back page is blank, it is, as you can imagine, not overloaded with reading matter. An editorial and features on Mitty Collier and Billy Stewart take up the first seven pages, with the remainder containing the US R&B Hot Forty, new releases, a feature on 'The Originator' - Bo Diddley, news, singles in depth - Denise LaSalle 'A Love Reputation'nd Irma Thomas 'Cheater Man' - and the first part of a history of the Chess label.

Issues No.2 and No.3 were identical in size, with the former containing articles on Laura Lee, The Dells and 'The Game of Chess', part two of a history of the label. There were also album and single reviews. The latter issue featured Etta James, Willie Dixon and Little Milton, with part three of the Chess story.

Jumping to issue No.8, again there is no date, but the editorial by 'John' mentions a forthcoming Muddy Waters album entitled *Electric Mud* being issued in April. This came out in 1968, so I think it is safe to say that this publication first sprang to life the previous year – 1967. Within that editorial 'John' also writes: "*First off I must thank you all for your patience in waiting for the magazine. I've now found it impossible to publish a mag each month, but I'm hoping that you will all think that each issue is worth the wait. Those members who were with*

us at the beginning will remember our old magazine and I'm sure they will agree that this one is worth waiting a little longer for. Nevertheless, I will publish a magazine as near to every month as is humanly possible."

That eighth issue was a slightly bigger publication (20.5 x 25.5), but contained only twelve, let's say, sparsely filled pages. There are articles on Koko Taylor and Ramsey Lewis, three pages of reviews and Keith Yershon's column, which strangely enough looks at non-Chess/Checker/Cadet releases. Unfortunately, I cannot find any information as to any issues beyond number eight. There might not even have been any!

Around the same time that the Chess publication appeared, another 'appreciation society' dedicated to a particular label made its bow – BELL VIEW, and although I have issue No.1 sitting here beside me, there is no indication as to when it actually appeared. The best I can do is guesswork again and say 1968, as a featured artist, Merrilee Rush, has her latest single 'Reach Out I'll Be There' reviewed on the previous page and that cover version of The Four Tops classic was issued in 1968, as was another reviewed single, James and Bobby Purify 'Untie Me'. Neither is there an indication as to who was behind this publication, as despite there being a brief letter enclosed with this first issue it is simply signed 'Gloria' with an address in West Ewell, Surrey.

The twelve-page publication itself, as you can imagine, is basic. There was the feature on Miss Rush, another on James Carr, recent releases reviewed, snippets of label news and a listing of the Bell UK catalogue.

Anyone care to guess what that first issue - Bell 1001 - was and the label it was released on in the States? No! It was The Box Tops 'Cry Like A Baby' which came out on Mala in America.

1968 would also see the Sue

record label receive its share of the limelight with **THIS ISSUE**, but it is unknown as to what was published in the way of newsletters/publications, or indeed how many, as I know of only one, dated July.

All those previously featured publications were labours of love for those involved and would like to class themselves, like *Blues and Soul*, as 'magazines', although they were really fanzines, as by definition a fanzine (blend of fan and magazine or -zine) is *a non-professional and non-official publication produced by enthusiasts of a particular cultural phenomenon (such as a literary or musical genre) for the pleasure of others who share their interest.* According to Wikipedia, the term was coined in an October 1940 science fiction fanzine by Russ Chauvenet and first popularised within science fiction fandom, and from there it was adopted by other communities.

It is up to the individual as to how they categorise those pre-*Blues and Soul* publications, but the first 'soul' fanzine is arguably the one published by Tony Berry of Gloucester with the title **COLLECTORS' SOUL**. The 'blues', were suddenly vanquished,

although a hint of R&B remained in the form of a very brief mention of Etta James in regards to an article and discography which would appear in issue No.2 - but didn't!

"*Thank you for purchasing the first copy of 'Collectors' Soul' and I trust you will enjoy reading the contents,*" began Tony's editorial, and he continued: "*The title was chosen because the information outlined in this magazine[?] has been compiled with the collector in mind. Where possible, record numbers have been given, so that you may attempt to obtain any record which is subject of a column or sentence, even if that particular item is now deleted.*

"*I feel that the true collectors of R&B records still retain their independence even though their collections are jeopardised by re-issues, because there are still many rare singles which continue to elude the enthusiasts. Examples of those are – 'At the Discotheque' Chubby Checker. 'Just A Little Misunderstanding' Contours, 'Call On Me' Bobby Bland, 'Tell Her' Dean Parrish, 'Come On Over To My Place' Drifters, 'Sweet Thing' Detroit Spinners and 'What's Wrong With Me Baby' Invitations.*"

Tony finished by adding: "*It is always a good thing for the readers of a magazine to participate in its activities and I trust that you will forward letters, articles and details of records for sale, which will then be considered for publication. A whole page could be dedicated to readers' letters if the need arises.*"

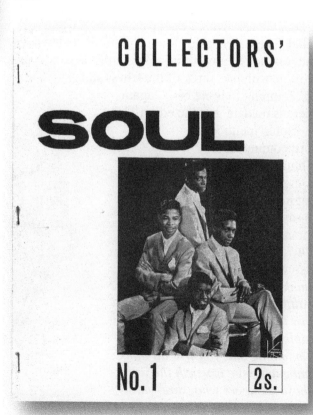

That initial issue contained eighteen pages, including the cover, measured 20.5 x 25.5cm and featured a wide assortment of articles, everything from 'The Temptations Without David' to 'Deleted R&B Giants', 'A Collector's Guide to the Best Re-Issued Singles', 'Discotheque News', 'Motown Looking Back' and much more.

Issue two was expanded to twenty-two pages as Tony got his wish for readers' letters and records for sale, with the former containing much in the way of praise for the new publication, and by issue seven, when The Showstoppers had

in which Tony wrote the following: "*You will no doubt notice that I have not outlined details of this voting business that we arranged, the main reason for this being that 'Collectors' Soul' will probably finish after the next issue and I am planning to return all outstanding subscriptions.*

"*The reason for this rather drastic move is purely financial. I have already invested about £30 into the magazine fund but each issue costs £40 to complete and there just isn't enough money coming in to cope with this heavy outlay each month. The only possible way out would be to double the price of the magazine and make it 4s. including postage, but I am not keen to do this unless all the readers were in favour.*

"*I will be getting married next month and I just cannot afford to plough any more money into the funds – the magazine has got to support itself because I am working hard enough as it is.*
"*What do you think?*"

I have no recollection as to what my reply was, but it would have been one tinged with disappointment, but also one telling Tony that he had to do what was right by him.

Issue No.11 duly appeared and looked at first glance like any of the previous ten, but it was indeed the last one, with Tony explaining to everyone, much as he had done in the letter to me, that the magazine was no longer a viable proposition, and once he had paid all the outstanding bills, "*There might be one- pound left, and that is too thin a margin to exist on when running a publication.*"
He added: "*Perhaps some future creation in this direction will one day bring us all together again so that we may continue to share our views and beliefs – I sincerely hope so. In the meantime, I would like to thank from the depths of my heart the regular contributors who have done such a good job and also those readers who have purchased copies of 'Collectors' Soul'.*"

Although its lifespan was relatively short, *Collectors' Soul* left a void, although this would very soon be filled by countless others, but as Keith Rylatt was to write some thirty-four years later in *Manifesto*: "'*Collectors' Soul' wasn't involved in any snipping or egos or show casing the more 'respectable' Soul acts*

COLLECTORS' SOUL   EDITOR: A. R. BERRY
(A MONTHLY MAGAZINE FOR COLLECTORS OF NEGRO BLUES & SOUL RECORDS)
29 WESTFIELD ROAD, BROCKWORTH, NR. GLOUCESTER, ENGLAND
24TH May 70

COLLECTORS' SOUL
GENE CHANDLER
• Articles on Top R & B Artists
• Records for Sale or Exchange
2s.
REGULAR FEATURES INC R&B
ARTISTES, NEW RELEASES REVIEWED, ...ANCE REPORTS AND NEWS ITEMS

been replaced on the cover by Gene Chandler, the page total had increased to twenty-six and content had certainly improved, continuing to include a bit of everything and something for everyone.

However, despite the following that *Collectors' Soul* had built up since that inaugural issue, I received a letter, dated May 24th 1970, with my copy of issue ten *and wasn't afraid of promoting Alvin Cash & the Registers, The Showstoppers, Motown, small town clubs, shops and collecting – stuff that was of direct interest to its grass roots readers. If 'Shout' was a broadsheet in Soul journalism, 'Collectors' Soul' was a successful tabloid."*

Like the many that followed, it was basic, but, it must be added, much better produced, not having the look of a hastily put together 'bedroom' publication. It was certainly missed.

There are not many publications that I haven't been able to find and add to the collection, library or whatever, but one is **SOUL TO INSPECT** from around 1968 and edited by Keith Lax. So, what do I know of this one? Issue one consisted of half a dozen pages, not including the cover, with the rather sparse content covering Bobby Bland and, well, little else.

There is a single sheet of a publicity shot of the Lamp Sisters, but I don't know if this was with issue one or issue two. It matters little I suppose, but that second issue had doubled in pages. Issue four had something of a 'Stop Press' sheet mentioning that from September 6th, Duke Peacock releases would be on Action Records.

Not much to go by, but a publication to look out for.

As you have read earlier, **SHOUT** was born out of *Soul Music*, changing its name as 'soul' had not only been mentioned in a *Record Mirror* article on Cliff Richard, but now there was a seemingly constant stream of cover versions of American recordings being churned out by British bands; some passable, others an insult to the original.

The initial issue under the new name, No.34, featured Joe Simon on the cover and it proceeded where *Soul Music* left off, providing its readers with a comprehensive guide to black American music. Priced at one shilling and six pence, it was a photocopied cover, blank on the opposite side, followed by twelve or fourteen pages on the music.

A complete collection of this magazine would provide its owner with something akin to an encyclopaedia of soul music. There were articles and discographies of various artists and listings of tracks issued by somewhat obscure labels – where else could you find mention of the likes of the Rex, Flip, Aladdin or Palos labels? There would be reviews of various concerts, often accompanied by an interview with the artist, countless record reviews and so much more, as there was certainly no wasted space in this publication.

From issue No.44, it was edited by Clive Richardson, who wrote in his book *Soul Citizen*:

"Filling twelve pages was simply a matter of copy-typing the various record and concert reviews, interviews and discographies, though the latter was fraught with complexities because of the format, abbreviations, master numbers, disc numbers and the like. All of this was fronted by an editorial page and the front cover, which remained single-sided for several years because of the physical problems of running art or photocopy paper through the duplicator." Clive also added: *"The circulation and subscription was small. I don't think the paid subscriptions ever went over 200, and distributed shop sales were a couple of dozen, courtesy of Dobell's record shop in Charing Cross Road. The print run was a fairly constant 250."*

Issue No. 51 saw the cover price increased to two shillings and the publication going monthly, while No.52 saw 'Formerly Soul Music' dropped from the cover and it was from now on simply *Shout*. No.53 saw the first actual photograph grace the front cover – Tammi Terrell, who had recently died.

Advertising at this point was minimal, half a dozen small one-line ads at three pence per word for a private one, or six pence per word for trade, which wouldn't have brought in a life changing fortune, so it was with open arms that Clive welcomed his first full-page trade advert – Ember Records Speciality label, in issue No.56.

General articles were few and far between, whilst the editorial was often seldom more than a few lines. Breaking the norm, however, was the editorial of issue 71 (November 1971), which saw assistant editor Roy Stanton put pen to paper as regards a proposed trip by a coachload of 'soul fans' to the Blackpool Mecca.

Enquiries had been made prior to the visit as regards 'restrictions' and they were briefed by the manager as to dress and age, but upon arrival at the Mecca, four were refused entry due to the length of their hair – something that had not been mentioned in 'the brief'. One of the four had actually been in the premises a few weeks previously. Stanton went on to mention that a reliable source, close to the management, had informed the organisers of the trip that a certain London journalist, with a grudge against one of those travelling, had contacted the Mecca and warned them that there might be 'trouble' on the night. It was information that was totally wrong and unjustified. Interesting times - and rumour has it that the 'informant' was none other than Dave Godin! True or false, I have no idea.

The cover price of *Shout* increased to 15p with issue No.75, while ten issues further on came the first 'wrap round' cover, along with a different print layout, and so it continued until the landmark No.100 when the print format changed again, with Clive also paying tribute to the original editorial board of Tony Cummings, Dave McAleer, Roy Stanton and Dave Godin.

In that 100th issue Tony Cummings wrote: "*It still seems a charmingly naïve dream…starting one's own magazine indeed! The idea wasn't mine, of course. When, in the early 60's R&B first became the religion of the few, Mike Vernon started his archetypal 'R&B Monthly' followed by Pete Wingfield's 'Soul Beat'. In 1965, at the tender age of sixteen, I and a friend, Derek Brandon, commenced publication of 'Soul' magazine. A frenetic 18 months saw various issues and a couple of name-changes, to 'Soul Music Monthly' and 'Soul Music'. Those early days now, predictably, seem golden days. Images abound; chaotic editorial meetings in paper-strewn bedsits…. losing an entire issue on a bus, necessitating a scrambled re-print… falling into exhausted slumber covered in duplicating ink.*"

Of the magazine that was born in a small bedsit in Soulful Streatham back in those psychedelic days of 1966, Dave Godin penned: "*At a time when soul music is in a critical and crucial state, being subverted by enemies from within and without, it is particularly vital and heartening that magazines like 'Shout' continue to flourish and it is truly a joyous occasion that the 100th edition has been reached. Any tribute paid to the magazine must also contain a hefty measure of praise for Clive Richardson for his tireless and unstinting work on behalf of the music we all love. In the highly corrupting and seductive world of records Clive's dedication stands out like a beacon amongst the trendies and whizz-kids, the pseuds, careerists and weekend revolutionaries, and because of this, one knows that issue 100 will be as much a labour of love as issue 1 was.*"

Issue No. 100 had consisted of twenty pages, the biggest issue to date, and *Shout* continued in its usual format until issue No.105, when it was transformed into 21 x 29.5cm in size and thirty-eight pages of content. Okay, the cover price had increased to 50p but…

This, however, was not to be the norm. Issue 106 consisted of forty pages, as did 107, but by 112 it was back to a meagre twenty-two.

"*Well, we finally made it with another issue, thanks mainly to the stirling* [sic] *typing performances by Tony* [Bourke] *and Rob* [Hughes], *while once again indebted to Paul* [Pelletier] *for undertaking the post-typing production and distribution. It now seems that you're gonna have to resign yourselves to bi-monthly SHOUTS (it happens to the best of us – Blues Unlimited, Living Blues, etc..) since as the years go passing by my 'spare' time is becoming increasingly occupied with other commitments. Fear not, tho' SHOUT may be a little tardy at times, but it ain't dead by a long way!*" read the opening few lines of Clive

Richardson's editorial for that issue No. 112 (July 1977), but despite giving hope to the future, this was to be the final issue of *Shout*.

Clive was later to write:" *It is likely that Roy and Paul saw the magazine as a source of revenue, and in theory the production element could have combined into the schedules of Paul's label listing projects. Once the production chores had been taken from me, I was left with time and inclination to expand into the wider journalistic opportunities provided by the launch of 'Black Echoes'. However, when it was realised that there was little profit to be made from 'Shout' and that the production was somewhat laborious, the magazine reverted to me. My circumstances had changed, though, and perhaps the era had ended anyway.*"

Many of the fanzines/magazines, call them what you like, had a limited life-span. Some failed to exist beyond the initial rough draft, others withdrew from the race at the first hurdle, while the odd one persevered, only to decide after another couple of attempts that enough was enough and they would leave the world of soul music publications to others.

Few were actually missed if truth be told, but there were the odd ones that had found a niche in the market, drifted away from the usual run of the mill stuff and added some quality amongst the ordinary. One such publication surfaced in the summer of 1969 and it is a shame that EARSHOT is only to be found in a printed format over three issues.

It was edited by Roy Simonds and Peter Burns, who had decided that they "*wanted to deliver a new concept for a time that would cover any form of music that they encountered and wanted to comment on.*" This was expanded upon by Peter when I asked him if it was their intention to drift away from the norm. "*Basically, after writing for B&S, Shout etc, I wanted to broaden the scope of my magazine to embrace other interesting genre such as reggae, modern jazz and anything else I found interesting,*" he was to explain. "*There were no magazines like Mojo, Zig Zag etc around in 1969, only tabloids like Melody Maker and Record Mirror, Disc etc and specialist magazines. But then I realised it would be good to have a partner to share the load (I was working full time as a graphic designer) and so I was talking to Norman Jopling (who was editor of Record Mirror at the time) and he suggested I talk to Roy Simonds who was also writing a column for RM called 'Disc info USA', As it turned out Roy only lived a couple of streets from me in Edmonton. So, I went around the corner and knocked on his front door. He was interested in my ideas but was also fully employed and said that he was getting a lot of*

mail for his column and doubted if he would have enough time to take it on. So, I suggested that I answer the questions that I knew about for his column and he jumped at the chance."

Did you find that because it didn't really cover mainstream soul, or northern soul, that your readership was somewhat limited? "*No. The first issue was done on a xerox printer where I worked, with a litho cover. We sold 400 copies. So, there was plenty of interest. Roy and I went to all the record shops in the West End in our lunch hours. Anywhere that we persuaded to take a handful of mags.*"

Earshot? Where did the title come from, I wondered? "*I was working in the Design Unit at the Wellcome Foundation in Euston Road and I met Tom Raworth who was in their transport department. He was ten years my senior and into modern jazz and especially beat poetry and was in the process of setting up a little poetry magazine called 'Outburst' which he persuaded me to help him design the layout for. (Years later he was highly successful with his poetry and toured American Universities lecturing on the subject). Working with him planted the seeds in my head. He and another guy at Wellcome Photography unit (Steve Fletcher) introduced me to modern jazz at Ronnie Scott's (old place in Chinatown) and other venues now long gone.*"

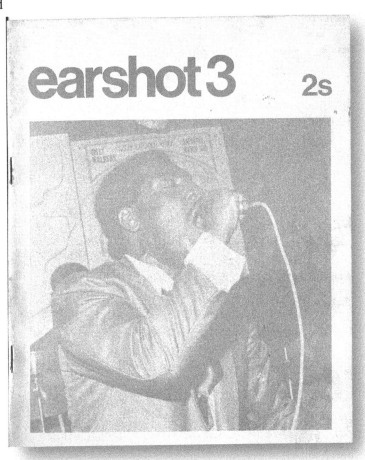

Although not an out and out soul magazine, *Earshot* was a publication that I felt had the promise to become something good and fill a hole in the marketplace. So, I asked, why did it stop after only three issues? *"Roy got married and moved out of London. I also moved house and didn't have room for the small second hand litho printer I had bought at the new place. So, we only issued three Earshots. Roy later started his own magazines, Boss - he was a big King Curtis fan and had compiled his KC discography which is now recognised as a classic and Solid & Raunchy which I wrote the occasional thing for."*

But back to the magazine. Both Roy and Peter had written for other publications - Roy with *R&B Monthly* - and looked at providing an alternative. An alternative it certainly was with its card cover (16.5 x 19.5cm) and its neatly printed contents. That first issue, published in July 1969, contained articles on The Intruders and Gamble Records, Dewey 'Pigmeat' Markham and Ritchie Havens within its twenty pages, and there was certainly nothing run of the mill about the latter two.

Two months later came issue two, with the promise of bigger and better things to come. Dave Godin for one. King Curtis, Walter Jackson, the Herald label, Alvin Tyler and even a film review were amongst the reading matter.

If issues one and two had whetted the soul fraternity's appetite then issue three certainly had them begging for more of the same.

Expanded to thirty pages, it had an editorial that read: *"The happy medium in print has always been one of the bug bears in running a minority interest magazine.*

"Our readership grows in spasms, as the magazine's reputation is passed from ear to ear and gradually more people support us regularly. Until a few issues have been around many potential readers shy away (after all how many mags have started full of promise and fizzled out after one or two issues). Most of the problems can be eliminated by sheer determination and hard work, but the biggest of all, and the most expensive, is the printing bill. We at 'Earshot' thought that by economy and effort by everyone concerned (i.e., PB handling layout and artwork, RS taking care of correspondence etc, Jaqui Burns and Angela Ranson doing all the finished type writing and John Hazell making the negs) we could keep the cost reasonably low.

"But we are happy to tell you that we have acquired our own printing machine and from January 1970 Earshot will appear on a regular monthly basis.

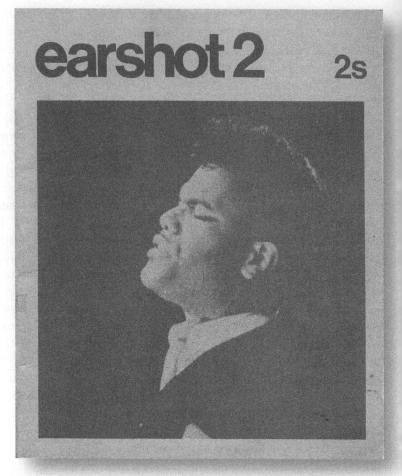

"In our efforts to get this machine we have really got behind with this issue, but we hope that our good news and the final appearance of number three will satisfy all readers."

J.W. Alexander, The Impressions, Otis Redding, single and album reviews, the usual general articles and, perhaps surprisingly, a piece on the Isle of Wight Festival, provided the bulk of the reading, while Dave Godin threw into the mix what must have been one of his most unusual articles in a soul related magazine. Under the title 'Eyeful', he writes about a film entitled *Woman of Darkness*. Not a mention of music to be seen anywhere.

Despite the promises of better things to come, along with the purchase of a printing machine and whatever else, issue four failed to appear.

But then, out of the blue, issue number four suddenly did appear in November 2005 – it was only thirty-five years late! It wasn't, however, in a printed format, but on the internet via 'SoulMusicHQ' and reading it, you wished for its return in that same printed format as the original three. Over the following seven years a further fifteen 'issues' appeared, consisting of highly readable articles – no more film reviews from Mr Godin, but once again, with the promise of *"Earshot 20 should be ready early next year"*, it failed to materialise and I am still waiting.

"It wasn't until many years later in my retirement that I relaunched Earshot in November 2005 online," said Peter. *"Roy didn't have any involvement in the later sixteen issues. I have another seven webzines ready for when I put up my new website which I hope will be this year sometime."* Something certainly to look forward to.

In the process of writing this book I have spoken to a number of editors, one or two I already knew, while a couple of others have become something like the modern-day equivalent to the pen- pals of yesteryear. Others, however, although it was never mentioned, may have considered me to be no more than a pest with questions on something they produced countless years ago!

One of those I contacted out of the blue was Sharon Davis, a familiar name to many due to her books on her beloved Motown and through her columns in *Blues and Soul* and other publications. Sharon was also responsible for the 1969 publication TCB, which was the official magazine of 'Motown Ad Astra', the official Motown Fan Club.

This, however, wasn't Sharon's first venture into the world of the printed word, as she had previously run The Four Tops Fan Club, but product wise these were no more than A4 typewritten pages of news on the group. *"I worked as a secretary for our local council and became obsessed with Motown's music and artists,"* commented Sharon. *"This interest was fuelled by Dusty Springfield, and her constant promotion of the Detroit sound via her interviews and live shows. I became the southern secretary for her fan club, met her several times, so my obsession grew."*

Sharon then joined the 'Tamla Motown Appreciation Society' run by Dave Godin, but *"When this Society closed, Motown in Detroit wanted individual artist fan clubs opened in the UK, so I*

applied to run one for The Four Tops, my favourite group of all time. With the help of Motown's publicity department based in Detroit, I got my wish and during the 1960s was able to help promote the music I loved so much from my parents' home in Uckfield, East Sussex. To this day, I remember printing stencilled copies of The Four Tops newsletters on the machine at work – after hours of course – and my mother and I enveloping them up and cramming them into the local post box, much to the dismay of our local post office!"

But how did *TCB* develop, I wondered? *"I lived with my parents until I was twenty-one years old when I moved to London to work for EMI Records, where I typed up one of The Beatles recording contracts when I worked as a legal secretary, then later on, the original contract when The Rolling Stones joined the company. That was typed on parchment too, so I was a bag of nerves trying to avoid making typing errors!*

"My decision to move to the big city coincided with other fan club secretaries doing likewise. From a flat in Ealing, London, and with Motown's blessing, the various fan clubs were amalgamated under one banner – Motown Ad Astra. It was an awesome task, operating this club during the evenings and every weekend. Not only did the Club provide an excellent service to members, but we also entertained visiting Motown artists. Either driving them around London, assisting with their touring schedules, and so on. By doing this, a personal and professional bond was forged – some which remain relevant today."

What about the names: where did the *TCB* and the *Ad Astra* come from? *"TCB, short for 'Takin' Care Of Business' - so named after the American tv special starring Diana Ross and the Supremes and The Temptations, was a fanzine produced by Motown Ad Astra in 1969. Motown Ad Astra, on the other hand, was named after a phrase on an R.A.F. poster, loosely meaning, Motown – Pathway to the Stars. It was run, as I mentioned, from a flat in Ealing by myself and five others, although I did the bulk of the writing. Both Motown and EMI generously supported us with merchandise and records, so we were able to generate money (but never enough to cover our costs). We were able to review records before their UK release, generating orders, and all the while offering a Motown service for fans on a global basis. When Motown artists came to London (some for the first time), they were given our contact number and address. We either met them at the airport or were contacted within a couple of days of their landing. We all had nine-to-fivers, so getting days off were hard to come by! We also enjoyed preferential treatment at concerts and built up a rapport with visiting artists.*

"After a year, the Motown gang split up leaving Jackie Lee and myself to solely run the fan club from a small Bayswater apartment. It was an impossible task, and sadly were forced to close Motown Ad Astra but carried on with our TCB magazine due to a healthy membership. When costs once again escalated and we could no longer financially sustain the fanzine, we reluctantly shut it down."

Copies of the magazine are few and far between and rarely appear. They consist of a dozen pages of various colours and are similar in content to general fanzines of the period - record and concert reviews, coupled with articles and interviews - but nevertheless they can still be considered an interesting insight to Motown.

As a matter of interest, Sharon Davis also produced *Motown Messenger*, which was a Motown/EMI leaflet/fanzine, (c. late 70s) which could sometimes stretch to around eight or ten pages measuring approx. 14 x 21cm. Sharon was to say that she had no idea as to how many editions were published, but a Motown collector in Canada was to say that he believed that there were fourteen.

The seventies were now on the horizon, but it would still be another decade further on before the floodgates would open to a world of soul music publications. From scrimping and scrapping for information on artists, their records and the emerging clubs, the 'in-crowd' would suddenly be well informed about the good, the bad and the often-ugly world of soul music. They had, however, to be patient and wait.

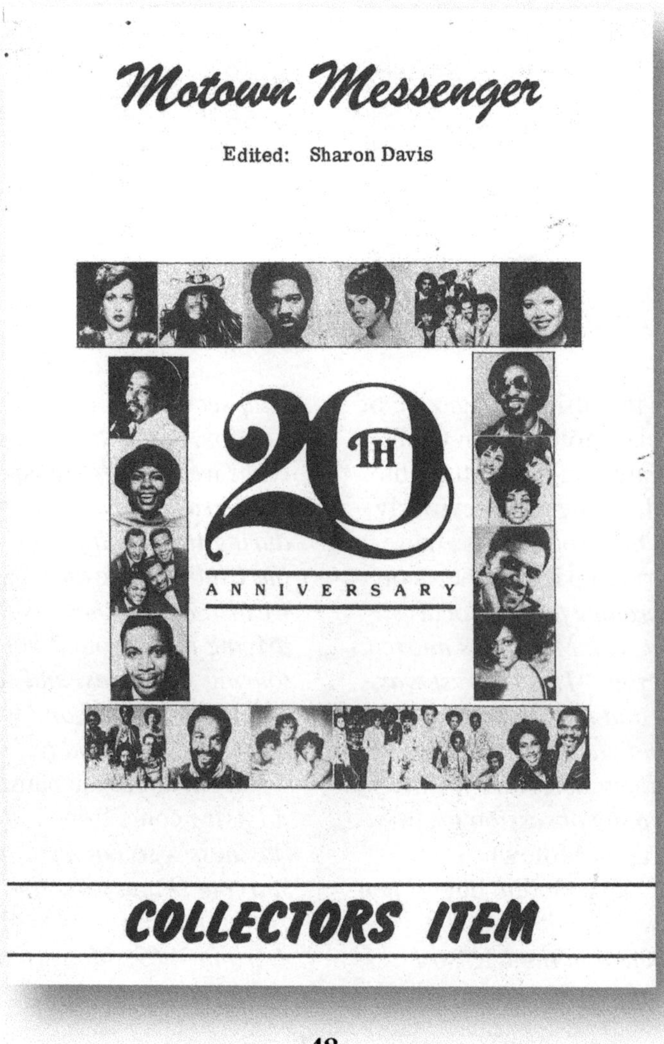

Motown Messenger
Edited: Sharon Davis

20TH ANNIVERSARY

COLLECTORS ITEM

THE SEVENTIES

As the new decade emerged over the horizon, there continued to be a constant trickle of reading material for the soul enthusiast, with 1971 seeing the first issue of a publication very similar to *Shout*, entitled HOT BUTTERED SOUL. Indeed, if you were to get a complete set of both, and bind them together, then you would have quite a comprehensive guide to soul music, one that would also take up quite a bit of shelf space.

Indeed, *Shout* No.71 mentions that initial issue of *HBS* – "*Hot Buttered Soul is a new mag centred on the Stax scene, but with plenty of other interest. #1 has Issac Hayes, Margie Joseph, Lou Johnson, Volt label list etc. 15p (18p overseas) to Chris Savory, 36 Scrapsgate Rd., Minster, Sheppy, Kent.*"

The finger clicking Stax logo was on the rather primitive cover of that first issue, dated October 1971, but there was certainly nothing primitive about the well typed out and neatly produced content. It was, in fact, better produced than its *Shout* stablemate, although similar in size, both in measurements and pages.

Chris Savory's editorial in that first issue rea: "*Usually at the start of a magazine there's usually a lot of guff about how the magazine is formed, what it's dedicated to, and what it hopes to do in the future. Well – here goes ....*

"*It's formed because I'm fed up with watching television, it's about SOUL, and we hope to be here next year.*
"*I told you it was guff.*
"*Seriously though the 1st issue is concerned with the Stax scene and although we would like each issue to concentrate on this, we would also like to feature a lot of other types of soul.*" Following a listing of William Bell's forthcoming tour dates, he finished by asking for any ideas or suggestions as to how the magazine could be improved.

Improve it certainly did, immediately increasing to twenty-two pages (not including the covers) for the second issue, jumping between that and twenty-eight by the time it reached issue number twenty. The cover also began to feature photographs of artists such as The Temprees, Bobby Patterson, Fontella Bass and Bettye LaVette. Contributors in those early issues included Tony Berry (of *Collectors' Soul* fame), Roy Simonds, Kurt Mohr, Martin Koppel, John Anderson, Barry Tasker and Ian Levine, amongst countless others.

Content was excellent, with the usual artist interviews, concert reviews and discographies, label listings for the anoraks and record reviews, but sales of *Hot Buttered Soul* would have been undoubtedly increased by the adverts, often over eight pages.

Present day floor fillers, such as Robert John - 'Raindrops, Love and Sunshine' on A&M and The Invitations – 'What's Wrong With Me Baby' on Dynovoice can be found as American imports at 25p each, or British label releases such as Barbara Acklin's 'Love Makes A Woman' and Edwin Starr's 'My Weakness Is You' at 25p and 45p respectively. Bargains or what? The editorial of No.19 mentioned that you never saw any back issues of magazines for sale! Quite similar to the present day when it seems to be the same ones that surface on the marketplace.

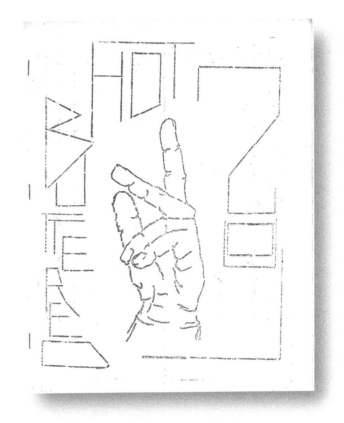

But the likes of *Shout* and *Hot Buttered Soul* had shied away from the innovative term 'northern soul', most probably as they were both southern based publications, but by issue No.19 (June 1973) of *HBS* Chris Savory realised that things would have to change and having mentioned in his editorial that "*the circulation of 'HBS' has doubled since last February. This is due to your continuing faith in us and to you helping to spread the message to all your friends*", he went on to add: "*If possible, I would like to get more sales in places like Blackpool; Nottingham; Bristol; Cheshire; Bolton and Burnley*". He went on to announce in issue No.22 (September 1973): "*As you'll see, we've also got a regular Northern column at last.*" This was something that did not go down too well in many places, but Chris, sensibly, stuck to his guns.

Issue No. 22 also carried a half-page advert each for two "soul nights". One was at the Wheatsheaf pub at 562 Kings Road in London which claimed to have been playing 100% soul on two nights a week for two years and where Terry Davis was DJ, the other being Keighley Soul Club – The Okeh Club at the Keighley Variety Club on the town's North Street where Pete and Flash played "all the Northern disco sounds".

HOT BUTTERED SOUL

And so, the 'new northern version' of *HBS* popped through the letter boxes in October 1973 (remember, Wigan Casino opened its doors to all-nighters that September), with not simply a 'Talk of the North' column by Chris Bloor, but also review of a visit to Va-Va's in Bolton by Pete Fell, and so it continued in the months that followed as 'northern soul' was here to stay.

A series of articles entitled "What is Northern Soul" in issues Nos. 26, 27 and 29, written by Soul Sam, Chris Bloor and Russ Winstanley respectively, seemed to hit a nerve with some, as 'The Road to Wigan', which appeared in No.32, was related to the mixed response that had been received at the magazine headquarters "*regarding the problem of when it's soul and when it's dance music, or whether the feud of funkies versus dancers is as great as it's made out to be.*"

It was clearly a serious north versus south thing.

The adverts became more 'northern' related, while

Dave McCadden, who was soon to become as big a name on the northern soul scene as many of the DJs, looked at the difference between Mecca and Casino sounds as 'Talk of the North' merged into 'Down at the Club'; but it was soon to be the magazine itself that was to merge into something different, as issue No.53 (August 1977) saw the final issue of *Hot Buttered Soul* as we knew it.

Into what did it transform itself? You will have to wait a few more pages to find out. It is also worth mentioning that the majority of issues of *Hot Buttered Soul* that I have seen nearly always have rusty staples, so if you want to own near mint issues, then you will really have to do some searching.

September 1971 brought us the initial issue of **RAUNCHY/SOLID AND RAUNCHY**, a title that you would perhaps expect to find on the top shelves in a newsagent's, but was perhaps taken from the Bill Black's Combo album title from 1960.

Edited by Roy Simmonds, the magazine started off as simply *Raunchy*, running for half a dozen issues up until March 1972. Later that year it was to reappear as *Solid and Raunchy* with a further thirteen issues appearing up until mid-1974.

It was devoted mainly to reviewing albums and would perhaps be a much sought-after publication today as many sift through those LPs in the search for

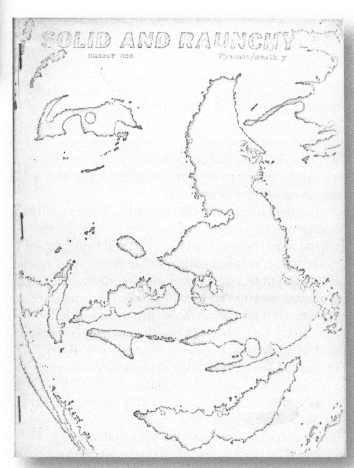

new sounds that were previously ignored or considered 'unsuitable' for playing on the club scene.

A year later came **BLACK WAX MAGAZINE**, similar in style to *Hot Buttered Soul* and *Shout*, with issue No.1 taking a bow in January 1973.

Edited by Roy Stanton, an ex-*Shout* disciple, with Tony Cummings as one of the contributors, Roy was to write in his opening editorial: "*Welcome to BLACK WAX MAGAZINE. But why another R&B magazine, what's wrong with the others? Nothing, of course, and I think it is most important to mention right away that BWM will not only be complementary to, but work in close conjunction with the other magazines, but more on that later.*

"*BWM was started mainly in order to print the encyclopaedical list of all R&B and Soul records issued in the UK since it is too much for the others to handle with their other commitments. In addition, we wanted to print some intelligent and valuable articles of the sort that is usually only found in 'rock' magazines.*" Was that an early dig towards the other magazines, suggesting that they did not include "intelligent and valuable articles"?

Roy mentioned that he would be working alongside the other publications that were out there and this

appeared to be so, as below the editorial is a mention of "*RHYTHM AND BLUES INC. an organisation devoted to the cause of rhythm and blues and soul music in this country. It was formed by the staff of the four leading R&B magazines in this country – BLACK WAX MAGAZINE, HOT BUTTERED SOUL, SHOUT and SMG.*" Another dig? What was *Blues and Soul* if it wasn't THE leading soul magazine in the country at that time?

Perhaps it was a dig, as near to the foot of that first page the readers are offered the opportunity to have their say on the soul scene: "*So let's have your comments on the following: 'Blues and Soul' often refer to 'our music' - how much is it ours and how much is it the artists? What is the relationship of the listener or 'fan' to the music? Does he have the right to criticise the work of the performer?*"

Issue number one of *Black Wax* certainly did not offer anything different from the others within its thirty-two pages, but according to the editorial in issue two, the publication was "*an unmitigated success*" and "*sold out*". So much so, that issue two had increased to forty pages and issue three to forty-six and although no different from the others it certainly provided value for money at a mere 15p. It certainly proved that the soul music devotees were desperate to devour as much information in the printed format as they could lay their hands on.

It did, however, fit in nicely alongside its 'Rhythm and Blues Inc.' stablemates with its well written articles, discographies and record reviews. The likes of Bill Millar, Kurt Mohr, Jim Wilson, Ray Topping and Neil Rushton were all amongst the contributors. Respected names all, with January 1973 seeing Neil Rushton penning a 'northern' column entitled 'Torch

Parade'; but by the time the article was published, the Tunstall based club was no more. A few months down the line, *Black Wax* was, somewhat surprisingly, to also disappear from view following issue No.6 (July 1973). There was no warning within the pages, nothing. What it did do was mark the end of the sixties and early seventies 'R&B' categorised titles.

Before moving on, amongst those titles that were part of the 'Rhythm and Blues Inc.' organisation was *SMG* and you may wonder why this has not featured previously. Making an appearance in July 1971, priced initially at 15p and edited by Barry Lazzell from Benfleet in Essex, this was not in reality a soul or R&B publication, but was classed as a magazine for record collectors, although it did feature a column entitled 'Hot Buttered Soul' by none other than Chris Savory – yes, he who started the magazine of the same name.

No idea how long it existed, but I do know there were at least six volumes and you could find articles covering Ric Tic records in Vol. 6 No. 2 as well as Stateside and Top Rank specials.

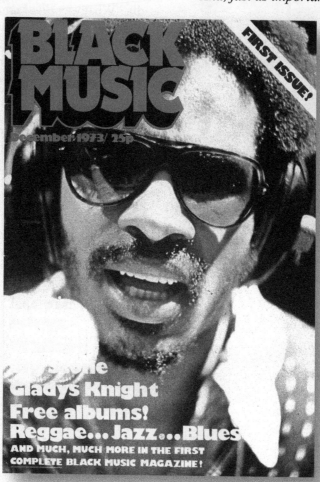

Then suddenly, *Blues and Soul* had a real rival, one that could be found nudging them aside for shelf space in the newsagents, whilst being competitive in size, price and content, as along came BLACK MUSIC.
"Black Music is the very foundation of pop culture. Where it all began. And where it's at today.

"Black music has given birth to blues, jazz and rock...to musicians of genius like Louis Armstrong, Billie Holliday, Charlie Parker, Chuck Berry, Ray Charles and Aretha Franklin. And black music is still setting the pace through the work of artists like Sly Stone, Stevie Wonder, Marvin Gaye, Thom Bell, Bob Marley, B.B. King and many others.

"From Harlem, New York, to Kingston, Jamaica. From London to Lagos. The music is as diverse as the people who make it. It's getting bigger and better every day and it demands a magazine to do it justice.

"We believe Black Music is that magazine. We aim

to be expert and factual, but never boring. Exciting, but free from uncritical hero-worship.

"We'll use top writers and photographers on both sides of the Atlantic to bring you news, reviews and interviews on the whole scene; soul, reggae, blues, jazz, gospel and African music.

"And, just as important, we want to include the voice of you – the musicians and fans on the street. It's your magazine, so let's have your comments – good or bad – so that we can make our next issue even better.

"Together we can make Black Music the magazine the music deserves."

That was the editorial from Alan Lewis in the first issue of IPC produced *Black Music* from December 1973. Fifty-six pages in a rather unconventional size of 29.5 x 21cm. They had Tony Cummings as a staff writer, who was to become editor after issue No.24, along with Dave Godin as a contributor, the latter not having picked up his pen in earnest for over a year. But was this really "*the magazine that the music deserved*" and a challenger to the *Blues and Soul* crown?

It certainly covered all aspects of the music in that initial issue – Stevie Wonder, The Detroit Spinners, The Isley Brothers, Grover Washington, Bob Marley, Eddie Grant and Limmie and the Family Cookin'. They had even captured Ian Levine to contribute in a 'Hey Mr DJ' column. It wasn't too comparable to *B&S*, they had their differences and could live side by side, allowing the enthusiast to make their choice, or even buy both. *Blues & Soul*, however, was well established and had the edge. Perhaps if *Black Music* had a fault it was in trying too hard, trying to encompass too many different styles of black music within its pages. Where *B&S* was more than happy to embrace the 'northern' side of the scene, *Black Music* appeared to keep it at arm's length. Ian Levine seemingly carried the torch and bemoaned the bootleggers, a constant thorn in the side of the northern soul movement, saying that they were using his column to pick out sounds and pressing them "*before I've hardly had time to play them.*"

Tony Cummings picks up the story. "*By 1973 soul music was so well established in Britain and reggae was rising as a significant underground that IPC, the biggest magazine and newspaper publisher in the world, announced their intention to launch a new magazine, 'Black Music'. There were two jobs being advertised, a soul journalist and a reggae journalist. I applied and much to my delight I landed one of them.*

"*Being plunged into the world of professional media proved an exhilarating thing. From day one I felt I'd reached my calling in life. Within my first week in Fleet Street, I'd conducted my first face-to-face interview with some funksters from London, Cymande, and by week two I was being asked to the CBS press office to conduct an interview with my long-time heroes The Isley Brothers. Their utterly stunning '3+3' album was about to be released and I excitedly wrote 'Surely those three vaguely seedy-looking guys in greasy processes and slick mohair suits who sang 'Twist And Shout' eleven years ago can't be the same cool dudes who are currently giving out with the super-70s wah-wah funk on 'That Lady'? You better believe it.' That same debut issue gave me the chance to write about Grover Washington, 'Bringing Jazz Back to the Charts'; The Detroit Spinners, 'From Ghetto to Gold'; and even a bunch of Chicago blues artists.*

"*After issue one I was bundled off to Capital Radio where I had my first experience of being on the other side of the interviewer's mic. I was there to talk to presenter Marsha Hunt about the magazine and the rise and rise of soul music. I did okay though I was a little taken aback when another guest, a militant black playwright, suggested that I was a 'cultural imperialist.' The bizarre idea that only black writers should be writing about black art was apparently out there in some places.*

"*BM's editor Alan Lewis – a wise head who'd learnt his skills with Melody Maker – gave me almost a free hand to write about whoever I wanted. I was living the dream. Invited again to the CBS press office, I was given an exclusive first play of the new O'Jays album 'Ship Ahoy' which turned out to be one of the greatest albums I'd ever heard while shortly afterwards a hotel interview was set up for me with Thom Bell, the brilliant Philadelphia-based arranger, producer and songwriter who'd brought us The Delfonics and The Stylistics.*"

April 1974 (issue No.5) saw 'northern soul' finally squeeze itself into the editorial – "*Britain's notorious Northern Soul scene is getting so much publicity these days that you would almost think they were MAKING the music up there.*" Strong words, but if they wanted to

nudge the north-south soul music scene even further apart, or perhaps just wanting to boost their sales, they went to town in issue No.7 (June 1974) with a seven-page special entitled 'The Strange World of Northern Soul' which covered all aspects of the scene, mostly from the pen of Tony Cummings. It would certainly have shifted a few more copies with the 'Northern Soul' tagline on its cover, but it also did itself no favours amongst the fraternity.

The report certainly did not hold back with its views, pointing a finger at the key figures (Richard Searling "*seems to play mainly discs supplied by bootlegger Simon Soussan*"), the venues, the tunes, and everything else in between; it certainly stirred a hornet's nest.

Tony did, however, use his two and a half pages to praise the Blackpool Mecca Highland Room, if not the town itself – "*the grossest, silliest, happiest, saddest, most glamorously tawdry place on earth*", writing: "*The Highland Room may have phoney Scottish shields and tartan décor but the music is pure soul. This is the stronghold of the connoisseurs of the Northern scene, those who look at their 'black bombing, bootleg playing, dull brained brothers from Wigan' with almost as much contempt as the teeny bopper masses.*"

It is not surprising that in the following month's issue of *Black Music* there were numerous letters of response, along with Russ Winstanley, Wigan's 'main man', accusing the magazine of creating a feud between the Casino and Blackpool Mecca. Others took a similar view, and the article is still talked about today - so let's bring Tony Cummings back into the picture.

"*The interviews and concerts continued to flow – the February '74 issue had me talking to Al Green, Dobie Gray and Willie Hutch. But then Alan Lewis asked me to go up north and write a piece on northern soul. I was reluctant. After all, didn't we have The Dave Godin Page? And hadn't Blackpool Mecca DJ Ian Levine been given a column to enthuse about his latest turntable plays?*

"*But against that there was something I found very appealing about northern soul. Maybe it was because I'd always been a supporter of the underdog. The entire record industry was, to me, clearly built on the methodology that if you throw so much mud against the wall some of it would stick. The harsh reality was that thousands, indeed tens of thousands of records were released that utterly failed commercially. Weren't some of my absolute favourite records of all time – 'Black Widow Spider' by Damon Fox or 'A Love That Never Grows Cold' by Jimmy & Louise Tigg – not hits brought to mass popularity through a well-oiled promotional campaign and careerist DJs? Rather, they were flop records, and the flipsides of flops at that.*

"*So up to Blackpool I went, heard some music,*

The music is black, American and obscure — ghetto English and fanatical — working-class kids in the tomorrow to records most of us will never hear. bad, of burning dedication and grubby exploitation. Underground. Tony Cummings reports . . .

sounds which never made it. The followers are mostly white, industrial heart of Britain who dance like there's no The Northern Soul Scene is a strange mixture of good and Despised by some, misunderstood by most, it is the ultimate

talked to some people, and on returning wrote my article. I'd found information about a San Francisco singer, Eddie Foster, in a fanzine called *Soul Bag*. And with that info I let my imagination run wild."

Tony certainly did let his imagination run wild as he imagined Eddie Foster having finished a gig in some unknown American backwater when, from the back of his memory, came re-collections of a record he had recorded in what now seemed like the distant past. He wrote: "*He'd always liked those Motown things... anything with a good beat.*

"*His hand freezes as it reaches for the ignition key and Eddie tries to remember the details of that record he cut two or three years back. The producer swore it had the beat the kids wanted and would make him into a big star. Never did happen! In fact, he only caught it over the radio twice. What was that damn record called? It was on In Records. 'I Never Knew', yeah, that was it.*

"*What the kids wanted?... S**t. So how come he's thirty-nine and still playing clubs no one comes to? Eddie suddenly feels very tired again. He'll catch a nap in the car before starting back home, he thinks, and slumps down in the seat. He'd turned the car radio on when he climbed in but he can't be bothered to switch it off. 'That was the Dramatics with their new super sound... Now we got a gasser which'll get all your feet dancin'...' With an effort Eddie flicks the dial to off and almost immediately slumps down even further as he drops deeper and deeper into unconsciousness.*

"*And as sleep enwraps Eddie Foster's aching frame with her welcomed, sensuous embrace something within stirs. His spirit unfurls its black wings and rises from the prostrate body. For a second it gazes at the unconscious figure and then up, up, up it shoots. Above the grimy San Francisco back street, above the surrounding slabs of office concrete 'til the city isn't a city but a few twinkling lights in a void of infinite blackness. And then the spirit starts to move outwards flying fast, faster, faster, out across the blackness of the ocean. Faster, faster. As the miles become hundreds and then thousands the spirit senses that tonight it has a purpose and a direction. As the miles scream by the spirit drops height and a faint glow, the recognisable sign of inhabited land, can be seen. It can make out land, then cities, then buildings, then people. It's in England, in London. There's St Pauls, there's Piccadilly.*

"*The spirit doesn't stop yet though; its goal is not yet reached. Out of London it speeds up the backbone of*

this small, overcrowded island. And as it moves up the centre of the land, the spirit sees the nature of the ground beneath it change. There are the scars of the Industrial Revolution. Factories, large satanic mills, the ugly grime and dirt of a consumer community. Now the spirit feels its goal is near. Yorkshire, Lancashire, The North. The strange unfamiliar names of the cities are no better known: Manchester, Wigan, Blackpool. But the spirit feels its goal is near. And as it flies over the chimneys of Newcastle it slows, drifting lower and lower. There are the shops, Woolworths, Wimpey bars, cinemas. There at last is the spirit's target. A concrete building brightly shining with twinkling, fluorescent lights. The Mecca says one, Tiffany's says another. And as the spirit settles and joins the young people pushing their way forward into the entrance an expectant excitement builds within, an excitement which reaches its culmination as the door is flung back and the spirit joins the milling crowds within, into the seething mass of dancers; drinking, laughing, digging the sounds. Dancing to music played over a hugely amplified discotheque system, dancing to the music recorded and forgotten in another world and another time... Dancing to Eddie Foster's 'I Never Knew'.*"

Tony adds: "*My northern soul article made a big impact. Northern soul fans by the hundred were writing in to Black Music; I was approached by a publisher for permission to reprint it in a book of essays on popular music; I won some sort of journalism award presented to me in a posh hotel by the IPC big banana Sir Keith Skinner. Then I was asked by book publisher Methuen if I'd be interested in writing a book for them on any subject I liked. As it had been a few months since I'd been so hugely impacted by the O'Jays 'Ship Ahoy' album and I had a growing interest in the long, long musical history of Philadelphia there was only one possible subject for me. I excitedly agreed and with a generous advance against royalties – more than enough to pay for a trip to the USA – I began planning my very first visit to a nation whose music I had idealised since my early teens.*

"*Helping me make my plans was Denise Hall. Denise had arrived in the Black Music office one day clutching an interview she'd done with a New York group called True Reflection, who'd made a lightning visit to Britain to play US air force bases. Denise was chomping at the bit to get to the States and interview more of her music heroes. I explained that Black Music* weren't going to finance a trip out to the States for her grand idea, a two- or three-part feature on Memphis 'legendary Stax Records. But Denise came up with a proposal. With some of the advance the publishers Methuen had given me for the Philadelphia book I would pick up the tab for her plane ticket and both of us would fly to Memphis. For a couple of days, we'd interview every Stax artist we could then I'd get a Greyhound bus to Philadelphia where I'd interview as many people as I could there for the book while Denise would spend a couple of weeks talking to more Stax artists and starting to transcribe the interviews. When we returned to the UK she would get freelance payments for The Stax Story and she would transcribe all the interview cassettes I'd brought back from Philly.

"It was a convoluted plan but it worked really well. My time in Memphis was enjoyable. However, I picked up the vibe that the once mighty Stax empire who'd given us all those Otis and Isaac Hayes classics was beginning to wind down. And my time in Philadelphia was a head- spinning adventure with every day crammed with interviews, visits to the legendary Sigma Sound Studios and revealing talks with the legendary masterminds of Philly soul, Kenny Gamble and Leon Huff.

"On our return to the UK Denise and I were able to put together the Stax Story, the first part of which was published in the March 1975 issue and by the time the fourth part was published in June I was getting close to completing 'The Sound of Philadelphia'. The publisher had brought in an American editor Judy Holland to pull together the four books marking Methuen's move into the exploding music book market. I liked Judy a lot. She had something of the Californian hippy about her and with some weekend meetings in the flat above the Black Wax shop where Hilary and I were living she patiently coaxed the final chapters out of me."

Things seemed to subside a little - perhaps too much for *Black Music*, as it brought in 1975 (issue No.14) with yet another Wigan slag-off from Tony Cummings, with the reporter more or less insinuating that the Casino and the likes of Richard Searling played Blackpool Mecca cast-offs.

Saturday nights would see many embracing both venues, starting off at the Highland Room before heading over to Wigan, unconcerned about the difference in music policy, but *Black Music* - or was it simply Tony Cummings? - would not let matters rest, as September 1975 (No.22) stirred the pot once again with the 'After The Goldrush' article.

"Sometimes a magazine really KNOWS when it hits the target. In June 1974 Black Music carried its first survey of Britain's Northern Soul scene – the first in-depth account ever published and the one which,

arguably sparked off the whole explosion of mass-media interest in the Northern phenomenon. In January 1975 we carried the follow-up 'Northern Soul Revisited'. Both features reaped a whirlwind of reader response.

"Letters poured in, telephone calls threatened to jam our switchboard and writer Tony Cummings was even stopped in the street by readers inflamed by the articles. Never has BM encountered such a phenomenon before or since."

The article went on to say "many claimed extreme bias on Cummings part", while apparently the man with the big spoon was supposedly only too prepared to admit that his earlier features were flawed, but was comforted by the fact that in general content, history was proving his assessments and predictions right.

But if Cummings did admit to his flawed comments, he gave them little thought when he continued to play Wigan Casino against Blackpool Mecca, only this time stereotyping those who went to the former as being "rail workers from Crewe, packers from Preston, steel workers from Sheffield and factory hands from Burnley". Just because you had to wear a collar and tie to gain entry upstairs at the Mecca…

Opinions were certainly divided when it came to Tony Cummings, but no-one could deny his impact, and indeed longevity, in the world of soul music, and he remains one of "the" names when it comes to soul in print.

"I felt I had a soul man's dream job," Tony Cummings continued. "Each month Black Music gave me the chance to talk to my long-time musical heroes. I interviewed the soul legend Ray Charles. Then, a month later, one of my favourite groups The Chi-Lites. But there was still plenty of hard toil involved each day. When each issue came up from the printers Alan Lewis and I had a little tradition. Phoning, typing and page layout would stop and for half an hour or so, trying to spot errors that had slipped through. Proofing was never my strong point and there was usually a typo or two plus things that the printers had failed to rectify. Checking over the July '74 issue was particularly nerve-racking for me because of something that had happened a few days before – something that showed me that as well as the pampered life of booze-fuelled press receptions, big stacks of free promotional albums, going on the door for any club gigs one wanted to attend, and an expense account to pick up the cost of taxi rides, there was a great deal of prosaic hard work. It took hard work to deliver, on time, a monthly music magazine to Joe Public.

"On a rare day when Alan wasn't in the office our editorial secretary had fielded a call from the printer. They had an emergency. The issue was set to go on the machines to begin the print run. But the artwork for the advert on the outside back cover hadn't arrived. Normally it would have been something Alan would have effortlessly handled – as well as being BM's editor he dealt with all the page design work with its to-ing and fro- ing of galleys from the printers which, when checked, were pasted into position with spaces left for the assigned positions and headlines done using a primitive form of transfer known as Letraset. The printer's demands were urgent. I had to get a photo and a caption to them that morning, otherwise the mag was going to be printed with a blank outside back cover. I hurriedly found a photo in our filing cabinet, rather inexpertly Letraseted the words Edwin Starr and got photo and words to a bike rider to speed to the printer in Luton. I was relieved to see my one and only Letraset experience didn't look too bad.

"In the autumn of '74 Blackpool Mecca DJ Ian Levine went on a trip to Miami. He came back not only with thousands of records for his legendary huge record collection but also numerous interviews after he'd presented himself at Henry Stone's renowned TK setup as a Black Music reporter. On his return, by interviewing Ian himself to glean his sights-and-sounds memories of his days at TK I was able to give BM readers in the November '74 issue the Miami Sound lowdown on George McCrae, KC & The Sunshine Band, Little Beaver, Latimore and many others.

"The December '74 68-page issue of Black Music taking a First Anniversary Bumper Issue cover flash showed the width and breadth of the magazine's coverage. I wrote about Denise LaSalle, Syreeta and Ann Peebles; Alan Lewis talked to Minnie Ripperton; BM's reggae man gave readers an in-depth account of Dennis Al Capone; Dave Simmons weighed in with a column trailered 'Britain's only national black music radio show' (every Saturday on BBC Radio 1); Vernon Gibbs filed his New York Report; and Bob Okenedo waxed lyrical with a three page article that began 'If ever there was an occasion when blacks in Britain could say 'Yeah, we've arrived' it was last month's Black Arts Festival in London.'

"But seemingly northern soul was something that wouldn't let me or Black Music go. The following month's BM featured my long Northern Soul Revisited piece. Its first paragraph showed that the scene – once a tightly knit band of obscure soul record idealists – was now deeply divided. The BM article began 'Russ Winstanley behind the spinning decks at a Saturday Wigan Casino all- nighter: I see someone from Black Music is here but we don't give a damn.' The article went on to chronicle the Wigan Casino's willingness to play pop records by Gary Lewis & The Playboys, Keith and the notorious Wigan's Ovation. If they had the right dance music drive Wigan's disc spinners simply didn't

care about the pigmentation of the singer's skin.

"The BM interviews continued to roll on and I continued to enjoy them. In the September '75 issue I'd gone to the luxury hotel suite of crooner Johnny Mathis who had suddenly come onto the soul fan's radar when he unexpectedly released an album produced by sweet soul icon Thom Bell. My article about the quintessential easy listening singer began, 'Well, I've been black all my life'. This was Johnny Mathis' response when asked whether he was surprised a magazine called Black Music was interested in talking to him. It was difficult to stifle my impulse to reply that it had hardly shown.

"In October Methuen published 'The Soul Book' which featured essays by me, Ian Hoare, Clive Anderson and Simon Frith while the following month my 'The Sound Of Philadelphia' book came out. However, the planned CBS Records compilation album tie-up didn't happen. TV's The Old Grey Whistle Test called 'The Sound of Philadelphia' 'the best music book of the year' and I was told by the pleased publisher that initial sales were 'very good'.

"I'd left Hilary to go and live with a journalist, Vivien Goldman. But neither of us had the will or the habits to establish a stable relationship and within months we had broken up. I took up with Vivien's friend Cathy Usiskin, a some-time art designer living in a luxury flat in Holland Park. Then to my surprise I was asked by IPC to take on the editorship of Black Music. Alan Lewis had been head hunted to become the editor of weekly rock paper 'Sounds'. Within days I found myself with a new role at the magazine. I wasn't able to carry out quite as many interviews as I'd previously done but much - records, gigs, receptions and more records - remained the same. IPC brought in an amiable young man called Philip Gorton to handle Art/Production and though my first editorial meeting with Sir Keith Skinner and the other IPC executives revealed that BM's circulation was a bit down from its glory days, by reducing the quality of the paper on which it was printed a little money could be saved and the mag was still making a small profit for the IPC monolith.

"Things weren't just changing for me; soul music was changing. Disco was now so dominating the soul scene that there was only one obvious choice for the January '76 cover story – my first as editor. We offered a disco special. I rather overdid it. A piece by me on the history of dance music and interviews with Van McCoy, BT Express, The Fatback Band and remixer Tom Moulton took up so much space that along with Part 1 of Carl Gayle's special report from Jamaica there were only three subjects in that issue - disco, reggae and northern soul.

"On the northern soul front there were intriguing

developments. Writing about three singles by Barbara Pennington, L.J. Johnson and Evelyn Thomas, *Black Music* reported, 'Ian Levine, the Blackpool Mecca disc jockey turned record producer, has readied a further fusillade of newly recorded Northern Sounds to infuriate the bigots so annoyed at the (pop) chart success of his co- production 'Reaching For The Best'. (Said Levine,) 'My idea was to find three artists who had the talent but not the breaks and put them in a Northern soul setting.'

"Levine did so with some success. Two of the three singles made the pop charts and were featured on the Beeb's *Top of The Pops*. Vivien Goldman and I had signed a contract to write a book, *The Strange World of Northern Soul*. But after one trip up north to do some interviews I'd begun to wonder whether I had the stamina to pick my way through this labyrinth of squabbling DJs, never ending piles of newly discovered floor fillers, obsessive commentators, bootleggers and music which often seemed a long way from the music I enjoyed listening to. The music on my stereo - The Blackbyrds, Sam Dees and The Soul Children weren't northern soul. Neither was it music that had been sucked into disco which with every passing month was becoming increasingly vacuous and stylised.

"For the December '76 issue I had conducted an intriguing interview with Barry White and also wrote about British 'n' black artists The Real Thing and Tony Jackson. That issue also ran Pt 2 of a piece titled 'Lamb In The Wolves Den' where Ian Levine wrote about his adventures and misadventures in producing records for The Exciters, Evelyn Thomas and Sheila Hart, the latter a white girl from Blackpool whom he had recorded with the US servicemen *Towards Tomorrow*. They were the group my eccentric reggae-playing friend Mike Dorane had months previously recorded during my disastrous money- losing spell trying to establish Mike's Island-distributed Rockers/Movers labels.

"That December issue also had something I'd been planning for months – Critics Choice, a piece where I would wax lyrical about what I thought was the best album of the year. I thought that album was going to be by Harold Melvin & The Blue Notes or maybe Undisputed Truth's latest. But when it came to writing the piece the album I chose was almost as big a surprise to me as it might have been to *Black Music's* readers. Once or twice in the past I had been asked by record companies to compile and write sleevenotes for albums of old recordings and had worked on compilations by blues man Buster Brown and old doowop tracks by the Dells. But nothing quite prepared me for when Pye Records, then licensing Stax Records, asked me whether I'd compile an album of old Rance Allen Group tracks. The music they sent me was the most heart-pumpingly soulful I'd ever heard. Okay, so the lyrics were religious.

But Rance's voice, from its exquisite falsetto and throaty screams, exuded such joy and conviction that I simply couldn't stop playing his timeless songs of faith. So this particular Critics Choice was the 'Sanctified' album by gospel's Rance Allen Group.

"Then out of the blue came a phone call which was to sweep away all my thoughts of deadlines, cover stories and future issues of *Black Music*. Denise Hall phoned to tell me that an opportunity had come up that could transform my life. She had become very tight with two black record executives and with them had evolved a plan for a TV series that could potentially take the music we loved to a gigantic mass audience. What they proposed was a TV documentary series taking in the whole history of black music – from its African roots, its slavery songs, jazz, blues, city shouters, rock 'n' rollers, doowop, gospel and the whole panoply of modern soul music.

"To demonstrate this was no pipe dream, to script and co-produce the project the guys were offering me a contract, a reasonable salary and would pick up all my travel costs, my shipping of possessions, installation into a house with Denise and her daughter and the purchase of a car. All I would have to do was hand in my notice to *Black Music*, prepare an initial shooting script and they would send through a plane ticket and money.

"It was an amazing offer and I leapt at it. In April '77 I put together my last issue of *Black Music*. I went out with a cover story detailing the long history of the British soul scene, The Good The Board & The Plastic – which covered everything from the Tamla Motown Appreciation Society to the latest wave of British funk acts. And after a goodbye-UK party where friends gathered to wish me a fond farewell, I left for the US to begin a whole new soul man adventure."

By 1976 northern soul had all but disappeared within the magazine's pages and it had changed its name to *Black Music and Jazz Review*, something that did not fit in with the evolving scene, and although it continued for a further six years, its final issue appeared in April 1984 when it merged with *Blues and Soul*.

Suddenly, the floodgates were open. Northern soul was reaching its zenith, for the time being at least. Messers Levine, Curtis, Jebb and Freeman had given Blackpool more than its illuminations, projecting the Highland Room at the Mecca into the forefront of the northern and modern soul world. Winstanley, Searling, Roberts, Evison et al had given Wigan more than its pies to boast about by creating the legendary Casino. Other venues such as The Catacombs in Wolverhampton, The Torch in Stoke, Va-Va's in Bolton, Samantha's in Sheffield, Cleethorpes and many more pulled in the dancers and churned out the sounds. The birthplace of it all - Manchester's Twisted Wheel - was also never far from one's thoughts.

Those clubs, DJs and records, along with the whole culture of the northern soul scene, inspired many to put their thoughts, memories and whatever else into print, turning bedrooms into offices-cum-print rooms, bringing out a seemingly endless stream of publications dedicated to northern soul. Even the national music publications were now getting to grips with the northern phenomenon.

In an issue of *Disc* from December 1974, Beverley Legge wrote: "*The time has come, my friends, to talk about Northern Soul. If you've never heard of this type of music before, then may we suggest you pay close attention to what we have to say. Because, without doubt, Northern Soul is the most dramatic and most exciting thing to happen to British music in the past ten years. And we are not exaggerating*", going on to salute Wigan Casino as the *"soul centre of the north"* and Russ Winstanley as *"Mr. Northern Soul"*.

Roger St Pierre of the *New Musical Express* perhaps hit the nail on the head in writing: "*One thing's for certain, if a cult of such epidemic proportions was happening in London, rather than far off Blackpool, Keighley, Warrington and Manchester, the pop press would be full of it and the record industry would be rushing up the records like peas from a pod.*"

October 1974 brought something completely different in the way of soul publications and in all honesty something that would only appeal to a certain few – the record collectors, along with perhaps the anoraks of the scene. SOUL SOUNDS had no record reviews, nor venue reviews. Neither were there any in-depth articles on those artists who had given everyone so much pleasure over the years. There was no insight into the record labels, articles on 'how I got into soul music', or tales from the journeys to the various clubs. No, this was, as editor Tony Bourke was to say: "*to provide for the enthusiast, a comprehensive catalogue of rhythm and blues and soul music recordings issued in the USA.*" He continued: "*Over the years interest in this type of music has grown steadily and although there are many excellent publications now available, there has never been an attempt to produce such a reference volume. In compiling a work of this nature*

there will inevitably be many shortcomings, errors and omissions and it is hoped that these will not detract too much from the significance of the publication. The complete catalogue will be issued alphabetically in monthly instalments of about forty pages, with corrective supplements at regular intervals.* To say that Tony was taking on a task of titanic proportions is being polite about it, but he should have been given credit for even thinking about such a venture in the first place, never mind actually putting it into motion. If ever a publication was doomed to failure then unfortunately this was it.

Personally, I only have issues one to twelve, but I have scribbled down that there were sixteen in total. There is also a note from Tony, to whoever bought the original copies, that number six was temporarily out of print, as were some of the back issues, but it was hoped to do a re- print at a later date. It must have been popular then!

It must also have taken Tony an age to research, never mind type up, and he only charged 20p per copy! Cheap for a forty-page publication and for the information contained within.

Listed by artist, in alphabetical order, issue one covered Abaco Dream to Ernie Andrew; issue two Ernie Andrew to Mickey Baker; and so forth. Issue four was a corrective supplement, but the system of including additions was considered to be "*rather messy*" so it was decided to make issue eight nothing but corrections. Issue nine took on a new format by listing the 'A' and 'B' side in one row, instead of the 'A' side first then the 'B' side underneath.

As mentioned, I only have up to issue number twelve, undated, but Tony mentions that it was the magazine's first birthday, so he must have stuck to his word of issuing monthly. Even so, Tony had only reached 'Courtship'!

So, let's say that there were only sixteen issues, my notes saying that it came out in late 1975 - there was no way that the project could possibly have been completed. Had he managed to do so, then I wonder just how many issues of *Soul Sounds* would have been produced.

As I said, it was one for the connoisseur and the record collector.

With *Blues and Soul* and *Black Music* now available on Britain's high streets, there was soon to be a third vying for the punters' hard earned cash – **BLACK ECHOES**. This was no glossy publication like the other two, but more of a tabloid newspaper.

First published on January 30th 1976, edited by Peter Harvey and Alan Walsh, *Black Echoes* saw its two dozen pages cover all aspects of black music, but where it had the edge over its competitors was that it was published weekly.

At 15p it was good value for money and something to look forward to, even although the 'northern' section was often limited to one page, with some of that given over to various adverts for events and record sellers. On occasion, it would drift into two pages.

If it was northern that you were into, you got articles such as 'Northern Soul – Alive or Dead' by Neil Rushton and 'Weird and Very Wonderful' by Peter Harvey (February 28 1976) – a two page feature on Cleethorpes; Soul Sam's current top ten spins and 'All Change on the Northern Line' - the changing style of Northern Soul (October 9th 1976); 'Shop Around' by Chris Savory and loads of bootlegs and pressings (November 20th 1976); and Richard Searling's top ten sounds of 1976 (December 25th 1976).

It moved with the times, and by the nineties it had incorporated colour and was re-named simply *Echoes* in 1981, going one step further in January 2000 when it became a full-colour magazine, stretching now to anything up to eighty-four pages, with hip- hop, dancehall, house and garage all being found within the content. But by now, the northern soulies were long since gone.

Credit, however, is due in regards to its longevity and today it can be bought in either a printed or digital format, under the editorship and joint owner-publisher of Chris Wells, with up-to-date news on its own website.

Having begun in 1976 and developed from the newspaper format of then to the glossy magazine of today is quite an achievement, so I asked Chris how he thought *Echoes* had managed to do this? *"Echoes was always about current music. In the beginning that meant largely soul, funk and reggae. It took in hip-hop and house during the eighties and, when I became Editor in the mid-90s, I made sure it also included jazz.*

"As a weekly we were pretty big with Northern Soul fans because we were - in pre-internet days - the scene's regular noticeboard for events and our charts (reggae/soul) were often pinned to record shop walls. By the turn of the century, when the internet provided instant access to everything, we changed tack to become a more considered, grown-up read. There was no real way to make money out of purely an online publication, but repositioning ourselves as a longer, more intelligent read on black music - and going monthly - paid dividends."

Like the music itself, it has continually changed. So, I wondered, did Chris feel that the magazine catered for every avenue within the world of soul music, or was it now perhaps more geared to the more modern side of the scene?

"Echoes was never just about soul music - it has always covered reggae. As a mere reader since the first issue - and mainly a soul fan - I can't say the reggae coverage never interested me much back then. But we did cover soul, funk, Northern and deep soul, so it had most bases covered (for me) back then.

"We have never been an 'oldies' mag, though we do extensively cover reissues these days. In general, we spend the majority of our pages looking forwards

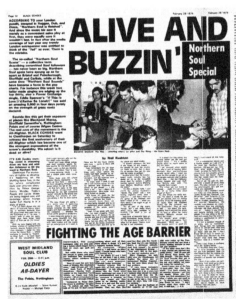

include reviews where possible. We now take the two-cover approach: usually it's soul/R&B on one end and reggae/jazz/hip-hop on the other. This offers two opportunities rather than one for artists to get on the cover - and, for us, two opportunities to extract advertising support out of those artists. The Echoes cover is still a prized asset amongst both major and indie record labels.

"We also gave up having a central London office in about 2003, thus saving thousands on rent, business rates, electricity costs etc: we've all worked de-centrally since then. (Very green of us!) The move meant we were insulated against the post-internet music biz crash and so were able to ride the downturn out - unlike several other music mags, some of whom went out of business."

rather than backwards, but since my own heroes are people like Marvin Gaye, Bobby Womack, Curtis Mayfield, Al Green and Sam Dees, we never forget where we came from. I'm as into Jarrod Lawson and, say, the Australian soul/jazz scene as I was the seventies and eighties guys."

But what about circulation figures? Whilst not looking for you to reveal your actual figures, has there been a rise or fall in the readership in recent years and how does it compare to what could be considered the heyday of the 70s/80s period? "All music magazines, in every genre, sold a lot more during the sixties, seventies and eighties. It's been fairly constant since the nineties. However, we have built up an online readership too, and as older readers drop off, new ones come in to replace them. Our core audience isn't exactly teenage - more the mature, committed black music fan who still buys vinyl and CDs as well as streams; still goes to concerts and buys merchandising; still likes a print magazine in the hand as well as news and stuff online."

Looking at what's listed in the recent digital issues, Echoes appears to be very much, let's say, 'up to date' with current tastes, featuring the likes of Stefflon Don, Jarrod Lawson, Aloe Blacc and Ledisi. Is this the case, or do you also retain a 'vintage' look and encompass the 'northern soul scene'? "During the Covid crisis we have published with a slightly reduced number of pages. This has meant dropping the Northern Soul section as a separate entity, though we have tried to

Sometimes when you pick up a 'job lot', there can be the odd publication that you already have, or have little or any interest in. It doesn't happen often, but it does now and again. One lot brought me copies of two publications produced by the **RECORD INFORMATION SERVICES**. One was a forty-page issue, covering almost all the articles and discographies that appeared in the early editions of Soul Music. Obviously, there was a bit more at times between its pages, but this was really the bulk of what could be found in that publication. Entitled as being 'Volume One', it came out in July 1976.

At the same time as I obtained the above, I also received a forty-two-pager covering the Brunswick label. This was published in October 1978 and was publication number fourteen. This was a straightforward listing, and like the above, it was compiled by Paul Pelletier, who owned the Beaten Tracks record shop in Bromley, Kent.

I have no idea as to how many similar listings Paul produced, but I have seen one from 1975 covering Top Rank, Stateside, Triumph and Palette labels. There is a website, with numerous publications listed; some, however, might be reprints, as number fourteen is a British Motown one, rather than the Brunswick one I have.

Not for the reader, but ideal fodder for the record collector.

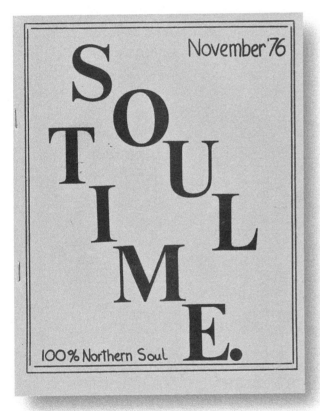

We previously found Dave McCadden putting pen to paper for *Hot Buttered Soul*, but in November 1976 the nineteen year old branched out on his own with SOUL TIME, announcing *"Welcome to SOUL TIME. The first ever magazine that contains 100% Northern Soul.*

"We intend to become a guide to record collectors, Northern enthusiasts and just anyone who is interested in Northern Soul. SOUL TIME is not a profit-making venture, and if any profit is made then it will be used to buy records to give away in competitions. All articles used in the mag. are given voluntarily by people who want the magazine to be a success. For a long time, there has been a market for a magazine to cater for the North, but finance and a general apathetic attitude have been the main reasons why such a mag. has never surfaced."

McCadden went on to say that *Soul Time* would come out in the months that *Hot Buttered Soul* didn't, as he was not trying to rival this *"highly respected magazine"*, adding that he wanted the readers to contribute articles, adverts, club details and record shop details, in fact anything that was related to the northern movement.

That first issue, A4 in size and consisting of twenty-two pages, saw contributions from Rod Shard, Tim O'Keefe, Richard Searling, Martin Koppel and Dave Withers, as well as the man at the helm who revealed a few cover-ups and a list of 'pressings', whilst poking fun at the 'International Northern Soul Club' with a spoof advert.

Fun was certainly to the fore in Dave McCadden's *Soul Time*, and all his future publications for that matter, as were the serious, well written articles. No one was safe from his pen and this became more obvious in the magazine's second issue, where on page two he wrote:

"We've had a few requests for a section dealing with books, so here's a few books that we think are worth reading: 'Bootlegging as a hobby' – Kev Roberts, 'Friends aren't everything' – Russ Winstanley, 'Sex with a French bootlegger' – Richard Searling and 'How to Make Enemies' – Dave McCadden." These came below Dave's 'Northern Soul Top Twenty', which was certainly one with a difference as it included *"'You Got to Pay Your Dues' - Inland Revenue; 'Job Opening' - Ministry of Employment; 'Better Use Your Bread' - Mothers Pride and 'Gonna Be A Big Thing' - Errol Flynn."* But away from frivolity, the undated issue two contained venue and record reviews, New Northern Noises by Chris Savory, a feature on Lou Johnson by Derek Howe, Wigan Casino by Dave McCadden and the New York Connection by Dave Withers.

Adverts for *Soul Time* in other publications would read: *"Features the inside story of the Northern Soul scene as it's never been featured before! The Private Eye of Northern Soul."*

Issue three, again undated and like issue two consisting of only twenty pages, had an editorial proclaiming that *Soul Time* was here to stay, which turned out to be untrue as this was the final issue. Of the magazine that is, and not Dave McCadden.

Away from the silly side of things, the actual articles (in all three issues) were good. In the last of the trio, we had 'A Look Back At The Northern Scene in 1976', 'Still In The Shops – Motown Special' and 'Mr M's – The Time Warp In A Time Warp'. The advert section was also beginning to bloom, with Dave inviting one and all to visit his record stall in Bury Market every Saturday.

Some might have been pleased to see the back of Dave McCadden but *Soul Time* left a small void, whilst at the same time it had not just sown the seeds from which we would see countless publications sprout, but it had set the bar high for those who followed. Many would try and aim for it, but few would succeed.

Further issues of *Soul Time* were certainly planned, but were never to appear; instead, it was NEW SOUL TIME that was now available at nights, all-nighters and via mail order. Edited by Siz, he explained in his first editorial as to why the word 'New 'had now appeared in the title. "*Welcome to the first edition of New Soul Time. Of course, you are probably be wondering what has happened to Dave McCadden's Soul Time, well to answer that, I will just have to say that due to outside pressures he has had to give up the magazine and he has asked me to pass on his apologies for any inconvenience caused whatsoever to anybody, and thanks everybody concerned who contributed to his magazine.*" Siz was to add that *New Soul Time* was taking over where *Soul Time* left off, featuring much of the same along with a few new ideas of his own. He added that it would appear on the first Friday of every month to coincide with the Wigan oldies nights.

Issue No.1 of *New Soul Time* was issued in June 1977 and carried a cover price of 30p, retaining the A4 size format of its predecessor, but only containing eighteen pages, although the best part of two of those was taken up by a crossword! 'She's rated 'X' says Prince Robinson' - six letters - anyone?

Amongst the articles was a J.J. Barnes discography, a report that insisted that Blackpool Mecca was not dying, records to watch out for with Ian Levine pushing 'I Feel Love' by Donna Summer (!), Derek Howe with an article on CBS recordings still available in the shops and another on CBS rarities by Tim O'Keeffe. Dave Evison wrote a piece on the Torch all-nighters.

In his editorial Siz did warn that having a full-time job meant the magazine might not appear with the regularity that he aimed for, and so it was to be, although issue two was delayed due to a printer's holiday. He did, however, manage four issues before the end of 1977.

Any irregularity in its publication was certainly cancelled out by the reading matter on offer. Venue reports on the likes of St Ives, the Ritz, Wigan, Yate, Belle Vue All Dayer and the Blackpool Soul Festival, with a look back at Va-Va's with Richard Searling, Derek Howe's 'In the Shops', features on labels such as Grapevine and Soul Sounds, reviews and much more kept the readers happy.

Unfortunately, *New Soul Time* failed to appear after issue six, disappearing off the radar without any prior warning, not even giving you the answers to yet another two-page crossword!

But for those who really needed their fix of soul reading matter, there was little to be concerned about, as two other publications had surfaced during 1977 – *Deeper and Deeper* and *Soul Cargo*.

The soul and R&B publications we have seen began in the south and only recently managed to venture north to the scene's Lancashire hot-bed. There was always something of a vast football rivalry within the county and none more so than that between Manchester United and Liverpool. Whether or not that rivalry continued into the world of soul publications I have no idea, as I was unaware of the mere existence of the fanzine side of things, but was only too aware of the dislike when it came to the round-ball game. But in the world of the soul scribes, we venture from the Stretford home of *New Soul Time* to Birkenhead, Merseyside for DEEPER AND DEEPER.

If you look at issue one of *Deeper*, which came out in July 1977, the comparison between the two publications was vast, with Merseyside on this occasion failing to match its Manchester rival. But it soon gathered momentum and by issue No.2 editor Kevin Murray had found his feet and the direction that he wanted to go in, and his publication was now a more than worthy addition to the soul library. What else could it be, with the likes of Derek Howe, Gary

Cape and Chris Savory all contributing? It even began carrying an ISSN (international standard serial number) on the cover, something really unusual for an early fanzine.

Full page adverts I imagine helped with the costs - Spin Inn Records and Radio City - but the content would also have attracted readers. In the first handful of issues, you would find Bettye LaVette, the closure of Stax records, Clarence Carter, 'Recent Singles', 'Overlooked Sides', George Perkins, an interview with The Commodores, reviews, adverts and more within the usual twenty-eight pages.

Issue No.6 brought a distinct change of format, moving from a large 20.5 x 25.5cm to the smaller A5. As Kevin was to explain in his editorial, the move was simply "*to cut costs*", the bugbear of all fanzine producers.

Going for a smaller size publication did see an increase in pages and it now consisted of thirty-two, although issue No.7 also brought an increase in cover price from 25p to 30p. This was to increase again for No.8, up 10p to 40p, but it was also to see a decrease in pages to twenty-eight, and it was perhaps due to costs that a ninth issue failed to appear despite a mention that "*a second-hand typewriter had been purchased*" and that "*work was already underway on issue nine.*" So, another one bit the dust.

Out of the ashes of *Hot Buttered Soul* came SOUL CARGO in October 1977, but this was no rising of the phoenix, no slap-bang up to date publication but simply the continuation of what was *HBS* from a matter of weeks earlier. Why mend something that didn't need fixing? All that had changed, in reality, was the name on the cover. Oh, and the appearance of a crossword.

Chris Savory remained at the helm, welcoming everyone back on board with: "*Welcome to what we hope will be the first of many successful issues of SOUL CARGO – the magazine for the facts & info soul fans. We plan six major issues per year (which will be available to subscribers and shops) and three supplements (which will be available only to subscribers). Costs for the nine issues on subscription is a mere £1.70 in the UK; £2.30 in Europe; and £3.50 elsewhere.*"

As I said, nothing really changed. Reviews, discographies, adverts, they were all here within the twenty-six pages. Why Chris insisted in not numbering from cover to cover, along with the pages of adverts at the back not being numbered at all, I don't know, but the content began on the inner front cover and finished on the inner back cover (with an advert for record sales on that back cover).

Soul Cargo adopted what had become something of a standard size for fanzines - 20.5 x 25.5cm - and it retained its popularity amongst the soul reading fraternity with its info-filled pages. The 'Northern Trax' column kept those north of Watford happy, whilst informing the rest of the country what was happening in the heartland, and in issue No.4 (April 1978), it also helped those newcomers to the scene identify between a bootleg, a pressing and an original.

An ISSN had appeared on the cover of issue No.3, while issue No.5 (a UK special) took fanzine covers in a different direction with its 'hand drawn' illustrations. Some may have considered them crude, but they were certainly different and effective.

Derek Howe had by now become a familiar name in the world of fanzines, appearing as a contributor in almost every publication, and here in *Soul Cargo* he was responsible for the 'What's Going On Column' from issue No.5 onwards, throwing together little snippets of information, gems such as the *Irma Thomas Live* album appearing on top of a pile of albums in Coronation Street and someone coming in to the shop where he worked (HMV in Manchester) and while looking through the 'northern' section asking "What does three before eight go like?"

What *Soul Cargo* did do that was different from the rest was to produce a 'supplement' in addition to its normal publication. In reality it was simply a smaller version of the fanzine, with supplement No.1, issued in November 1977, consisting of twelve pages and given out free to subscribers, with others following in March and July 1978.

In the editorial of issue No.9 (February 1979) Chris wrote: "*Magazines are springing up left, right and centre with a round dozen soul magazines now being issued in the U.K.*

"*So, what does the future bring? We hope to be here in the years to come but our future survival depends on circulation and although we do have the largest of all the fanzines, Soul Cargo still would like to increase its sales via shops and in clubs; and in increased subscriptions. Perhaps some of you out there might be in a position to help?*"

Continue it did, but only for another six months as the editorial of issue No.12 (August 1979) announced: "*Issue No.12 marks the end of our second year of publication, and sadly the end of Soul Cargo as a viable concern. Doubtless it will come as a blow to some of you and it is not without a great deal of hard thinking and long discussion that I have at last decided to call it a day. There are, however, a number of other magazines already doing good work and I feel sure that you, as soul collectors, will continue to give them the kind of*

support that you have given to Soul Cargo.

"*I'd like to express my sincere thanks to all who have contributed, bought, written, sold, or helped in any way with Soul Cargo. I've made some great friends and had a good time, but I feel the time is now right to call it a day.*" It was disappointing that *Soul Cargo* was to become a thing of the past, but as Chris Savory had mentioned in his editorial, there were by now others out there to take its place.

"*I was the guy who started Soul Time, way back in November '76, there were only three issues printed and then I had to pack it in due to pressures from work demanding too much of my time. However, having moved to another department I now have plenty of time to carry on, BUT, there is another magazine using the name New Soul Time, so I can't really use the name again can I? If The Jades don't object (wherever they are) I'll call it Nite-Life....*" So wrote Dave McCadden in the editorial of what was to be the one and only edition of **NITE-LIFE**, which appeared in late 1977.

Nite-Life was A4 in size, although it didn't look it. Perhaps it was the rather tall, skinny guy on the cover than gave it the illusion of being bigger, but had this publication continued, then I am certain that it would be up there with the best. There is, as expected, the McCadden humour, but only in very small doses, and as always there is also quality within the twenty pages.

Record reviews 'I Can't See Him Again' - The Twans and 'Sweet Sweet Music' - Christopher Serf being two of the twenty-five to come under the spotlight, while a trio of articles cover 'Press Coverage of the Northern Scene – What Do you Think?', 'Wigan Casino – After the Punks', 'Pressings – Where Do We Go From Here?' and 'Backing Tracks'.

In The 'Press Coverage' article, Dave calls *Blues and Soul*'s coverage of the northern scene "*a charade that keeps going on issue after issue, as the whole scene sits back and laughs*", with its correspondent Frank Elson being "*a joke*". Then it's the turn of *Black Music*, whose coverage is considered "*non-existent, yet when they started, they were all too quick to stir up the shit and peddle all sorts of untrue stories, wildly exaggerating facts and deliberately inciting confrontations between DJ's and dancers alike. Nowadays of course they don't even bother doing that, little realising that the market for accurate coverage of the north will bring forth fanatical support and interest in an otherwise boring mag, still living in the shadow of B&S. All they need is someone who knows the score to write for them."*

Black Echoes is considered *"middle of the road"* and has *"none of the snobby ideals of the glossy ones"* and *New Soul Time* also receives a couple of lines, saying that it covers the Mecca type tunes rather than northern ones and needs to go either one way or the other. The 'Pressings' article is also quite eye-opening, even today.

Just for good measure, there are also a couple of venue reports and an interview with Tony Middleton, a page on English Cameo Parkway releases and the lyrics to 'By Yourself' - Jay D. Martin and 'That's No Way To Treat A Girl' - Marie Knight. All good stuff for only 30p.

Just like the music, the north had begun to monopolise the publication world, but the south struck back with a vengeance in January 1978 in the form of SOULED OUT.

Edited by Steve Bryant out of Ilford in Essex, with Ian Clark, Rob Hughes and Roy Simmonds amongst the contributors, it had a more professional look about it, was printed on quality paper, and was certainly value for money with its 40p cover price.

A4 in size, that initial issue began with a detailed discography of the Hot Wax label, which filled just over five of the sixteen pages. There was a look at the Van McCoy owned Share/Vando labels, followed by a few paragraphs on the man himself and his 'most prolific artist' on those two labels – Chris Bartley, an article on Walter Jackson with discography, and another on The Continental Four, along with front and back cover photos of Messrs Jackson and Barkley, making up this initial issue.

A stunning photo of Ruby Andrews was the cover shot for issue two, a much better choice than the other featured artists, Hoagy Lands and The Montclairs, who claimed the space within the pages along with a Music Merchant label discography.

From issue three onwards, the cover was card, rather than simply paper, but although the content remained the same, it took on a new format, being printed in two columns per page, giving it a more compact look. A couple of full-page adverts were also sneaked in. The content was of a high standard, with each artist profile being well-written, with the likes of The Whispers, Tammi Terrell, The Soul Children, The Charades, Chris Clark, Dee Edwards and Fontella Bass filling the pages.

RUBY ANDREWS

abc Records

Somewhat strangely, issue seven saw an increase to twenty-eight pages, and the fans were excited. Forthcoming interviews with Joe Stubbs, Roquel 'Billy' Davis, Edwin Starr, J.J. Barnes, Rose Battiste and Laura Lee were promised, as were label specials on the likes of Spring, Malaco and All Platinum, but they were never to appear, as that seventh issue from May 1984 was to be the last.

Edited by Iain Stewart out of Weybridge, SOUL SYMBOL was a distinct mixture of serious articles and fun poking nonsense, something that was confirmed in the editorial of issue three, but if you didn't like the latter you could have skipped it and simply read the interesting bits, or not bothered buying the magazine at all.

In all honesty, it is something of a strange publication, as there is no real page numbering, although every now and then you would find a number at the top of a page.

Take for instance issue No.4. Forgetting the card outer cover, page two is indeed number '2', but then the ten- page record listing of Brunswick 45s has pages two and three numbered but no others. A 'Soul Weekends' article has number two on its second page, as does an article on Al Green. Such bizarre numbering continues in future issues. It appears to be that each article had its own numbering sequence. That aside, the majority of the content was good and even the non-serious stuff would often raise a smile.

By issue No.7 (April 1979) the format had changed to a smaller 20 x 26.5cm with centre stapling having replaced the side stapling and it was now a forty-four-page publication, continuing to sell at 30p. But there were to be only two further issues before *Soul Symbol* disappeared amongst the also-rans.

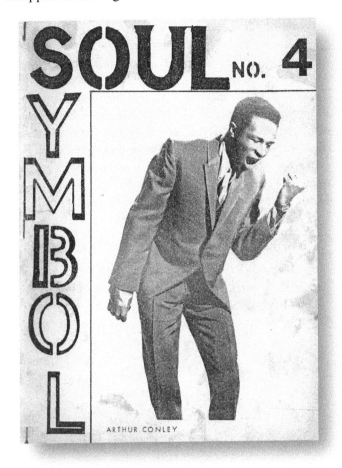

ARTHUR CONLEY

From Yorkshire came **TALK OF THE NORTH**, a publication that, despite its name, professed to *"cover the full spectrum of the soul music scene"*, and was also registered with the Registrar of Business Names, yet another 'first'.

Edited by Pat Brady, who gave a special thanks to Chris Savory in his first editorial, it was A4 in size, priced at 40p, with the customary side stapling, and from the outset it was going to *"report in a realistic, impartial and professional manner on all the major events on the Northern Soul and Disco Funk music scene."*

Issue No.1 appeared in the summer of 1978 and had a promising look about it. There was a report on Angels night club in Burnley, where Richard Searling was said to be developing into *"a stylish, tasteful, funk spinner, proving many people wrong, who openly said that Richard could not make the change from 'Northern Soul' into 'Disco Funk'."*

Siz, (remember him from *New Soul Time*?)

contributed with a look at how the northern soul scene could embrace changes over the next couple of years. There was a report on things down Wigan Casino way, another on Leeds Central and a look at soul in the Midlands, along with 'Memories of a Northern Soul Jock in Hibernation' by Ian Dewhirst, 'Sounds of the Seventies', a couple of quizzes, reviews and letters – how they materialised is anyone's guess as this was the first issue.

So, was this seen as a long-term project by Pat? *"Really, it was a case of timing"* he replied. *"I had got some very good journalists on board: Stuart Cosgrove wrote his first published article there; Timothy Brown of Todmorden waxed lyrical on those pages and the likes of Neil Rushton, Guy Hennigan and Bub all wrote articles. I must also add, that I owe a great debt to the late Chris Savory, one of the true gentlemen of soul, who printed the magazine for me.*

"Lots of our writers became significant contributors to the scene, so in that sense it was great to have these people involved.

"Although I loved putting the fanzine together with my then girlfriend Lynne (whom I've now been married to for 40 years!!), she went to Barcelona University for a year abroad, and the task of putting it together became a bit too much because I was also a full-time DJ by then.

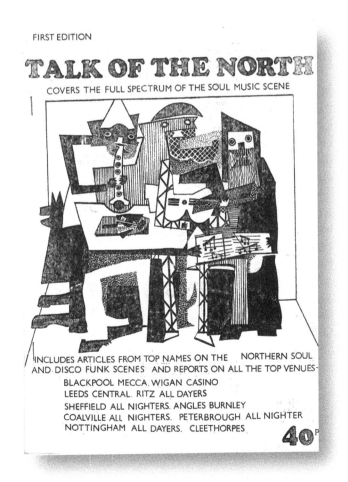

FIRST EDITION

TALK OF THE NORTH

COVERS THE FULL SPECTRUM OF THE SOUL MUSIC SCENE

INCLUDES ARTICLES FROM TOP NAMES ON THE NORTHERN SOUL AND DISCO FUNK SCENES AND REPORTS ON ALL THE TOP VENUES-BLACKPOOL MECCA. WIGAN CASINO LEEDS CENTRAL. RITZ ALL DAYERS SHEFFIELD ALL NIGHTERS. ANGLES BURNLEY COALVILLE ALL NIGHTERS. PETERBROUGH ALL NIGHTER NOTTINGHAM ALL DAYERS. CLEETHORPES

40P

"It turned out that it was a springboard for Black Echoes and we actually sold every copy out!"

Issue two brought an increase of two pages, while the content remained much the same, as it did in the two that were to follow, although for some, there was the welcome addition of adverts. It was noticeable, however, that prices were beginning to creep up. You could get J.J. Barnes – 'Real Humdinger' and 'Please Let Me In' on Ric-Tic at £1 post free from one seller, while another had Bobby Paris – 'I Walked Away' at £60. Too expensive? Then there was always Dobbie Gray- 'Out On the Floor' and Eddie Foster – 'Do I Love You' at £1.25p.

It had originally been planned to publish *Talk of the North* on the first Friday of every month; whether that was adhered to is unknown, but what is certain is that December 1978 - issue No.4 - was the last one published. There was no warning, it was gone, Pat Brady had been headhunted and joined *Black Echoes* to do their weekly northern soul column. Their gain was the fanzine world's loss and it remains amongst the sought-after publications of today.

As 1978 drew to a close, Chris Fletcher threw SOUL SOURCE into the ever-evolving world of soul music fanzines. Like others, it took a couple of issues to gather its momentum, but over the course of its rather short life- span - one year - it did provide some good reading.

If there was one aspect that saw *Soul Source* differ from its rival competitors (although having said that, there appears to be a genuine camaraderie between the editors as they were all quick to mention each other's publications) it was to come to the fore in issue two, with a full- page (excellent) caricature of Russ Winstanley. Issue three had Richard Searling, while four featured Alan Rhodes. The only others that were included were Brian Rae, Stewart Brackenridge and Derek Gallagher who featured alongside an article on Wigan Casino's Mr M's in issue No.8.

Content in the nine issues that surfaced between December 1978 and December 1979 was the basic diet of fanzines – record and venue reviews, with a considerable number of records for sale to whet the appetite. Page content slowly increased from twenty-six to thirty-four, with the first real article coming in issue three, when Soul Sam put pen to paper and wrote about the 'Sad State of Northern Soul Today'.

Sam wrote: *"As an insider who has been a fan of 1960's soul for over ten years, I feel compelled to write* [about] *its sorry state at present and try to explain how this has happened.*

"Since 1963, I have been buying new soul releases and going to clubs like 'The Scene' and 'Wheel' in Manchester to hear the new sounds – my interest was always in NEW material, and this led me in later years to the the 'Torch' and Blackpool Mecca, where the atmosphere was electric, the floor full to established and brand-new sounds of varying tempo's. Everyone looked forward to the new 'Monsters' and 90% plus of these were good soul records. At this time, I became a DJ as well as a collector and customer, and in the early 1970's the scene was at its best– people enthusiastic on the floor and off it, plus few commercial pressures.

"Since 1974, certain changes have occurred, all of which have worked against the scene in general, and 'NEW' northern sounds in particular. The split between funk and northern took a lot of old Mecca fans into funk, leading them to reject nearly all northern apart from the Mecca oldies they remember. The one's who remained loyal to northern attended the new all-nighters, especially Wigan, latched on generally to the faster stompers (I wish I'd never used that word) among the newies, and the oldies scene developed, many of the sounds of course, not being oldies to people just joining the scene. These two things taken together have led to the 'oldies explosion', which to me is so very bad - and personally boring) for the scene and can lead to one of two things – it will disappear up its own backside or remain in a 'time warp' like the 1950's rock and roll scene."

Sam went on to write about there being too many venues and commercialism, finishing his piece by saying: *"Finally, unless some of what I've mentioned in the last paragraph happens,* [finding the right venue

to play the 'new' sounds and the willingness for people brainwashed by regurgitated oldies and 'pop' newies accepting them] *I shall seriously consider leaving the scene, despite being just as enthusiastic when I hear a good new sound. I do though feel it's a waste of time travelling, if you're inundated with requests for pop crap or the same 'oldies' – however good some of these are, the magic has gone on the 1000th time of hearing, surely!"*

Strangely, Sam is still on the scene today, sometimes found playing Motown sets at what are generally 'oldies' events; but he also stuck to his guns, by playing some excellent sets in the 'modern' rooms. Even more strangely, Sam's 'outburst' saw only one letter arrive at the editor's home and it came from Chris King of whom Sam had written: "*The Midlands is suffering a massive overdose of King disease."* Chris hit back with: "*He did not think that when I was paying him £25 to £30 a time to DJ for me a couple of months ago, but since I have not used him so frequently, his attitude has changed."* Chris went on to say that he picked DJs who would fill the floor and play what the crowd wanted as he ran events purely to make money.

Record and venue reviews continued to fill the majority of the pages, which were all very well, but perhaps a few more general articles might have helped *Soul Source* along the bumpy road. As it was, Chris wrote in issue nine that "*We have made very little money, if any at all, in fact we've subsidised heavily*

from our own pockets", going on to add that the cover price was going up "*as most of our income is based on that. We are raising it from 35p to 50p, it may sound like a steep rise but we hope to keep it at that for at least a year. If you don't want to pay it you don't have to, and eventually we will have to cease publication."*

I have yet to see an issue ten, so perhaps, disenchanted by it all, Chris simply decided that enough was enough, leaving the publication world to others.

You can't keep a good man down - and that saying certainly applied to Dave McCadden, as March 1979 found him back in the soul in print marketplace with his latest offering – IT'S THE BEAT, A4 in size like the majority of current publications and consisting of twenty packed pages for 40p.

Three pages on the Carousel All-Dayer in Manchester; a crossword where you could win an album took up a further two pages; a review of some stompers takes up another three; followed by two pages of Richard Searling's current big plays: Joe Matthews – 'I Don't like To Lose', Jay Traynor – 'Up and Over' and 'Cross Your Heart' by Yvonne and the Violets being only three of many mentioned. There was 'What Northern Soul Means To Me', a few old adverts, a full page promotion to buy *Soul Symbol* and strangely on the second last page comes Dave's editorial. His usual sense of humour can also be found scattered through the pages.

For some unknown reason there was no second issue of *It's The Beat*. Perhaps there was never intended to be one!

When you don't have a copy of the first issue of a particular fanzine/magazine it is not so much annoying, but it does make it difficult to actually tell when that particular publication first came out. That was the problem I encountered with OKEH NORTHERN SOUL, so I made that my first question to editor Glyn Thornhill. "*First issue, if memory serves me right, was late 1979,"* came the reply. Great stuff, as the first issue I have is number two and the others I have, although numbered, are undated. "*Issue two! Wow,"* exclaimed Glyn. "*I don't hold a copy of that myself, as during a house move circa mid-80s, I lost all but issue four onwards."*

Originally, *Okeh* was some dozen pages stapled together, but when issue four came out, it had materialised into a creditable A5 size publication, printed on light blue paper, with the content listed on the front cover.

As mentioned a few lines back, I don't have a copy of issue number one, and only have four of the seven issues that Glyn published; unfortunately issue number three is also one I have missing, and apparently, some of the comments within the pages of that third issue had upset "*certain DJs/promoters*" according to the editorial in issue four. So, Glyn was put on the spot and asked to throw some light as to what he had said that ruffled a few feathers. All he would say was: "*Won't go into too much detail but the 60s Stafford Mafia brigade and a certain DJ threatened to have me shot…*"

Must get a hold of that third issue!

Anyway, Glyn survived, adding in the editorial of that fourth issue: "*I have even had people telling me what I should write. Personally, my involvement in the scene is purely sheer enjoyment, and, I suggest that people getting uptight about certain issues to go and…*

"*This magazine is portraying a point of view, whether praise or criticism of current aspects on the soul circuit. In my opinion journalism of this nature has been lacking for a number of years.*"

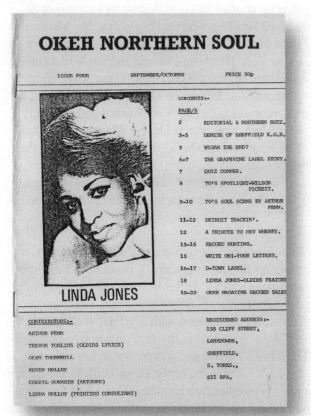

Overall, it was a magazine that carried a good mix of articles, and if you could get Richard Searling into contributing you were certainly doing something right. Richard could be found in issue number five giving a brief look at 1981. Other 'names' to be found within the pages of *Okeh* were Soul Sam, Arthur Fenn, Richard Domar, Rod Dearlove and Keith Rylatt, quite a line-up. You would find reviews, both records and venues, individual artist features, letters and much more, so I wondered about circulation figures? "*Issue*

one had only fifty and each issue after we upped the print run. If memory serves, issue number two was one hundred, issue three two hundred and so on…

"*I think at the height of Clifton Hall, Rotherham's all-nighter scene, we had a circulation run of five hundred for issues six and seven, with many selling at venues rather than mail order in those days.*"

The last issue I have is number seven, but with the infrequency of many of the publications available and not actually being around the scene at the time, it is always difficult to tell if the last issue that I have is actually the 'last' one, or if others surfaced but have disappeared from sight altogether. "*No, issue seven was the final issue - the fanzine was consuming lots of time and effort. I'd also started a new job. However, the main reason was the printing firm we used - a Women's Co-Operative, and they were moving premises, or couldn't commit to printing any more, so with exorbitant costs elsewhere, it seemed time to call it a day.*

"*Looking back, I'm proud that the music we reviewed has stood the test of time and many of our Top 20 chart, circa 1981, are staple classics on the rare Soul Scene today.*

"*If I had to pick out any low points, the politics in hindsight being controversial to gain sales was a bad move, creating lots of animosity and threats. But we are all passionate about the music no matter what and that enthusiasm shone through.*"

It's September 1979 and Wigan Casino had been pulling in the crowds and churning out the sounds for six years. It had become something of a place of pilgrimage. If you were into northern soul you just had to go and be one of many sweat-drenched individuals in that cavernous dance hall. As I have said elsewhere in the book, I didn't, as football was my number one priority. I did do the Twisted Wheel and the Mecca, but, to my regret now, not the Casino.

Anyway, back in September 1979, to celebrate those momentous six years, it was decided that the time was right for the Casino to bring out its own magazine and so NORTHERN NOISE was born. Today, like many of the sounds that pulled the attendees onto the dance floor and attracted the crowds to Wigan like moths to a flame, the magazine is very collectable and sought after.

This thirty-two-page A5 size magazine is, I suppose, one of the 'must haves' for any soul magazine/fanzine collector. It certainly was for me, but I wasn't so enthusiastic as to want to pay the prices you would find it listed at on the internet. I was eventually grateful to get all four issues together for less than the price of one internet copy.

Northern Noise

NUMBER 2

40p

HAVE A STOMPING CHRISTMAS

AND A
NORTHERN NEW YEAR

Here it is - The Poll you've been asking for - who REALLY ARE the best and worst!

YOUR CHANCE TO VOTE!

plus Mr. M's Special

plus COMPS - LETTERS - FEATURES, ETC., ETC., inside just for you!

But what about content? Issue one has Richard Searling writing about being on the road with Edwin Starr, along with listing his current Top 25 tunes.

Northern Noise

NUMBER 1   40p

SPECIAL TRIBUTE TO SIX INCREDIBLE YEARS AT WIGAN CASINO
Plus THE MOD REVIVAL - WHERE WILL IT END?
PLUS LOTS MORE INSIDE

No.1? 'Where I'm Not Wanted' by Eddie Holman. There is an article on Grapevine Records, Roger St. Pierre writes about the Mod Revival, and Russ writes about the past six years at the Casino. Mike Walker, the Casino manager, tells of how he came to know Wigan. Russ appears again, listing his Wigan all-time Top 20, with Tobi Legend's 'Time Will Pass You By' edging

out Frank Wilson and, perhaps more surprisingly for some, Eddie Spencer's 'If This Is Love'. *Blues and Soul* make a contribution by promoting their publication and there is detailed look at the DJs who spun the tunes in the main room – Russ, Richard, Dave Evison and Pat Brady, and in Mr M's – Kenny Spence, Brian Rae, Stuart Brackenridge, Derek Gallagher, Martin Barnfather (aka Soul Sam), Steve Whittle and Keith Minshull. There are, as could be expected, numerous adverts, for record labels, the Casino and also Spencer trousers.

It was edging towards Christmas when issue two appeared with much of the same. Kev Roberts found his way onto the pages promoting his Destiny label, while Richard's top all-nighter sound was now Carol Anderson's 'Sad Girl'. A letters page had also materialised within the pages.

Despite offering a six-month subscription for £3, only four issues were to appear. Issue three came out in January 1980 and issue four a few months later, both retaining the same format as the previous two. All, as mentioned, are very much sought after today.

There was, however, one other Casino related publication – **THE WIGAN CASINO STORY**, again A5 in size and put together by who else but Russ Winstanley – "*a souvenir booklet available in a very limited edition to the thousands of members of the legendary Casino*". Limited edition? Thousands of members? Wonder how many were actually printed and, perhaps more to the point, how many are still around?

Twenty pages of mainly photos and a couple of adverts. Three pages on the 'Russ Winstanley Story'

Wigan Casino Story

RUSS WINSTANLEY

and Mike Walkers' piece from that first issue of *Northern Noise* reproduced is all the reading matter. Nothing excitable, but for those who hang onto the memories of the Casino, very collectable.

Desktop publishing was still, like the resurrection of northern soul itself, to come spinning across the dance floors, leaving those prospective editors-cum- designers to come up with their own cover ideas and page lay-outs. Many opted for label scans or a particular artist's photograph, but others were like Steve Guarnori and Kevin Griffin, who were a little more artistic when it came to their publication **NORTHERN LINE**, which first appeared towards the end of 1979. Not only did the covers take on a completely different look to their stablemates of the time, the article headings were also often hand-written in various fonts and with different pens. It was certainly different, although so similar in style – A4, photocopied and side-stapled.

For those who don't have any issues of *Northern Line*, there are not many to go looking for, and if you only have issues one, two and three, then you have the full set. But then again, you don't, as will be explained.

Before I do, let's drift back to the beginning, and I asked Steve how *Northern Line* came into being. Did it have anything to do with the fact that he had contributed to other publications and simply fancied doing one of his own? "*Yes. Kev Griffin and myself started off by producing a newsletter for northern soul fans in West Kent, a double side of A4 with sounds on it, news about venues, gossip, piss takes, that kind of stuff, and 'The Northern Line' was an extension of that. We only did fifteen copies of the first issue and gave them out to the locals! After that we went up to fifty copies and we would sell them at places like 6Ts.*

"*I did most of the typing, and used to throw the office secretary off of her typewriter, so to speak, at lunchtimes to type up the articles. I was printing them off on the works photocopier in my lunch hours and Kevin was responsible for some of the articles and subscriptions and promotion etc.*"

Kev was to add: "*It was called the Northern Line, because we used the Northern Line tube to get to Euston station and then on to Wigan.*"

And now, explanation time.

There were only three issues of *The Northern Line*, but in the editorial of that third issue Kevin wrote: "*This will be the last edition of the Northern Line in its present form, why? Because we're changing the name. Steve and I have had a serious chat, which makes a change 'cause we usually row, and both of us have agreed that by calling the mag. 'Northern Line', we were limiting ourselves to much in the things we wanted to put in it. It's also a sad fact that the Northern Scene is in many respects shrinking and for this venture to be any sought [sic] of success we need to appeal to a wider field, the soul scene in general. "So, having said that, let me tell you what's in store for the future. We are changing the name to 'Black Beat' (Steve's suggestion, sadistic aint he?), incorporating the Northern Line, so the N.L. won't be lost for good, it's just shrinking somewhat and becoming part of 'Black Beat'. Got it? Good, 'cause I aint.*"

But before we move onto *Black Beat* – we might as well continue with it here instead of fitting it into the actual history in July 1980 when it first came out, let's have a quick look at what *Northern Line* had on offer for those initial purchasers.

For the anoraks, there was 'Matrix Marks', a guide to what to look for when buying in respect of what was an original or a bootleg, articles on the likes of The Impressions, Steve Cropper, Edwin Starr, Eddie Holman and the Grapevine label. Almost forgot to add that there was also a giant crossword – with its unusual numbering sequence stretching to 276 across!

But the one that grabbed the attention more was Steve's piece on the current northern scene. He had spoken previously on the split on the scene, not the Mecca/Casino one from 1975, but the soul tunes/pop tunes one that happily seemed to disappear. He was voicing his concern about the music being "s*lap bang in the middle of its biggest ever, if not its biggest ever, transition period. The falling attendances and empty spaces on the Wigan dance floor show that. Thankfully the atrocities of Muriel Day, Petula Clark and Anita Harris have bit the dust, as have most of the people who went for that sought [sic] of thing. What's left now is a smaller circle – albeit a better one – one that now contains more or less exclusively, the fans of Black American music (as opposed to anything that goes stomp). Despite this seemingly 'purified' state at which we find ourselves, I feel that the scene is in the most dangerous position ever.*" Thankfully that 'danger' subsided and the scene today is as strong as ever.

Oddly, you might actually still hear Muriel Day at certain venues!

Continuing in the same format, *Black Beat and Northern Line* No.4 had a map of the Harlem area of New York on its cover - told you it was different - while the actual content was much of the same, although minus the crossword, as everyone was still trying to complete that first one! A note on page two told those who were after copies of the first three issues that they were out of luck as they had all been sold. Such was the popularity of the magazine that issue four was also to be a sell-out.

EDWARD HAMILTON   CARRIE RECORDING CO.

FULL POLL 84 RESULTS

Packed with Soul info news & reviews

Issue five had something of a Detroit ring to it, with a social history of the city, a piece on the riots of 1967, part one of 'Detroit's Soul Music' and 'Motown the Early Years'. This issue was also to see the first regular column from Rod Dearlove, a name that will surface more prominently later on, although his article in issue No.6 on 'bootlegging' was worth the 10p cover increase alone.

That sixth issue had seen 'Northern Line' disappear from the cover, but it was to make a fleeting appearance on the front of issue eight, which heralded not so much a new dawn, but a new size, as it was now a journey back in time to the 20.5 x 25.5cm size of old. This slight reduction in size gave the publication a more 'compact' look, something I liked, while I also consider this issue to be Steve and Kev's best one yet, one that included 'Starting to Collect Records? A Few

Tips For Beginners' by Steve and 'Modern Soul Scene', the first contribution from Soul Sam. Among his selected tunes were Shirley Brown 'You've Got To Like What You Do' and Daybreak 'I Need Love'.

If the change from *Northern Line* to *Black Beat* was to cause a little confusion, then the appearance of 'The Soul of Black Beat' on a cover was to do likewise when it came to my attention. Was this yet another change of name or a completely new publication altogether? Even with 'Special – 2nd Anniversary' printed along the bottom there was some uncertainty, but thankfully Kev welcomes everyone to issue number twelve in his editorial, so the problem was solved.

Reaching issue twelve was indeed something of a milestone in the world of fanzines and the guys at the helm took up just short of two pages to explain: '*how they got it together*'. Kev wrote: "*I guess it started about four years ago; there was a lot of mudslinging and backstabbing on the northern scene. Too much cloak and danger is bad. Info withheld from people who are willing to learn causes resentment, and that's when the rot set in. The scene is full of a lot of people who've given up their search for info on artists, records etc, because their questions were not answered by people who prided themselves on what they knew and others didn't. At this time there was little in the way of fanzines; the media press was, and still is a complete waste of bloody time. Most people on the scene have been around years, gaining their knowledge thru years of experience, but that's a long time for people who haven't. Info must be readily available. Two years passed; things went from bad to*

worse. 'Soul Cargo' and 'Symbol' were coming to an end, and 'Souled Out' was soon to disappear. When they sunk it left the soul scene with a big hole in the information department."

Steve added: *"After issue three, we sat down and had a long debate, at the end of which we decided to change the mag name to 'Black Beat'. By calling it 'Northern Line' it limited us as regards subject matter i.e. Deep Soul, 60's, 70's, 80's R&B etc. Issue four came out as 'Black Beat' taking our name from the Houston label (almost), we thought it a better name than calling it Soul something.*

"Up to No.6 the mag was going out free to anyone sending an SAE – we wanted to give people an insight into what we were doing, let people know we weren't rip offs. So, we decided to charge from No.6.

"The other big problem was how to get it printed – commercially, cost would be sky high. Up to now the mag was produced off a 'borrowed' photocopier. We decided to get our own printing gear and be completely independent. Kev borrowed a few quid, bought the necessary equipment. With this, a thirty-two-page mag could then be produced for 25p."

Both Steve and Kev were quick to point out that there was little or no money to be made from producing a fanzine, and any money that was made, was simply ploughed back into the publication. They were also to dwell briefly on circulation figures, saying that they *"cleared circa 500 copies an issue – very good for the state of the soul scene, far larger than any other fanzine today"*, whilst adding that the likes of *Black Echoes* would clear 15,000 a week. A far more important comment centred around the question of "Why not offer more advertising space?" to which came the reply: *"We don't withhold advert space; we don't push it. We could have pages of adverts – live off our advert fees for cost of production; but this cuts down on the amount of space for info. Info is far more important."*

It was little wonder that *Black Beat* outsold its rivals: even the letters were thought provoking, or just plain provocative, with Soul Sam having doubts about the integrity of the Wigan Casino management (No.12) and an un-named reader questioning the Casino's accounts (No.13). This was better than any soap-opera.

Issue number sixteen (July 1982) saw Rod Dearlove give his thoughts on 'Running A Mag', looking back on his experiences of time doing *Midnite Express*. His first tip was *"A shotgun to the forehead is much safer, less money and easier on the pocket"*, going on to say that a two hundred print run for issue one was the most to do for that first venture, until you were established. He then moved onto the choice of printing method, either duplicating or photocopying, as either of the two allowed you to use correction fluid and also enhance

copied headings and record labels with a fine nibbed pen.

One interesting fact that Rod added was: *"There are about seventy-to-eighty magazine freaks who buy all the soul fanzines etc. Those people will be the backbone of the sales."* Something that perhaps explains - alongside the small print runs - why some of those early publications are so hard to find today!

Black Beat certainly showed no bias towards any form of soul music, even covering Beach Music, which could be found in issue sixteen, while it was not averse to change as December 1982 was to bring yet another change of name, plus a change of format. Both were somewhat minimal, as the name simply changed to *New Black Beat*, while the size reverted back to A4. But why change something that wasn't broke? *"What happened was that I moved to Peterborough,"* said Steve, *"and at the time Kev and I had different ideas for taking the magazine forward and I had a bee in my bonnet about the magazine needing taking to the next level. A friend of mine, Ian Clark, had a friend/work colleague who in turn had access to a litho-printer which to my mind would improve the quality of the end product no end. Kev and I fell out over something, I think it was over the number of copies of issue sixteen he sent me, something trivial like that, and one of those things that happen when you are young!*

"These days we are mates again, and it all seems a bit daft now, but at the time it was a bit of drama. So anyway, we went our separate ways. Kev did an issue eighteen of 'Black Beat' but after that concentrated on other things. Issue No.18 for me was Issue No.1 of 'New Black Beat'. Essentially there were two issue eighteens, one by Kev and one by me which was the first issue of 'New Black Beat'."

Despite the change of name, *New Black Beat* continued to deliver the goods.

Note that there is no number six of *Black Beat*, but two number sevens (October and December 1983), while I have two, slightly different, number twenties - one has twenty-six pages, while the other has thirty-two, and it is not simply a case of six missing pages. Also, the photos that appear on the back and inner back cover of one of those issues also appear on the back of issue twenty-one. Why, was a question that Steve couldn't answer!

It was nice to have something just that little bit different, but it was the actual readable content that mattered to those who parted with their fifty pence, or seventy when there was a slight increase. Like a couple of other publications, only a complete listing would do it justice, but in a nutshell, you got funk oldies, modern soul, blues review, smooth grooves, deep soul, jazz beats, 12" singles, jazz-funk, 70s disco, radio soul UK, letters, reviews. Photos, listings. There were even a few family trees! Not much else you could get, was there?

There certainly wasn't, and it remains one of the best publications that appeared, and not just in the eighties; and to reach such a level it must have taken a considerable time to put together. "*Thank you. Yes, I typed it all out, did the setting up of the pages, and reducing it all onto A4 paper in a local photocopier shop,*" replied Steve Guarnori. "*The finished templates were then sent to Ian, and his mate printed them in West London. When the mags were ready, I would go on the tube in my lunch hour with a fold up trolley, pick up the magazine in four or five A4 boxes - I was doing 650-750 copies by now - and take them back to work. Then after work I'd go off with the trolley on the tube to Kings Cross, get the train to Peterborough and load them all into a taxi to go home.*

"*Then I had to collate all the pages into complete magazines and staple them all together, and all that was before sending out a single copy! Yes, it was quite an effort looking back.*

"*I was a bit uncomfortable paying Ian's mate. He was a lovely guy Henry, but I got the impression that he was doing this job 'off of his employers' books' so to speak and one day Ian said to me 'If you get stopped leaving the building, say this...' After that I was always a bit worried about getting stopped going out of the place with all these boxes of paper. So, I got a Gestetner myself, this was issue No.12 onwards, but the quality wasn't as good, the thing was awful, ink on the kitchen table and the like. So, I asked Ian's mate if he would just do me the covers and I would do the rest myself, that made collection much easier - one box to pick up and lug across London, not five.*

"*That was the logistical end of things but what made 'Black Beat' for me was the quality of our contributors. Fortunately, I had managed to attract a fantastic set of writers, who were as passionate as I was and who always delivered the goods. To be perfectly honest it was their contributions that made the magazine what it was. At one point we had about twenty regular contributors and Black Beat's success was largely down to them, not me, that the magazine covered so many interesting articles.*"

If it was so good and so well liked, why did it stop? "*My first wife was suffering from schizophrenia after the birth of our daughter in 1985 and quite ill, being sectioned and in and out of hospital regularly,*" said Steve. "*I had a pretty demanding job in London which had long hours and was taking me to the USA for one week every month as well. I was literally getting these calls saying my wife had been taken into hospital and I had to come home and sort out caring for the children. In the end my children went into temporary foster care,*

as we had no family in Peterborough, so I could carry on working. After a while of this, something had to give as it was all getting too much. I also got into a mess with working out who had subscriptions and so on after the book with them all in got ripped up! In the end I think what was going on in my life at the time was reflected in the quality of the last couple of issues. Eventually, the something that gave was 'New Black Beat'.*

"*What must also be remembered, we didn't have the internet then, so everything was via phone, letter and word of mouth. The information and knowledge also wasn't there that is there today. Looking back, I thoroughly enjoyed doing it, and still write articles on soul music to this day.*"

"*At its height I think Black Beat sold 1,000 copies,*" Kev Griffin was to add. "*The cover price was 50p and we had quite a few annual subscribers from all over Europe and as far away as Australia, New Zealand and Papua New Guinea!*

"*The rest we sold around the nighters, all-dayers and the 6Ts crowd in London, which was in its infancy then. In fact, many of our contributors were the founder members of that movement. Namely Ian Clark, Ady Croasdell and the late Randy Cousens. I think Tony Rounce may have also written a few pieces.*"

Kev then went on to talk about the printing/production process that was used: "*By today's standards the production process was rudimentary and archaic. There was no internet in 1980 so research was good old fashioned journalism. Chasing down stories. Face to face interviews. We seemed to spend a lot of time meeting contacts in damp basement flats in South London! Lots of dirt was dished and scandalous stories offered. Most we didn't publish as were deemed too risky! Lots of telephone calls, no mobile phones so we were actually in phone boxes a lot of the time!*

"We read a lot of books and the local library was well used. Contacts were invaluable. All articles were typed on typewriters. There were no word processors. We went through a lot of Tippex!

"We were both holding down full-time jobs and still put out six issues a year. The work load a times seemed colossal and some nights I would literally fall asleep at the typewriter! It takes over your life. Myself and Steve were Evangelical.

"Printing was a mammoth laborious effort. Our print run was relatively small so getting it done professionally was unaffordable.

"Steve started off using the photocopier at his office but that didn't last long plus we soon needed to start producing more and more copies to cope with demand. I started using the Gestetner Printer in the office at the college where I was working. You had to turn the handle and feed the paper through. That ended up breaking under the load and I got a ticking off from the Principal! "So, I borrowed £600 from my parents and purchased an Automatic Gesterner Printer and Gestetner Picture Scanner. These were at the time state of the art desktop publishing. In reality they were a nightmare to use.

"Each issue was collated and stapled together by hand. It was a mammoth task. Most of this went on in my bedroom in the flat I was sharing along with thousands of 7" singles! It would be so much easier and cheaper today to produce Black Beat. But it seems that the printed word doesn't carry the same kind of value? However, Black Beat still has a presence even today on the Rare Soul scene and extracts get regularly posted on social media and there are plenty of collectors who have every single issue. I myself don't own one single issue.

"After Steve and I went our separate ways in 1983, I joined 'Soul On Sound' which was a soul magazine in cassette format; also a pop and rock one called 'Sound Wave'. We actually did the first ever UK interview with Madonna... But that's another story."

I had to ask Kev if he was the one who did the Madonna interview and he replied that he was, and *"she was a right cow, but if remember rightly has gone on to fulfil all the things she boasted she would do!"*

Before putting the seventies to bed there are one or two publications that I have not featured, as I have to date been unable to obtain copies. Information on them is also sketchy at best, but they merit a mention.

From 1970, there was the *Deep Soul Appreciation Society*, a publication edited by Terry Cooper; then from c.1971/1972 came *Disco Soul*, edited by Nigel Martin. I believe that there are at least four issues of this one. From around the same time, Veronica and David Day produced *The Peniman News*. There is knowledge of two issues of this one – March/April 1971 and January/February 1973. Rounding off the seventies is the *North Wales Soul Review*, published by the Bangor and North Wales Soul Club in January 1979.

THE EIGHTIES

The eighties were certainly a boom time for the fanzines covering mainly what was now cemented in stone as 'northern soul'. The beginning of the decade had outweighed the seventies on its own, but even that was surpassed in the 1986/87 period with an avalanche of publications, as many of those 'original soulies' began to return to the scene, having got married and raised a family, and were now joining up with those who had never left, boosting attendances at venues up and down the country. The marketplace was fresh and ripe.

I fell into the collecting world of soul music publications by accident, and in all honesty, I still don't go as far as to call it a collection; but when I find myself searching the various online sources for issues that I don't have rather than seeking items for my collection of football memorabilia, then I suppose it has become something of an obsession.

Collections of any form of memorabilia can never be considered complete, as there is always something new, and who knows what is out there from those days of yesteryear? I lived in something of a northern soul backwater and, as I mentioned at the start of this journey, I had a greater love for football and was not around on the scene when the vast majority of publications were initially available. Many of these publications, their origins and actual lifespan, have been reasonably easy to trace through having most or all of them, but there are the odd obscure ones that have sprung up out of nowhere, odd numbered copies that give no idea as to when they first appeared or when they died their ultimate death.

From the early 1980s and out of 'Auld Reekie' - Edinburgh for those who are wondering - comes **JOCK'S VIEW OF SOUL**, edited by James "Jock" O'Connor. On the cover, "*Issue No.1*" has been written in pen, as has the 50p price, but I suspect this has been done by the man himself other than a previous owner, as there is also a pen written note – "*See page 19 (what's on)*" and "*continued on page 17*" to be found inside.

The publication is typically 'home-made', with the editor stating that he had got his mother to type it all out, but content is good, as contributions from the likes of Pete Lawson would testify.

Reviews – record, concert and venues, listings, a piece on Ashford and Simpson and 'The Current State of Northern Soul' fill the pages, with the latter mentioning that Wigan Casino's Mr M's was "*the cess pit of Northern Soul*" and that the average punter proceeded "*to make a fool of themselves with regimental Casino wear, bags, badges etc.*" adding, "*The only hope*

for the Northern Soul scene (60s newies, oldies and modern) is for the scenes like Stafford to continue to educate the punters and covert newcomers into the scene and teach them the true and traditional ways of Northern Soul and places like Morecambe to either pack up or think for themselves and see what they are missing out on (although not financially). What we do today they will want to do tomorrow (or maybe someday)."
Sadly, there was no No.2.

As you will find, and as I have said, with some of the featured publications it has been difficult to give a definite date as to when they first appeared, especially for the month, not so much the year, with the editors never for one minute thinking that their meagre contribution to the soul music scene would be so revered in years to come, never mind documented in a book covering the subject of fanzines and magazines. Some of those early publication dates have been estimated by pure guesswork, not only by myself but also by those who produced the actual publications!

One such editor was Martin Scragg, who produced **THE SOUND OF SOUL**. Martin had originally got in touch with me as he had shown something of an interest in my articles in *Soul Up North* and I had enquired as to whether he still had any copies of his magazine, as up until that point I did not own any. "*Sorry – all back* *issues went almost forty years ago"* came the reply. Eventually issues of Martin's *The Sound of Soul* were to surface when I took a considerable number of publications off a well-known editor, so another blank space was filled.

Through writing for *Soul up North* Martin actually got in touch and I got to know him well, as he was also a keen collector of soul in print, so he was an obvious choice to contribute to the book and not just because he fitted the 'former editors' category. So, I simply let him tell his story.

"I first 'put pen to paper' back in 1981, with the reason being to promote the weekly Northern Soul nights that we were running at the Working Men's Club in Alsager, a fairly large village near Crewe in Cheshire. The original line-up of DJs was Dave Bell, Keith Williams, ex-Torch DJ Johnny Beggs, and myself – plus a few guests, such as Nick Cowan. We even got our faces on a page in 'Blues & Soul', after having received a visit from the roving reporter, Frank Elson. Northern nights carried on throughout 1981 and into 1982, with the only change in DJ being the arrival of Martin Meyler as a replacement for Johnny Beggs. Unfortunately, in the same year that they called time on the soul nights, the club was closed down permanently, due to the breaking of three deadly sins: serving non-members, serving after hours and serving under-age drinkers. A bad fire soon after finished the job.

"I was particularly inspired by Manchester's Dave

McCadden, who started his first fanzine with the simplest of titles – 'Soul Time'. He opened the proceedings in November 1976, the same month that I turned nineteen, went to a Wigan Casino All-Nighter, and started my first, and only, full-time job. I'm of the opinion that 'Soul Time' was something of a trail-blazer, mainly because it was the first fanzine that was aimed purely at the Northern Soul market. Apologies if I've forgotten any others that came out earlier.

"Dave's first attempt lasted for just three issues, and I wrote about all of them in some detail back in issue No.75 of 'Soul Up North'. When issue No.3 of 'Soul Time' marked its end around February 1977, some editors may have thrown in the towel. Dave McCadden, however, had an 'if at first you don't succeed' attitude. He definitely had a 'try, try again' motto – in fact he would try, try, try and then try yet again!!!! He soon bounced back later the same year with a one-off called 'Nite Life'. Next was 'It's The Beat' in 1979. The only one of Dave's fanzines that I could honestly have done without was 'Groovin' A la Go- Go', which mercifully was another of Dave's one-offs. It concentrated too much on the scene's seedier side (or should that be speedier side). There was very little of any soul interest at all. Fortunately, Dave bounced back in indomitable fashion with his masterpiece, entitled 'Soul Galore'.

"It's against this backdrop, corny pun intended, that I decided to join the list of budding hopefuls who had already taken up the editorial business, although my own small contribution to soul reading matter with 'The Sound Of Soul' was a bit different to other editors.

"As I mentioned above, I started work at the beginning of November 1976. I was a laboratory technician at the University of Keele. Of course, this was long before the buildings that made up the Students Union had become the home of the renowned Keele All-Nighters that still operate today, or would do if Covid hadn't invisibly threatened us all. My job gave me access to a photocopier – albeit a somewhat dodgy affair in the beginning. I still have the master copies of all five of the issues, which have given me hours and hours of memories – both good and bad. I didn't have the foresight to include an accurate date for my fanzine, but on the plus side, I always provided some recent venue reports, so at least I could estimate approximately when they first appeared.

"The first one was a free give-away to anyone who was interested. I didn't think of putting any dates in, but the editorial of the first mentions the imminent closure of the Casino, which puts it at some time around summer 1981. It had only six type-written single and double-sided pages, and was pre-dated by a double-sided 'Rare Soul Gems' leaflet.

"*The opening pages of that first issue featured number one in a series entitled 'Rare Soul Gems', and I'd chosen Alice Clark's evergreen 'You Hit Me (Right Where It Hurt Me)' for the privilege. I also printed all of the song's lyrics, which took some time because it meant listening to the track over and over and over until I'd deciphered them. This was about ten years before the invention of the internet in the early 90s, so there was no other way, and was the main reason why I opted for three instrumental titles when it came to numbers 10-12.*

"*I was still a relative novice, and never realised that my second choice in the 'Rare Soul Gems' series, 'Contact' by The Three Degrees, used a dubious counterfeit copy, albeit a decent one. To add to my mistakes, I didn't know that Lou Pride's 'Your Love Is Fading' and 'Another Day' from The Ascots were actually the real artists and titles, not covered-up.*

"*After a discography on the great Garland Green, and a list of twenty-five of the Verve label's dance 45s, I reviewed 'Five Timeless Gems' – some cheap singles that you could then pick up for a fiver, or even less in most cases. This was to become a regular feature in 'Sound of Soul', and the pick of my debut choices has to be 'I'm On To You Girl' by Skip Jackson & The Shantons (Dot-Mar). I didn't know at the time that Skip was then in the final year of his short life, so there wasn't any mention of the fact. That doesn't detract from the fact of the track being a masterpiece. And I still think that the lead-in vocals sound uncannily like Georgie Fame.*

"*The first venue report that I ever made was of an August Bank Holiday All-Dayer at The Bay Horse in Todmorden. This was my first visit to 'Toddy', so I took along a couple of friends who'd been there on several previous trips – Richard Shaw and Bob Germanek. It was still 'a bugger of a job trying to find', which is why I gave over a dozen lines of detailed route planning, ending with the helpful comment 'find your own way!' Mention of Bob Germanek reminds me of a 'Daily Star' headline that I read back in the mid-80s. I'd always assumed that the titles used by the 'Star' were total fabrications, along the lines of 'Freddie Starr Ate My Hamster'. I was therefore completely gob-smacked to see a photograph of Bob next to the title 'Alien Curry Monster Bit My Bum!' There isn't enough room here to give any further details, but you can bet that I quizzed him about the weird subject when we next met.*

"*The 'Farewell Oldies All-Nighter' that had been held at Wigan Casino on the night of 4th/5th September 1981 was the prelude to the venue's last ever All-Nighter - which was to come a couple of weekends later - at least it was advertised as such. I gave a personal review on this subject only recently in 'SOS', but time precludes*

much of what I had planned. Hopefully, Iain will find enough material to make up another volume – or at least a revision of this one.

"*Issue two contained the last Wigan report and a guide to cover-ups from the previous three years, while the editorial in issue three states that this particular issue should be out at the end of March 1982, which was 'about six months after issue two'.*" Martin also added that he still has copies of number one and two which he says "*didn't exactly sell like hotcakes. In fact, it was only encouragement from Rod Dearlove, editor of 'Midnite Express' that encouraged me to keep it going.*

"*For that second issue, Johnny Beggs had become the first of the additional contributors and my editorial included the news that Tim Ashibende had recently returned from one of his frequent record-hunting trips to the States, where he had found a copy of 'Try To Think What You're Doing' by Court Davis. At the time, this was still receiving a lot of dance-floor action at the Casino via Richard Searling, and he was still covering it up as 'Herbie Williams – The Lover Who Loves You Not'. Tim immediately sold his copy to Rod Shard for the staggering price of £100. That's not bad for a record that's currently valued by John Manship at around £2,500.*

"*The front cover of two was much better than one. It was nearly forty years ago, so it is very basic – it was all done with an old typewriter and the works Xerox printer.* "*The first issue of my fanzine wasn't much to look at.*

I had just done a Northern spot in Alsager, and numbers one and two were meant to be given away to everybody who was there. A few weeks later, I decided to start a fanzine, the shoddy No.1, and because I had a few of the 'Rare Soul Gems' left, [this was a leaflet that Martin produced highlighting various records along with the lyrics] *I attached them to every copy of the Sound of Soul issue No.1.*

"*I never really expected to make any money out of them, so I just gave them away to anyone who asked.*

"*So, we come on to 'SOS' No.3, with Martin Meyler being opted in to replace Johnny Beggs. This is my personal favourite issue, which could be improved upon with the benefit of hindsight, but at the time was a very fine read. No.4 is the only issue that gave a specific date of release, but how I could be so accurate I honestly don't remember. Although there's a May 28th 1982 date at the bottom of one of the later pages, that date is open to conjecture. This issue featured the addition of several further scribes, with Rod Dearlove, Nick Savory and Dave Evison joining Martin Meyler in giving articles. As far as venue reports go, I think No.4 had one of the most important of the time (IMHO). I've seen later articles that give my mammoth Top Of The*

World report a special mention, although I don't think that Soul Sam would agree! I filled an entire C-90 tape on the night, which contained the added banter of some of my niter-cohorts: Tony Cartlidge, Cath Oliver and Paul Thomas.

"Although I didn't realise it at the time, No.5 proved to be the final issue of 'The Sound Of Soul', I had rather hopefully expected that No.6 would be out 'at the end of October' 1982. But I realised that I'd bitten off a lot more than I could chew. Anybody who's ever tried putting a fanzine together will undoubtedly agree that it's a pretty gruelling task. I had never set myself a deadline for when the next 'SOS' would appear – which is why some issues of 'SOS' came out in such a haphazard fashion. No.3 being the best example. Some well-respected editors have taken even longer, and a good example is Graham Anthony's exceptional 'Detroit City Limits'. While issues Nos.1-8 appeared as regular as clockwork, in between November 1988 and April 1992, No.9 and No.10 weren't to be seen for well over four years, by which time the price had gone up from £1.75 to £2.50 and then £3.

"After issue five, I packed it all in, and started writing for Rod Dearlove's 'Midnite Express'. It was a lot easier to let somebody else do all the hard work!

"I had made some good friends along the way, including a few that were editing their own fanzine at roughly the same time. Rod Dearlove from Hull features heavily among them. When he stopped 'Midnite Express' after three issues, I was one of the people that persuaded him to have another shot. I also provided venue reports and record reviews in most of the subsequent four issues (1983-1984), which included accounts of a trip to Leicester Oddfellow's Club and to one of the Top Of The World niters. I didn't contribute to issue four, mainly because of Soul Sam's acerbic response to the previous issue's Stafford report, which he called 'Martin Scragg – Maggie's Minister of Sixties Soul?' I also ruffled the feathers of Sean Gibbons, when I woefully underestimated the turnout at

Gene Chandler's live appearance in Morecambe Pier ballroom on the night of 26th/27th August 1983. This faux pas was sorted out by a long phone call with Sean, and a grovelling apology from yours truly. A couple of years later, when Rod's next magazine appeared (1986), he sent me a complimentary copy of the first issue. This was the more famous 'Voices From The Shadows', of course. However, by that time I had become much more involved with a mobile disco I'd bought from my younger brother in 1977, and I didn't buy subsequent issues until several years later. These included the numbers that featured snooker legend Steve Davis, so I don't think that I was missed.

"Among the very first acquaintances that I made was the late Chris Savory, who sadly died in September 2009, at the age of 62. As soon as you heard his accent, it was obvious that he wasn't a Potter. His first mag was 'Hot Buttered Soul', which was a little ahead of my time, but when 'Soul Cargo' appeared, I became one of the first people to take out a subscription. This meant that not only did I receive all twelve of the official issues, but also the three supplements. His sales record boxes acted like a magnet at most of the Sunday All-Dayers being regularly held at the Newcastle-under-Lyme branch of Tiffanys. Chris later started the very first of the record fairs that soon became so common world-wide, and you can bet that I was at the first of them, which I think was held at the Y.M.C.A. in Hanley. Then there was Richard Radford from Brighton, who ran 'Soulside Rendezvous'. Although we never met in person, he was another that I swapped issues with throughout 1982.

"One of the local friends that I made at Tiffs in 1976 was the legendary Tim Ashibende. I would call in at his flat in Hanley on several occasions, and I usually came away with a few 7" that I'd never heard before. In 1995, Tim edited 'Tracks To Your Mind', although I never could work out the differences between an Introduction, a Foreword, and a Preface - nevertheless I bow to Tim's far superior knowledge. 'Tracks To Your Mind' was a very professional publication, which was among the best £2.50 that I ever spent. It was almost entirely devoted to Paul Kyser and his New Jersey rare soul set-up, which mostly meant Robbie Lawson and The Superlatives (the latter being the one-off group on Uptite, not the Detroit bunch). Issue No.2 was planned as a Detroit special – but the fact that it never got to see the light of day has to rank as one of the greatest losses in the history of Northern Soul fanzines."

When I finally managed to obtain those hard to find copies of *Sound of Soul* I sat down to read them and was surprised to find that the cover of issue four contained a prominent photo of Lyn Roman which was actually signed by her, but in her more familiar name of 'Linda Griner' – "*I photocopied the Lyn Roman photo from an early 1970s issue of Blues & Soul, so it's not first-hand,*" said Martin. "*I still think it's one of the sexiest publicity photos out there, and she's still quite a looker – even in her 70s. I didn't know until a few years later that her real name is Linda Griner of Motown fame.*"

Sadly, as Martin mentioned a few lines back, issue five was the last *Sound of Soul*; there was to be no echo, and yet another publication that had much going for it fell by the wayside and into relative obscurity.

The early months of 1980 saw Rod Dearlove take his first steps into editing his own publication; but where did the inspiration come from that made Rod put his feelings, his words, into print? "*I'm cycling home from school with a lad who is in my class but some months older than me and he is more worldly wise and advanced in joined up thinking,*" began Rod. "*He hangs around with the Paragon Skins. To the initiated of 70s working class culture, this is not an East Yorkshire equivalent of the Bullingdon Club, these are skinheads who hang around Hull Paragon Railway station. These are lads you don't attempt to stare out. So, we slow down at my house and he reaches inside his Harrington jacket and hands me a magazine. "Do you want to borrow this" floats on the air as he accelerates away but it isn't a question and it isn't a well-thumbed copy of Health & Efficiency, it's called Blues & Soul, and I haven't opened it but it will change my life forever.*

"*I have spent a large proportion of my life thinking about that magazine. I'm pretty sure I used to know who was on the cover, a female singer I'm sure and even the colour of her dress, blue, well, I think it was blue. I would while away motorway drives trying to focus the issue, date, anything really and then it would*

slip away again, lost in the mists of time.

"*As my life in records gathered momentum and I handled lots of records and wrote about lots of records, its precision point became blunter and blunter. But its impact on me never waned.*

"*I had sporadic pieces accepted by various publications including, incredibly, Black Echoes circa 1976/77 championing the likes of Kenny Carter and The Metros on RCA. It was an odd experience opening that issue and seeing my words in typeset and my name in print. You know that super-fast double take in Hanna Barbera cartoons? Trust me, that's how it feels. I think I'd probably sent the first piece in as a letter. But my first foray as an editor was Midnite Express.*

"*From memory I thought I just wanted to go my own way. Hard to remember 1980 now.*"

And so came the initial issue of **MIDNITE EXPRESS**, an A4 twenty pager which was priced at 50p. On the cover was a photo of Yvonne Vernee, who was to replace Saundra Edwards in The Elgins, and other full-page photos of Carol Anderson, Lorraine Chandler, The Inspirations and Mickey Lanay gave the content a rather sparse look, but there was decent reading within the remainder taken up with the likes of UK Cameo Parkway, part one of Ric Tic Relics, the Seventies Soul Scene and an all-nighter report.

That Seventies Soul Scene article came from the pen of a man who is still spinning those sounds today – Soul Sam, who went on to explain how he became involved in "*more up-tempo soul music and where to obtain such sounds*". He was to continue this theme in issue No.2.

When obtaining old back-issues of the publications featured within the pages of this book much time was spent scribbling down track titles which were mentioned within articles or in reviews that I was not familiar with. These were then listened to, and if liked, copies were obtained either for when I was DJing or to be played on my radio show. There were of course other tracks reviewed that were familiar and would be dug out, as it had been a while since I played them. Issue No.2 had three such tunes in 'Roly's Raries' – 'I Did It Again' by Bobby Cutchins, 'I Need My Baby' by Jackey Beavers and 'Love Is A Serious Business' by Alfie Davidson. Roly bemoaned that Mercury had still not released the latter and that Soul Bowl had it in bulk at one point, but that was so difficult to find now. Rod was to add that *"Roly, from Midnite Express, was our Labrador. He was also really good at football. Sadly, Music Hall has expired or we would have made our fortune from him..."*

Issue No.3 saw Rod lay the future of *Midnite Express* well and truly on the line in his editorial writing: *"Issue three of Midnite Express marks something of dilemma for the mag's future. Some, not all I hasten to add, of the people who sold the mag at various venues throughout the country have not yet returned their takings, despite being paid a commission and having numerous reminders. So, at present the magazine's future is in jeopardy. Hopefully, I will have received all monies by Xmas and will be able to continue with the mag. I have no wish to cause these people any embarrassment, but if the mag goes down, I'll be naming names so that others don't fall into the same trap as myself."*

Stern stuff indeed, but it must have hit home, as not only did issue No.4 appear, but *Midnite Express* appeared for a total of seven issues before it was added to the list of one-time publications in 1986. When asked if he had anything to add on the disappearance of *Midnite Express* Rod would just say: *"I think the printer I used had done me a favour and I couldn't afford the new quotes. A couple of people selling the mag for me also ripped me off."*

Deciding upon a title for your fledgling publication must often prove as difficult a decision as what to actually include within the pages. You want something not too long, but memorable. Many go for something including the word 'Soul', others for something familiar to the scene. That must have been Howard Earnshaw's thinking when he plumped for OUT ON THE FLOOR back in June 1981.

This was one of the few publications that had failed to come my way as I attempted to obtain at least one copy of every one that had appeared over the years, but Howard mentioned that he thought he still had at least one copy *"somewhere up in the loft"*. Lockdown did

have its benefits as unlike The Formations, who found darkness at the top of the stairs, Howard did locate that elusive issue of *Out On The Floor*. The publication was now there, all that was required was some background, so it was now up to Howard to cast his mind back in time.

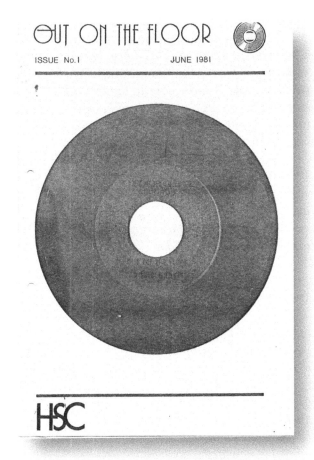

"At that time, I, along with Fred Ward, Alan (Spider) Turner, and Julian Frankland (Herbert) were DJing at a mid-week northern soul night in Huddersfield called The Coach House Club (situated at the bottom of King Street, which was sadly demolished later to make way for the Kingsgate Shopping Centre). It was reasonably well attended and we even got a coach full of fans to what should have been the final all-nighter at Wigan Casino (they had two more after that one)

"I had a hankering to produce a small fanzine/newsletter to promote the Huddersfield Soul Club, which we intimated was part of being a member of the Coach House!

"So, I had a word with my friend Howard Lockwood who had access to the print department at David Brown Tractors where he worked, and between us, we cobbled up a 'mock copy'. I recall it had a black circle on the cover, which Howard assured me would be so much better when we used the actual record, but it actually wasn't much better than the black disc!!

"I then approached the other DJs for their input. Herbert was keen to do a record write up on the newer

sounds that were being discovered at that time and Fred Ward said he would do venue reports. Alan Turner said he'd do something for future issues, and as a few of us had travelled to London to see George Benson in concert, I asked a lad called Dave Westoby to write about that.

"I decided to write a quiz which I again hoped would generate interest in the club.

"I collated all the contributions and typed them up on an old typewriter which I'd been given by another old name on the northern soul scene, Fred's brother Rob Ward who is sadly now no longer with us. I passed the typed-up pages on to Howard Lockwood who got around 75/100 copies printed, which were held together by a staple on the top left corner.

"I was rather unimpressed with the quality, and expected a lovely cover with a nice reproduction of the US Charger label of 'Out On The Floor'. Unfortunately, it turned out very poorly.

"We gave all the copies away at the Coach House over a few weeks, and of course, only a handful of people bothered with the quiz, which again disappointed us, although we did get a few positive feedbacks. Not enough for me to get enthusiastic about going ahead with it... so there it ended, or so I thought until I was promoted at work into an office which had computers, when they were in their infancy and a photo copier and the spark of being a fanzine producer/editor was reignited, and after a chance conversation with Dave Rimmer (Soulful Kinda Music) at an all-nighter at Knutsford Town Hall I decided to have a go... Soul Up North was born and the rest as they say is history!"

Out On The Floor issue No.1 consisted of six pages. Page two saw 'A Letter From The Editor', along with just over a dozen lines on the cover record and Dobie Gray. This was followed by a few record reviews by Herbert, who stated that Wilson Pickett's 'How Will I Ever Know' was his top tune of the moment. The review of the George Benson concert followed on page four, along with a quiz. Venue review followed on five and bringing up the rear was nothing more than four lines saying "so that's about it ..." and a mention of what was planned for future issues.

Were there future issues, I asked Howard? "I think I managed to produce two or three," came the reply.

Rod Dearlove was also responsible for another 1983 publication, the one-off A COLLECTORS GUIDE TO DETROIT. This is an A4, side-stapled, fifty-eight-page discography of everything Detroit, except Motown. "It appeared in between the two runs of 'Midnite Express'," explained Road. "I, with a collaboration of other like- minded souls, published what was an attempt to catalogue all the small and interesting labels operating in Detroit in the shadow of, though sometimes going toe-to- toe with Motown.

All the people credited within it deserve the same credit that has sometimes been solitarily heaped on my shoulders."

There are notes on each label, plus countless scans and an article by Keith Rylatt – 'The Detroit Sound On UK labels'. I'm not a record collector, nor a discography buff, but I did find the notes and info of interest.

The south coast continued to promote the music as if it were their own and out of Brighton came SOUL SIDE RENDEZVOUS edited by Richard Radford; and here is a title that forced a slight re-write to my original text, as at first I was uncertain if Soul Side Rendezvous and another publication called Soul Side were indeed one and the same. Let me explain. When I began the book, I had issues two, three and four of Soul Side, an A5 publication, with issue two having a card cover, while the others were simply paper. I was, however, also aware of a publication by the name of Soul Side Rendezvous, but not having seen it, or knowing anything about it, I was unable to make any connection, if indeed there was one.

Anyway, with my self-imposed deadline for this book approaching, I was offered a few publications and amongst them was issue No.1 of Soul Side Rendezvous. Upon its arrival, it confirmed that the two publications were indeed one and the same, with this first issue being totally different to the others that I already had.

Issue No.1 was A4 in size, consisting of fourteen

pages, but it must have been something of a hastily put together publication as the page numbers, where there are any, are all over the place. There are no numbers on the first three pages, but what should be page four is numbered 'ten'. Five and six are unnumbered, then seven is actually numbered 'five', then comes 'six', 'seven', an unnumbered page, then '11'; another unnumbered page, then '13'. Perhaps somewhat strangely, the actual articles flow as they should!

That content is quite a mixture, with articles on Gene Chandler, Edwin Starr and Ray Charles, record reviews by Ian Clark, more reviews under the heading of 'Brill Record', a review of a Jnr. Walker concert, a feature on the blues and an article on Brighton in the 60s, plus a crossword.

Richard Radford's editorial pays thanks to stalwart fanzine editors Rod Dearlove and Kev Griffin, the latter of the two being responsible for printing it, whilst stating: *"This is issue one and hopefully there will be an issue two on its way but nothing has been decided yet; yes, quite correct that this was a note of uncertainty, you may not realise the work that goes into producing a mag on a part- time basis, let alone the financial commitment"*.

A second issue did appear, but like that initial issue, there was no date to be seen, or anything within the pages to allow some detective work to be done in order to have a guess as to when it appeared. However, a fellow collector has dated issue two as being July 1982 and issue three from the following month.

Issue No.2, as mentioned, is A5 in size and has a card cover, while the inner sixteen pages, plus a one page 'stop press' supplement, have something of a glossy feel to them. Content was Betty Everett, New Birth, reviews, crossword, Ian Clark, Tony Ellis, Dave Thorley and much more. Good value at 40p.

There was no card cover on issue three, but it mattered little as it was the content that was of interest – 'Okeh Collectors', 'London Club Scene' and 'Fanzines' being only a trio of the articles that could be found inside.

In the editorial of issue four, Richard mentions that sales had gone up and that he was looking to sell 250 copies of this issue, which included features on Black Chess listing, Joe Tex and Johnny Taylor. Whether or not that target was ever reached I have no idea as I have not seen issue five; I don't even know if there actually was one. I do have a note that there were six issues, but no actual conformation as regards this.

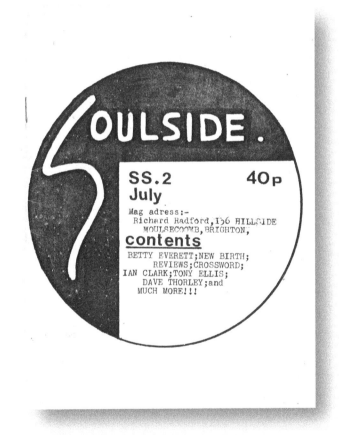

For a while in the eighties, the British media had something of a fixation with northern soul, and in September 1982 (No. 29), THE FACE magazine – *"a cultural trailblazer, covering music, fashion, film, TV, society, politics and current affairs"* - decided that here was a subject worth covering within its pages, pushing it out to the unknown in a six-page article, entitled 'Out On The Floor – A Primer For The New Soul Rebels'.

It began with Neil Rushton writing about 'Fans and fanatics' – "*Northern Soul is in THE FACE, instead of being dismissed as some extinct tribal ritual revolving around baggies and the Footsee (thanks NME), it is suddenly being taken seriously by outsiders.*" Neil continued his piece with a visit to the Cavendish Suite at the Old Vic Hotel in Wolverhampton, telling of how the fashions and the sounds had changed, of records being offered for sale at £40 and £50 a throw and Soul Sam receiving £20 for his DJ spot. He spoke to soul enthusiasts, with one admitting to spending the bulk of his £200 per-week wages on records, while another was to say: "*Tonight's the first Northern gig I've been to for a while. Tonight, I was going to see Kid Creole, but I decided to come here instead to see what the Northern scene is like now.*

"*I'm amazed. It was virtually dead a few years ago, but now the feeling of energy and something happening is back.*"

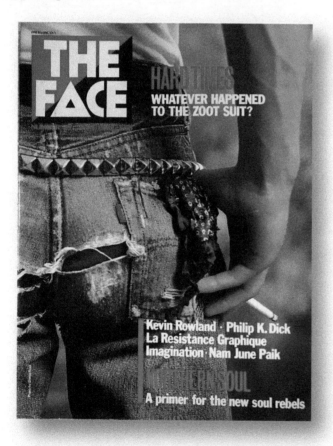

The magazine also carried an interview with David Ball of Soft Cell, spoke to a couple of others and carried a list of a of around two dozen 'in' tunes, including 'I Love You Baby' – Eddie Parker, 'Finders Keepers' – Nella Dodds, 'Next In Line' – Hoagy Lands and 'Kiss Me Now' – Florence Devore.

Not a soul related magazine, simply a one-off article, although it does find its way into the collections of many, but somewhat surprisingly, it

doesn't come cheap, even although there are numerous copies about.

Edging towards the end of 1982 comes **NORTH OF WATFORD** or simply *N.O.W.*, although it also had a sub-title of T.C.O.B. – Taking Care of Business. This glossy, twenty-eight-page magazine was what it said on the cover, all about events north of Watford, although it dealt more or less with events considerably further north of Birmingham, never mind Watford.

Published out of Stockport, it was compiled with the help of Spin Inn Records of Manchester, although there is no actual editor mentioned with the pages, and for 50p, it is a decent read. 'Streettalk with Kev Edwards', an article and interview with 'The Rude Lady Of Soul' – Millie Jackson, 'Rapping With Rick James', 'Jazz Breakdown with Colin Curtis', an article on Shalamar and 'Profile On Richard Searling' fill most of the pages. But just why there is a two-page article entitled 'Introducing Basketball', a handful of poems and a piece on getting a job is anyone's guess.

There are a number of adverts for events in and around Manchester, a 12"/LP chart and a look back at 1982 through the eyes of Greg Wilson, Mike Shaft, Colin Curtis, Richard Searling and Pete Haigh. There is also a listing of soul shows on various radio stations, one of which might surprise many – Radio Trent: for two hours on a Monday night you could listen to Dale Winton's Soul Show.

All of the above could be found in that first issue, but whether or not it stretched beyond that initial one, I have no idea.

It was spring 1983 when Gary Evans from Cockermouth launched THE DRIFTER out into soul world, and considering that Cumbria has always been something of a 'northern soul hotbed' it was somewhat surprising that it took the area so long to make its contribution to the scene via a fanzine. Many had contributed, but none had produced. So, why did Gary start *The Drifter* and was it something that he had previously given some thought to?

"I'm not sure why nobody had produced a fanzine in the area prior to the Drifter, but I had been playing around with the idea for quite some time before actually producing the first issue," came the reply. *"I've always enjoyed writing, English being one of the few things that I liked at school and marrying that with my interest in soul music seemed a natural step. My first 'published' piece was being on the letters page of Black Echoes. Sometime during late 1980 or early 1981 I moved away from Carlisle 'out west' which gave me two things - more free time and access to a typewriter, but it still took me until late 1882/early 1983 to produce number one. Looking back the magazine was probably a way of keeping in touch with people in those pre-internet/mobile phone days."*

In his opening editorial, Gary bemoaned the fact that there was a lack of *"new blood on the rare soul scene"*, but he was to be called to task by Kev Griffin, who was to write that the scene in the south was in good health, probably due to *"the re-birth of the mods some five years ago"* and went on to add that *"60's soul is now at its biggest since its hey-day nineteen years ago."* A second correspondent, Derek Pearson of Bradford, was also quick to tell

Gary that there was new blood coming through and they were more appreciative of some of the sounds being played than those who used to fill the venues.

"Our first issue went quite well" said Gary in the editorial of issue two, *"but one thing that did let it down was my below 11 plus standard spelling. This time I have invested in a dictionary and hopefully this has helped to some extent."* The spelling might have improved, but the content was still a little sparse, as it would have been in issue three if it had not been for a six-page article entitled '1969 – The End Of Soul's Golden Era'.

Were those first three issues all A4 in size, I wondered, as the five issues I have are not the same size? *"As far as I remember none of the first three issues were A4. They were kind of a strange size that the first printer I used decided upon. A strange hybrid somewhere between A5 and A4. Certainly, my copy of issue three is like this. Most of the fanzines about at the time (Midnite Express was a particular favourite) were A4 and I wanted The Drifter to be a bit different."*

But suddenly, *The Drifter* sprang to life, perhaps not so much with issue four, but certainly with issue five (March/April 1984), as it had changed in format from A4 to A5, but keeping to twenty-four pages.

It looked much better and with contributions from Kev Griffin and regular Ivan Ward, there was much to read instead of articles that would simply be glanced over.

Hoping that I wasn't going to offend, I put it to Gary that by the time he reached issue four, I thought it showed an improvement, and was heading to something good and long lasting. Why did he stop?" *I agree. Numbers four and five were*

head and shoulders above the first three, I had changed printer and settled on an A5 format. Although it was still very much a typewriter, Prit- stick and Letraset job I think it looked a lot more professional and, by issue five, they were going out to Japan and Scandinavia.

"The Drifter came to an end after I was reported to the taxman for running the mag! Although, in truth, most issues only just about broke even but the hassle of having to prove this just sucked the fun out of it. I found out later that it was my girlfriend of the time who grassed me up. It seems she thought that I spent too much time bent over a typewriter when I could have been out with her. Sad but true."

That fifth issue did not simply mark the first anniversary of *The Drifter* but also the last issue, although I thought it best to check. "*Yes, there were, sadly, only five issues. Number six was in the pipeline when I called it a day. I only have three, four and five unless the others are buried somewhere in the spare room!*"

Despite locking horns with the taxman and only producing five issues, there had to be some high spots. "*Interviewing Chuck Jackson for the magazine at Morecambe Central Pier was the biggest high.*" What about regrets? "*Not being a little bit more 'pushy' promoting the fanzine. I've always enjoyed the creative side more than the sales side and I think I could have done a lot more in this area.*"

Personally, I still think that *The Drifter* had the potential to become one of the better publications that surfaced over the years, so I put it to Gary that after he called it a day, had he ever considered doing another publication, or bringing back *The Drifter*?

"*Often. It still might happen yet! Post 'The Drifter', I did do one or two articles for other fanzines, including 'On The Scene' and a short lived mag out of Brighton but I can't for the life of me remember the title. I've also written/produced two books on Okeh Records, the second of which I've just had printed. I do get bored if I haven't got a project on the go so maybe now's the time?*"

1983 was also to see one of those publications that didn't really cover soul music in its entirety, but was still of interest to those who were inclined to digest every conceivable morsel that came their way.

PHILATELY was not about collecting stamps featuring soul or R&B artists, but covered the work of Phil Spector. Edited by Mick Patrick, it was A4 in size and consisted of thirty pages. As issue two came out in December 1983, and as I believe it was issued quarterly, it is probably safe to say that issue one was from October of that year.

Not having issues of this publication to hand it is impossible to give details of what 'soul' content could be found within the pages, but in that second issue there was a feature on The Blossoms. Other issues featured the likes of The Crystals, The Ronettes and Ike and Tina Turner.

Would I buy it if copies became available? Yes.

How collections are put together is entirely up to the individual. They can suit themselves as to what they collect in their particular field, whether to diversify into other areas, and how they present it. If soul music publications are your forte then you could try and obtain one copy of every publication, or every first issue, or even decide to leave one or two publications to one side as they are perhaps considered not worth the paper they are printed on – these, however, are few and far between, or of little general interest. One publication that could fall into the latter category, going by the title, would be **SOUL-SCOOT**; but it is one that has to be looked at closely before you make up your mind. From the pen of Newbury's Terry Smith and from late 1983, the cover of issue one might be the first thing to put a few 'soulies' off. Not just the title, and the image of a couple of people on a scooter, but the 'Lambrettas – a brief history'

and 'Review of the 1983 runs' written alongside. Pages two and three (or one and two as they are numbered) would also bring a negative reaction, as they contain a full-page advert for 'flywheels' and two scooter accessory suppliers. There are also similar adverts on a couple of other pages along with the two articles mentioned on the front cover. However, this twenty-six- page, A4, side-stapled fanzine is not just about scooters and the like, as there are eleven pages on the music.

But back to the editorial for a minute, where Terry welcomes everyone to *Soul-Scoot*, adding that it was previously called *Sounds From The Street*, a publication that I have yet to discover. It was planned to produce *Soul-Scoot* every two to three months and he was offering a five-issue subscription for only £3.

If that first issue had not been tempting then issue two would have seen many having a change of mind, as this was geared more towards the soul purists than the scooter boys. Page content had increased to thirty pages, with only two being scooter related. There was a review of a Style Council concert spread over two-and-a-bit pages, but the remainder was soul related – James Brown, Chuck Jackson, Black Magic and 45s reviewed. There was also just over half a page on 'Magazines and Fanzines', but this only mentioned *The Drifter*, *Midnite Express*, *Shades Of Soul* and *New Black Beat* with scooter and mod publications receiving more coverage.

Issues three and four were more of the same, but when issue five appeared in October 1985, it was now entitled SOULSIDE. *"I've changed the name of this mag"* proclaimed Terry in his editorial. *"There were several reasons behind this, but mainly because I felt 'Soul-Scoot' didn't really represent the contents of the mag, the majority of it was on the Soulside!! (good eh!!), although this mag is still aimed at*

* SOUL SELF SATISFACTION *

scooterists/mods as well as out and out Soul fans."

The title changed, but the numbering didn't, as this was No.5, something that might confuse the fanzine collector who could be looking for issues of one to four of *Soulside* when there are none.

Venue reports, articles, reviews – the scooter connection had been truly disconnected and the publication was much the better for it, something that should have carried it forward with the promise of a healthy future. It was mentioned that issue six would be out in February/March 1986, but it was June '86 before it appeared and in an A5 format, consisting of twenty-eight pages. The momentum that had been achieved with issue five continued, but it was also to come to an abrupt halt.

"Welcome to the last edition of Soulside" began the editorial. *"The last I hear you say! Yes, due to overwhelming outside commitments, mainly work, this is to be the last issue. But do not despair, I have a new project on the horizon. If you are a Bobby Womack fan, I am going to be starting a magazine devoted to the great soul survivor, which will hopefully lead into the start of a Bobby Womack Society."* Terry was to add that there were no back issues of any of his publications available, while also apologising for the poor quality of the copying of this sixth and final issue.

I have yet to see anything fanzine wise relating to Terry's Bobby Womack project.

January 1984 saw the first issue of a publication that is, for me at least, up there with the best, if not the best of the non-glossies. Derek Pearson's SHADES OF SOUL had everything that you could wish for in a fanzine/magazine, the same as numerous others really, but it was one that commanded your interest from start to finish and one that still makes an interesting read today, with articles of definite quality.

Around the time that I was beginning to do more than simply catch up on soul reading material, copies of *Shades* suddenly appeared on the Soul Source website, enabling those like myself who had missed it, or perhaps simply just missed odd copies, to read those back issues in their entirety. I went one step further and got my wife to print them off - yes, all thirty-two issues - on her work photocopier, not in their original A4 format, but in A5 with centre-staples instead of side-staples. They looked great and a handful accompanied me on holiday to Portugal for a read beside the pool. Since then, original copies of quite a number of the thirty-two issues have slowly come my way in various job-lots and, of course, been read once again.

From that first issue in January 1984 through to the last in June 2006 there was so much covered that, like one or two others, a full issue by issue content listing would be required to do this publication justice. Record reviews and cover-up's uncovered. Artist and venue features. Interviews. Countless one-off articles such as – 'DJ's, Why Do We Do It' and 'Hitsville USA, The Visit'. There was even a feature on fanzines and magazines in the first four issues.

The initial three issues of *Shades* quickly sold out and each subsequent issue saw the print run increase as its popularity around the scene grew. The number of pages was also to steadily increase, with issue ten having forty, issue eighteen appearing with fifty-two and issue twenty stepping in with sixty.

Three issues per year was standard up until 1988, when the output dropped to two over the next three years.

December 1993 saw the first issue for a year and between then and October 1996 only one per year was to surface. There was no issue forthcoming in 1997 and Derek apologised for this in March 1998 (No.27), saying: *"I think I lost my way somehow in the early part of the year for reasons that I'm not really sure why, but I am back on track now."* Lost his way perhaps, but the high standard remained, although there was to be no increase in the number of copies that appeared as it remained one per year through to June 2006 (No.32).

I rate *Shades* as one of the best fanzines to make an appearance on the scene, an opinion shared by many, and it was a pleasure to catch up with editor Derek Pearson for a chat about this highly rated publication.

As with speaking to most of the editors, I was curious to know why Derek decided to venture into the world of soul fanzines. *"I don't know if there was any sort of exact trigger point that made me decide to start doing a fanzine – at the time I was buying and reading each and every soul related fanzine I could get my hands on,"* came back the reply. *"My background context was that I'd only started going to northern soul all-nighters in 1977 and was rapidly immersing myself in the culture of a soul boy in the late seventies.*

"What's that old saying about 'the devil is in the detail'? Well in the early eighties I was actively buying as many records as I could from any, and as many places as possible, including various American based sales lists and scouring every month the fine print in the sales adverts in the American music magazine of its time - 'Goldmine'. And believe me, when I say fine print I mean fine print – anybody that used to get and/or read the magazine at that time will know exactly what I mean. "The first issue of Shades Of Soul was aired in January 1984 only a few years since I first got involved

in this fascinating scene. It was actually my girlfriend of the time Gillian Sutcliffe (who was later to become my wife) that actually came up with the name for the magazine. I seem to recall we were sat in a bar in the Little Germany area of Bradford city centre and I was running down a long potential list of names for the mag all ending with 'of Soul' (ha ha ha) when suddenly Gillian said 'Shades Of Soul' and the suggestion was quickly cemented in place."

So, having decided to produce a fanzine, and given it a title, what were your initial aims? Publish a few issues to pass the time, or was there a long-term view? "I doubt very much I would've had a long-term view regarding the magazine, as bear in mind at the time I never really had a long-term view of where I wanted to be or to go in life in general, so the magazine would have been no different. Once I'd started doing the mag it sorta snowballed and took on a life of its own."

As I have already mentioned, Shades is arguably up there with the best of all the fanzine type publications, so obviously you set your sights high. Were you surprised as to how well it was received and how long it lasted?" I don't think I had intentionally set my sights high for 'Shades Of Soul' per se, it's just that I intentionally wanted to pack in as much information as possible into the smallest amount of space.

"I've always been a believer that everybody has got a voice that should be heard; now whether they're saying anything of any value is open to question. So, I had pretty much an open-door policy to printing any and all articles that were sent to me. What qualified me as a fit person to judge what was either a good or bad style of writing? "With hindsight I honestly don't think I ever rejected any articles that were sent in to me over the 20 years life span of the magazine. Some sort of critical editor I was eh? [laughs].

"To give you a crystal clear example of what I didn't know what I was doing, I'd typed up a four page article on J.J. Barnes and printed the first two pages in No.3 which ended completely abruptly and un-announced on one page (with not even a cursory 'to be continued on') then completely abruptly and un-announced started again in the following No.4 as if nothing had happened [laughs] and I don't think anybody noticed, or if they did nobody said anything!"

It was obviously hard work maintaining the standard? "Because I'm pretty obsessive though it wouldn't have been described as that then, more likely that I was just very keen and like gathering facts and figures together and writing stuff down. At the time I was a perennial list maker and my life history and memory confirm this thoroughly. Whilst I threw masses and masses of stuff away like everybody does I kept tons and tons of weird and wonderful stuff that perhaps

many other people wouldn't have done [laugh]. Whether I'm just some sort of extreme collector or some sort of mad hoarder is open to question to those that know me well."

But all good things have to come to an end, so what made you decide to stop? "Well by the time it was the year 2000 I'd been doing the magazine continuously for twenty years producing one issue every twelve to eighteen months non-stop. I'd started the mag in 1984 when I was a young, energetic, something year old, but by the end of the decade I was getting older and life was so much harder mentally and physically, but the sunshine on the horizon was I'd just met the love of my life after all these years. Every woman I'd ever gone out with before, every woman I'd ever lived and loved with before, was just a practise, just a trial in leading up to this beautiful woman."

Did you ever regret stopping and did you ever think about starting again?" No, I never regretted stopping it for one moment. I had served my shift in the world of fanzines and it was time to let somebody else take the mantle should they wish. But the age of the physical paper fanzine was rapidly coming to an end with the dawning of a super shiny new digital age. Fanzines continued to exist but not as we used to know them. Think blogs, Twitter, Facebook and all that sort of merry-go-round."

There was no hint that Shades was going to disappear completely, although David did say in his editorial to that thirty-second issue that he could only produce the magazine infrequently, and suggested to anyone who subscribed that they could have a long wait between issues.

The disappearance of Shades was a huge loss to those on the scene who enjoyed the written word and its demise is still lamented today.

I have to thank a two page insert in issue number three of **THE OTIS FILE** to help me define the exact date that this particular publication first saw the light of day, as inside there was not simply an application form, but also illustrations of the first three issues of the newsletter/fanzine/magazine, call it what you like, with issue one dated May 1984, issue two September 1984 and issue three dated January 1985, the latter also having '1st Anniversary Edition' on its cover.

Going by the application form, the 'Appreciation Society' was formed in December 1983 by Swindon based John Stuart and in January 1984 the first four-page newsletter was issued. As the membership grew, it was decided that a 'magazine would be a more appropriate medium'. Membership was £4 per year UK and £6 per year overseas. For your outlay, you would receive three 'Society Magazines' each year, regular newsletters, a membership card and a badge. There was also the opportunity to buy a T-shirt and photos, plus a 10% discount from Soul Survivor Records' mail order lists.

The only copy of the magazine I have is a decent A5, twenty-eight page publication, but it isn't all about Otis, as this particular issue has features on Doris Duke, ZZ Hill, Clyde McPhatter and Syl Johnson. This was also the final issue of *The Otis File*, as from May 1985, the publication was re-named SWEET SOUL MUSIC.

From that first issue of *Sweet Soul Music* I learn that the third issue of *Otis* that I have is actually a re-print, as the editorial states that due to it selling out, it was re-printed but in A5 format, and that would be the format going forward.

The difference in the two magazines is like night and day, black and white, or whatever comparison you wish to make, as *Sweet Soul Music* now ranked alongside others of the same style and format. It was now, however, a forty-eight-page publication, and Otis was reduced to simply appearing on the cover, an interview from 1967 and a video review. Issue two still carried the sub-heading 'Issued by The Otis Redding Appreciation Society' on its cover, but this was the last time it featured as it simply became *Sweet Soul Music – Independent Soul Magazine*, although there was still an association with the 'Otis Society' and the man was remembered in a regular column within the pages of the new styled production. But with four dozen pages, there

was huge room for expansion, and the editor made the most of it with features on everyone from Jackie Wilson and Bobby Bland to Martha Reeves and Fontella Bass.

Issue number six took the magazine up to 1987, and the editorial of that issue stated that it would be a year of change for the magazine, as a complete overhaul was planned for issue seven. And sure enough, there was; but it only really extended to a glossy cover, as content was simply more of the same!

There was no hint that this seventh issue (April 1987) would be the last, but it was. The 30p price increase and the glossy cover was all for nothing.

Although 'northern soul' is a UK manufactured part of the extensive 'soul music' umbrella, with the enthusiasts also being more appreciative of the music of black America than many within its homeland, it doesn't have a stranglehold on the publication side of things, as a handful of examples within these pages will prove. So, let's for the time being, leave the darkest corners of the United Kingdom and cross the Atlantic Ocean to Canada, where 1984 saw the world of soul music publications take another massive stride forward with the publication of SOUL SURVIVOR.

Edited by Richard Pack, along with editor-in-chief Martin Koppel, they put together a thirty-two-page glossy publication of excellent quality, interesting articles and top-notch images. This was as far a cry from the bedroom produced fanzines as you could possibly get. Professionalism with a capital P.

That 'Beginners Guide' began as follows:
"*'Northern Soul music has got nothing at all to do with Soul Music today. They're all living in a time-warp up there, always harping back to obscure sounds from the mid-sixties. Most of them are technically a right load of bilge. And a lot of the big dancing numbers could hardly be termed soulful and the artists aren't even black in a lot of cases.' The above is a quote from the 70s from a soul writer from the south of England and it shows how the south viewed the northern scene. Northern soul was and still is to a certain extent a scene – a cult which revolves around a way of life involving a certain style of dancing, dress and most of all music. The following is the beginners guide to this phenomenon.*"

The four-page article was divided into small subsections: *DANCING - At the start of the evening, dancers can often be seen putting talcum powder on the dance floor to make sliding and spinning easier; THE SOUNDS*
- The pop records were far removed from the rare Soul Sides originally played and were generally called 'STOMPERS'; THE FASHIONS - Northern fashions were centred on baggie trousers, which had wide legs with up to 36 inch bottoms. One black glove was often worn on the right hand; TAILOR MADES - 1970 saw producer Biddu trying to create the Northern sound in Britain, he was the first to produce an acceptable custom-made Northern dance record. [Jimmy James 'A Man Like Me' and Ian Levine's 'Reaching for the Best' by the Exciters are both mentioned] *LEGAL RE-*

There was a mention of there being a separate advertising section, printed on newspaper type paper, from issue two, but whether this materialised or not I have no idea, as none of my issues contain such a thing. It might have been interesting to cast the eyes over, but as I didn't collect records, I wasn't shedding any tears or bemoaning its loss.

But what was within the pages of *Soul Survivor* were well written articles, discographies, reviews and more by contributors of the calibre of Robert Pruter (whose 1991 book *Chicago Soul* is a must read), with issue one containing enough to persuade those who bought it to do likewise with number two and also spread the word to others.

In that first issue, and remember it was on sale and catered for soul enthusiasts on both sides of the Atlantic, were articles on The Radiants, Linda Jones, Irma Thomas, Ric Tic Records, The Fascinations, an interview with James Brown, 'Motown Oddities – a look at early recordings by artists who were later to make their names on the Detroit label', 'Twenty of the Rarest Northern Soul Records – No.1 – The Magnetics – 'Lady In Green', No.20 - Darrell Banks – 'Open The Door To Your Heart' and for the benefit of those across the pond – 'Northern Soul – A Beginners Guide To This English Phenomenon' (which was perhaps not politically correct!), but it would certainly raise a few eyebrows and muttered comments.

94

ISSUES - Selectadisc!; FANZINES - Many Northern

ISSUES - Selectadisc!; FANZINES - Many Northern fanzines have been issued over the years, these were mostly poorly duplicated mags. containing club and record reviews. Among the many were 'Nitelife', 'Soul Source', 'It's The Beat' and 'New Soultime', which left no-one in doubt of its content with its sub-title – 'for stompers, by stompers, about stomping'. Wigan Casino had a short lived magazine called the 'Northern Noise' this was the only professionally printed magazine and lasted only two issues [sic]*; UK NORTHERN LABELS - Inferno, Disco Demand ..; CLUBS - Drugs were widely used on the scene and drug abuse led to the closure of many clubs including The Wheel and The Torch; ENDERS - Although the Northern scene was based on the fast dancing numbers, a few slower numbers would be played towards the end of the night. One of the biggest was the Bacharach-David number, 'Long After Tonight Is All Over' by Jimmy Radcliffe on Musicor; UK COVER VERSIONS - At the height of the Northern Soul boom in 1975 record companies who were unable to track down the original versions of Northern favourites, would record cover versions on unknown English pop groups in an effort to cash in on the craze.* [Wigan's Ovation and Soft Cell are mentioned]*; BOOTLEGS - There can be few collectors who do not have bootlegs among their collections, whether they know it or not. Selectadisc, the Nottingham record retailer, alone issued near to 200 bootlegs; COVER-UPS - The DJ's cover up obscure records to try and keep the record secret and to stop it from being bootlegged. The records are given fictional titles and the artists also are given false names often that of well-known Northern Artists, to give extra appeal to the punters.*

I have not reproduced everything which appeared alongside the heading, but enough to give you an idea of what was written (no idea by whom), and I wonder what the Canadians/Americans, or others in the *"twenty-five different countries"* where the magazine was apparently copies in the likes of

Manchester's Beatin' Rhythm record shop, here in the UK, where I bought mine?

The photographic content within all ten of the issues of *Soul Survivor* was excellent, while the articles ranged from Otis Leavill, Felice Taylor and Roy Hamilton to Sylvia Moy, Denise LaSalle and Kim Weston. There was even an A-Z of blue-eyed soul in issue number eight.

Sadly *Soul Survivor* wasn't true to its name, as it didn't, and issue No.10 (March 1989) was the final issue. It had sold well and by the time of that final issue, only numbers three, four, seven and nine were still available. Today you can still pick up odd copies, like those of many other titles, some being easier to find than others.

One of those 'obscure' publications that has materialised is SAILORS DELIGHT, a glossy covered, 20.5 x 25.5cm publication which was edited by Paul 'Sailor' Vernon from Mill Hill in London, with issues stretching from anything up to seventy pages. Turning the pages though, it could certainly be considered something of a strange publication. Some of the content was akin to the odd fanzine with its jocular tone and spoof articles, but it also carried some excellent well researched material such as a piece on DJ Mike Raven in No.12A circa September 1982 (the editor was apparently superstitious and didn't want an issue No.13) and 'A Buyer's Guide to Post-War Gospel Records' in No.14, circa May 1983.

But such articles were few and far between as the majority of pages were taken over with record sales and auctions which included everything from blues, R&B and soul on 78s, 45s and albums. Looking through the lists, there were bargains to be had, such as Barbara Acklin's 'Love Makes A Woman' on USA Brunswick for £1.

There is not much info to go on

for this publication, but I did manage to find out that it ceased to appear after issue No.17, prior to the appearance of *Blues & Rhythm* magazine.

As something of a postscript, Paul Vernon was a noted blues fanatic and rare record dealer and went on to write an autobiography entitled *Last Swill and Testament* in 2008.

Mentioning that *Blues & Rhythm* magazine, it is worth noting that although the music had developed from R&B of the early sixties to predominately 'Northern/Modern Soul' there were still many out there who preferred the blues and R&B and *Blues & Rhythm* magazine certainly catered for them.

I have a copy of this Tony Burke edited publication from 1988 and it is certainly a well-produced magazine, A4 in size, containing articles, discographies and reviews, and in the latter, you could find albums by the likes of The Showmen, Robert Parker, Chris Kenner and Solomon Burke. It was priced at £1.85p.

Another eighties blues publication was *Pickin' The Blues*, a small, compact A5 read, published by M.S. and F.A. Harris from East Calder in West Lothian. The first issue, dated January 1982, was no more than eight pages for 20p, but by the time it reached issue five, June 1982, it had increased to a healthy twenty pages and was now priced at 30p.

It was full of classic fanzine material and should certainly have appeased those who favoured that type of music.

But back to soul, and another early-eighties publication that found its way north to south-west Scotland long after it first came out was GROOVE WEEKLY. This is yet another 'down south' publication and was the brain-child of twenty-year-old Ralph Tee, who was later to become assistant editor of *Blues and Soul*. Ralph was to inform me that *Groove Weekly* "started in May 1980 and inside it was the very first issue of my abbreviated name Ralph 'Tee', It ran for 100 issues, the last being October 1982 when I was seduced by Pete Tong at 'Blues and Soul' to go and work for them instead."

Unfortunately, despite there being 100 issues, I have been unable to obtain the majority of them, but in one that I did stumble upon, issue No.30 (December 19th 1980), Ralph mentions that along with friends Marios and Nigel they initially produced a weekly, four-sided newsletter with a print run of fifty, which cost nothing to produce, while the current sixteen page, A4 size publication, which sold at 10p, cost £240 to print. Much if not all of that cost I imagine was clawed back through the numerous adverts. Having said that, turning the pages of issue No.51 (June 19th 1981) there is a mention that if you paid postage and packing of either £2.50 for ten weeks or £4.50 for twenty weeks, you would receive the magazine for free!

Content was, as could be expected, London linked, but credit must go to Ralph and co. for putting such a publication together, more so as they appear to have managed it on a weekly basis through the passage of time.

Venue reports, concert and record reviews, letters - they were all there in what would range from twelve to sixteen pages of this very creditable publication.

Ralph is still heavily involved in the soul scene as I write, as a DJ, radio presenter and also as co-owner of Expansion Records.

One other 'unknown' publication came out of Birkenhead, the Jon Williams produced SOUL BLOWIN.

A4 size, priced at 25p and printed on glossy paper throughout, this was a sixteen-page read and was, according to Jon in his editorial of issue No.2, "*the North's rapidly expanding soul funk and jazz-mag.*" Page seven goes as far to proclaim that *Soul Blowin* is the "*North's No.4 soul mag*", but unfortunately there is no mention of what the other three were!

Again, I don't have a copy of issue No.1 so it is difficult to be exact as to when this one first appeared on the streets of Birkenhead/Liverpool, but there are a couple of references to 1983 in issue No.2 so we will simply leave it at that.

Jon certainly knew what he wanted to do - interviews, reviews etc - and what direction he wanted to take with the magazine, but as I have never seen another copy it is difficult to tell how long he managed to keep this publication going, or if he achieved his aims.

Something that did stand out in this second issue was the back-page advert for Soul On Sound, a London based company in Mayfair no less, who were offering "*a new concept in soul music entertainment – a fortnightly stereo cassette magazine – featuring news, reviews and star interviews*". A new concept indeed and I wonder how many wandered into Cheverton Records in Liverpool or Spin-Inn in Manchester and bought one, or sent off their cheque or postal order for £1.50 to obtain a copy?

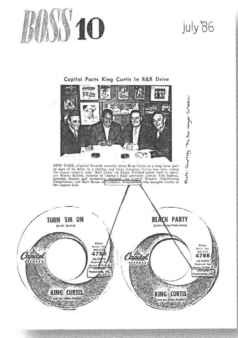

Time to slip in yet another publication which is both obscure and only of interest to a select few – BOSS, from March 1986. Edited by Roy Simonds, a name already familiar to many, this was yet another of your 'Appreciation Society' type publications, being everything King Curtis.

There are some eighteen issues of this fanzine, with numbers one to fifteen being published in A5 size, with the others in A4. Issued bi-monthly, printed in black and white and averaging twenty pages, content was as it said on the label, with reviews, photos and label scans.

As I said, obscure and only for the select few, although an issue for the collector who requires one of everything soul related that appeared.

Another candidate for the 'Soul In Print Top Ten' appeared in the summer of 1986, but there was no hint from its initial ventures into the soul music world of just how good this publication was to become. That, however, does not mean that the undated, A4, side-stapled, twenty-eight-page first edition of VOICES FROM THE SHADOWS, which was priced at 60p, or the first three or four for that matter, were not up to expectations. Far from it actually, as Rod Dearlove's publication could sit comfortably alongside its stablemates, nudging some of them into the 'Donkey Derby' whilst *Voices* was out on the track at Ascot.

Having learnt the ropes, so to speak, and had a couple of ups and downs with *Midnite Express*, what made Rod venture once again into the world of soul in print, I wondered? "*I'm just an enthusiastic person,*" came the reply. "*I was buying a lot of really good records no-one seemed to be mentioning. There was a group of us all buying and tape swopping.*"

'The Complete Sam Dees', 'Guide to Gospel', 'Stateside Connection', 'Men Behind the Music', 'Japanese

Issues' and reviews made up the bulk of that first issue, but it was all enough to whet the appetite of the faithful. They couldn't even complain when issue number two appeared towards the end of 1986 with a cover price of £1, as the number of pages had increased to thirty-two, it was now centre-stapled and looked considerably better than that first issue.

Voices, however, may well have become yet another of those one-off publications, disappearing without trace, as Rod explained in his second editorial saying: *"Forty pence is a hefty increase, I know. And it wasn't without a great deal of thought that I decided to press on with 'Voices' after that fateful Saturday morning when our initial printing deal fell through. Devastation is not a pretty sight. Spending the remainder of the day banging on doors – and my forehead against several walls – (perks of the job?) I eventually gained 'Voices' not only a stay of execution, but a new deal which will guarantee our future. Admittedly, it makes the mag more expensive to produce, but it is a dam sight more reliable, it takes more than love."*

Rod continued: *"If your response had not been so positive my decision would have been made a lot easier, thank you sincerely for your letters of encouragement and calls, all of these made me realise just how much you enjoyed our first issue. I can assure you we are here to stay. There is so much quality black music not covered in sufficient depth, we hope, in our small way, to re-address the balance."* This was akin to attempting to break a record to the dancers at a soul night - you had belief in the tune and kept plugging it until it was accepted.

Struggling to keep *Voices* going seemed ongoing for Rod, but he was to recall a stroke of luck that produced something of a boom in sales." *It was the ultimate irony that after John Lias paid Blues & Soul a backhanded compliment of sorts in an issue of 'Voices' in 1988, saying it wasn't as good as it was in the 70s,*

SUPPORTING QUALITY SOUL, GOSPEL, R&B. INDEPENDANT LABELS A SPECIALITY

we were banned from advertising in it. If I could have planned this Machiavellian twist any better I would.......well, no, I couldn't have planned this any better, because the response to the ban was a landslide compared to the modest uptake from the actual first advert they'd ran. We'd paid for an ad to run over two consecutive issues of B&S and the first advert provoked a modest amount of enquires, about fifteen to twenty from memory, but the ban meant everyone, or at least it seemed to me, wanted to see this new magazine that B&S found so offensive. After the ban, 'Voices' really took off."

Despite issue three reverting back to side-stapling, it was centre-stapling for issue four and then suddenly Rod's persistence paid off and *Voices From The Shadows* went glossy. The punters realised that here was something of quality and there was no looking back or remembering that 40p increase.

Voices number six hit forty-eight pages of reading, but it was the following issue, the fifty-six page (including the cover) number seven, that really set the tongues wagging and pushed the magazine to new heights, and it wasn't because of the new regular cover price of £1.50.

There had always been a list of contributors' names under that of Rod's own as editor, luminaries such as Tim Brown and Glyn Thornhill amongst others, but now there was a 'Managing Director', a first amongst fanzines, and it was none other than noted snooker champion Steve Davis. There was no fanfare of trumpets, no 'keep the faith' logo on the waistcoat at snooker championships. Davis came in unannounced and allowed Rod to continue in the manner he wanted to, bringing quality with a capital Q to the world of soul music publications.

Was Rod willing to reveal how Steve Davis got involved, I wondered? *"Robbie Vincent told him to read Voices. After issue six I was in so much debt with* the mag I couldn't go on. I don't tend to think things through. Steve rang me one Saturday morning from Monaco and said issue six was great so I had to tell him that was the last one. I was on the point of selling records from my collection to cover the costs of it. He told me to do nothing and then he came to see me and told me his intentions to keep it going. I do remember that call from Monaco going on for hours, I dread to think what it cost."

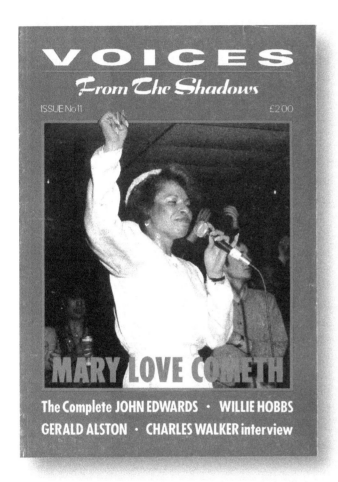

The editorial of issue number six had carried a veiled hint at what was to come, with Rod writing: "When I initially founded 'Voices' I never thought I would be in a position to write this, but I can now report that the magazine is in a viable financial position that it will appear more regularly and become far more professional. We will be appearing every three months initially. At a future date, we hope to publish 'Voices' bi-monthly. We will also be launching a record label later in the year."

No-one would have called *Voices* anything but a professional publication, but No.9 (Winter 88/89) took UK soul publications to a new level – eighty pages, full colour cover and not a staple in sight as it was now perfect bound. Soul Music's answer to *Readers Digest*. There was even a full-page advert for Miller lager on the back cover!

Content was an excellent mixture, perhaps edging towards the Modern side, but there was always something for everyone. Where else could you get 'Soul In Scotland', 'The Complete Jack Montgomery', a twenty-one page 'Modern Soul' special (issue No.13) and what bordered towards a 'page three' colour image of Jo Armstead (issue No.14).

By issue number nineteen, the cover price had risen from £2.50 to £3.50 and had risen again to £4.00 for issue number twenty-two. When issue number twenty-five appeared it was £5.00, but it was still value for money. It was also, however, the end of the road, the last edition of the quality publication.

"I started the magazine with four words I wrote on a scrap of paper – VOICES FROM THE SHADOWS" said Rod in that final editorial. "We were as near penniless as a young married couple with a family could be. I wanted to produce the best soul music magazine in the world. It was, of course, pure bravado. Nonsense; a reverie; a pipe dream. This issue of VOICES is not about me. It's about all the people I've worked with; all the people who've contributed in any small way; even those from whom I've since parted company. Friends who've died; friends who have loaned me money; friends who've offered me support through times of personal trauma and family illness. Thank you. Thank you sincerely."

Rod finished by saying: "I'd like to think everyone connected to this magazine will look back on it and think like I do. It was worth it."

He was also to tell me later: *"I had massive health issues that I don't want to put in print, and I was badly let down by a number of people and badly ripped off by people I thought were my friends. In 2000, I severed my ties with the soul scene. I won't be back. I was actually still trying to work on the mag as late as 1988 or 1989 from memory."*

There was obviously never any chance of Rod resurrecting *Voices*, but there must have been some good memories and high points?*" Every issue was a high point. The waiting for the design, the waiting for the mag to be printed. I used to put one copy on the passenger seat for the drive home and would keep glancing at it. If I caught a light, I'd read some of it. The next day we'd mail them out and then the phone would ring for days with people saying how much they enjoyed it."*

Voices From The Shadows is certainly something that Rod Dearlove can be proud of, and although some of the content is a little dated today, it is still an interesting read and a publication that should be part of the collection of anyone who enjoys soul in print.

The summer of 1986 was to thrust yet another new title into the ever-increasing list of reading material for the soul devotees, with the appearance of **MOVIN' UPTOWN**. It was edited by Nick Cull, who felt the need to publicise real soul music at a time when numerous groups used black backing singers and a *New Musical Express* poll saw names such as Paul Weller and Simply Red appear in the Soul/Funk section.

So, what did *Movin' Uptown* offer the soul public? Sixteen A4 pages, crammed with record and venue reviews that jostled for space with the odd article, and I do mean jostled for space, as Nick used up more or less every inch he could without making his brainchild overloaded.

Issue two appeared in October 1986 and actually brought a reduction in price and an increase in pages, something as rare on the soul market-place as some Shrine forty-fives! Not only did the price and page numbers change, but the whole format of the magazine did as well. It was now A5, giving it a much better look.

Content, however, didn't change and it was much of the same, and this carried through to issue number four, which was at one point said to be the final one. However, thanks to a friend of the editor, a fifth issue was confirmed to have been published, although missing from the files at this end.

Early 1987 saw **THE OWLS EFFORT** make its nocturnal, no sorry, initial appearance on the northern soul scene. Edited by Richard Domar from Wolverhampton, this was an A4, side stapled publication, priced at 80p, consisting of thirty pages, well twenty- seven if you take out the crossword and clues and a quiz, but then again if you managed or could be bothered to give it a go, there was the opportunity to win one hundred 'seventies' singles for both. Strange prize for what professed to be a northern soul publication, but Richard did mention within the pages that he would probably include articles on the Modern side of things if anyone wanted to contribute. He also added if the winner of the quiz and the crossword wanted to change his or her prize to 'sixties' singles then they would only receive ten! Think I know what I would have chosen.

The Owls Effort was stencilled and duplicated, so it was text only, which wasn't a bad thing, while the inclusion of a film review plus a couple of joke-like articles were thankfully overshadowed by decent reading – 'A Night Out at the Catacombs'; 'Future Monsters'; 'Detecting a Counterfeit' and an article by the ever- readable Tim Brown.

Issue two had an excellent cover illustration, something that was repeated to a slightly lesser degree on all but issue seven, while Richard apologised for the "*poorly printed bits*" which was down to the duplicator, along with having a moan about the pathetic response to the crossword and quiz in issue one.

The film reviews continued in issue two, but this time around one of the two under the spotlight was *Quadrophenia*, which does feature a few soul tunes, while the other, *Coast To Coast*, starring Lenny Henry, was originally shown on BBC2 and is still available to view on YouTube. This film, or whatever it was classed as, features no less than eighteen Motown tunes in the soundtrack, and to be honest is quite passable.

Issue three of *The Owls Effort* saw the cover price rise to £1, while issue five was £1.5p, six was up another 20p and what was the final issue, No.7, was priced at £1.50p. The number of pages, however, had not shown any increase.

Content continued to be on a par with, if not better than, some of the other publications in the marketplace with issue No.5 containing a twelve-page article by Pete Smith on *Black Music* magazine. In all, there were seven issues published.

'The Best In Motor City Soul' was the sub-title of **DETROIT CITY LIMITS** issue No.1 in November 1987, thirty A4 good old side-stapled pages for a mere £1.50, and it wasn't all about Motown. In fact, very little of it was; a couple of pages of 'Gordy's Groovers' and that was about it. But as we all know, there was more to the motor city than Berry's hive of industry.

"Detroit City Limits is for the dedicated Detroit soul collector and its aims are simple – to gather as much information about the artists, labels, producers, writers etc. into one authoritative source. Originally the magazine was to be a general soul mag. but that would have proved an impossible task as Soul is an ongoing musical form still creatively active" wrote Graham Anthony in his first editorial.

What then did the latest publication on the scene have to offer? Gino Washington plus discography, The Thelma label, Cody Black, The Magictones, Carol Anderson, The Geneva label, The Fantastic Four, Sport Records, The Detroit Connection and a Jimmy Scott discography.

And so it continued, with more of the same in issue two, issue three and issue four - or was four different?

101

Well, it was and it wasn't. Let me explain. At one point I only had the one copy of *Detroit City Limits* – issue four. This wasn't A4, but measured 21 x 24cm and it showed signs of reading by its previous owner(s). I was then given a complete set of the magazine, issues one to ten, (thanks again Dave) and every one was A4 size, including issue four. The only difference is, as you could expect, is that the printing etc is smaller and there is no mention in issue five of a reprint or anything. What issue five did contain was an additional ten pages, but it was back down to thirty-four for issue six and Motown continued to be kept at arm's length.

By issue nine the printing had changed, although not completely, and looked better for it. All back issues had been reportedly sold and the magazine looked to be on a strong footing. But even with the usual subscription rates being printed in issue ten, an eleventh one sadly failed to materialise and *Detroit City Limits* was no more. For many it was yet another greatly missed publication.

One-off publications can be something of a nightmare as they can appear and disappear in the blink of an eye. A small print run, perhaps sold at only one venue, and that's it, gone. Something that does help is the editor being well- known and if he was, and if he had previously appeared in print, then word would get around and copies of the magazine, should any still be available, would filter throughout the scene in general. One such publication is GROOVIN A LA GO-GO by

that effervescent scribe Dave McCadden.

Groovin is a forty-page A5 publication and within its pages no-one is safe from McCadden's pen, as his 'Northern Soul Hall of Fame' shows, with Soul Sam, Martin Koppel, Ian Levine, Simon Soussan, Russ Winstanley, Richard Searling and Dave Evison all being put up for ridicule by the editor. There is more nonsense within the pages, but nothing that would see Dave McCadden receive a solicitor's letter, or a visit from the local constabulary; it was all tongue in cheek.

It was not all jocular though, as there were record reviews, and Pete Lawson writing about the 'State of the Scene', while there was not one but two crosswords. What was it with crosswords in these soul publications?

Although a one-off, I don't think it was intended to be so, as Dave seeks contributions from writers, whilst Ivan Ward, writing about a soul night in Carlisle, mentions that it is his first column in the long-awaited magazine.

Dave McCadden also offered something that no other editor ever did - "*If anybody feels this mag is not worth the money, send it back to me and I'll refund your money.*"

It's the summer of 1988 and it saw SOUL FILE, a twenty-two page, A4, and need I say it, side-stapled publication, materialise from the Preston home of J. C. Orritt. That first issue consisted mainly of record reviews and an Arctic label listing, with perhaps the

most interesting feature appearing on the back page, an advert for the 100 Club and an application form to join the '6Ts Rhythm and Soul Society'. According to the accompanying note, the police were unhappy with the previous membership scheme not being strict enough, so it was decided to cancel it and start a brand-new system for everyone.

Soul File offered much the same as countless other fanzines over the years and yes, it must have been difficult for some editors to find new angles and different artists to write about, but with the world of soul music being so wide, it wasn't an impossible task, it just required time and patience.

Over the months that followed, it showed an improvement and by issue six (August 1991) it was centre-stapled and contained twenty-eight pages, but perhaps just lacked that special 'something' to take it onwards. Like countless others, there was no prior warning as to its demise and it disappeared without trace from the scene.

As the nineties edged that little bit closer, along came **SOULFUL KINDA MUSIC** in March 1989, a publication that would outlive almost all its competitors and one that would be accepted as a 'must read' by many who frequented the venues up and down the country. An ideal companion on those often long journeys back home. Edited by Dave Rimmer, *SKM* as it became commonly known was to last for seventy-two issues and I wondered if, in those early days, Dave thought it would last so long?

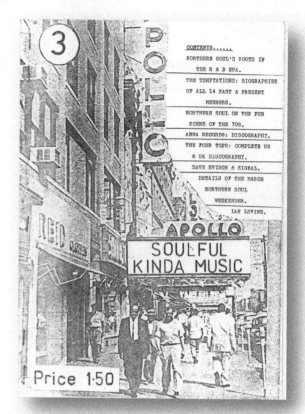

"Never in a million years lol. You don't plan how long these things are going to last when you start them though do you? It just kept going."

It certainly did, but where did that inspiration come from to kickstart it in the first place? *"Two things made me start it: buying a copy of Derek Pearson's Shades Of Soul, and complete disillusionment with Blues & Soul. I kept going for so long because I enjoyed doing it, and at its peak I was selling 800 copies an issue, which meant I was making quite a lot of money out of it."*

Issue No.1, which was undated and priced at £1, was obtained whilst in the process of putting this book together and consisted of thirty-four A4 pages, with features on Edwin Starr, Garnett Mimms, J.J. Barnes, Ric-Tic records and others. There is also a list of 'periodicals' from both the UK and the States, a couple of which I found unfamiliar.

In his first editorial, Dave wrote: *"This mag. represents my first attempt at writing about soul music, so as the editorial, I thought I'd try to sum up my feelings about the music we all love.*

"To me, soul music is defined by the emotion expressed in the singers voice. I'm not one of those people who believe that you have to be black to sing with soul. If that were true you would have to be black to appreciate it."

Having gone on to explain how he got into the music and expressing further thoughts on how he left it and got back into it, he added: *"If you've waded through my personal memories so far, perhaps you'll go on to enjoy the mag. I hope so, as I said, it's my first attempt* so I can only judge how successful it is if people buy it and reply with their comments. Even the rude ones." Needless to say, Dave passed the test and *Soulful Kinda Music* was not simply accepted by the multitude but went on to be one of the best publications around.

Those early issues were somewhat basic in style, as could probably be expected from the time – A4 in size, with the customary side-stapling, but looks aren't everything and what *SKM* lacked in style, it made up for in content. That 'basic' look, however, was soon to disappear and Dave commented in the editorial of issue five: *"I think things have started to come together with this issue"* and it did look a better produced publication, but it wasn't really until issue No.17 - a Wigan 20th Anniversary Special - that the layout moved up a few rungs.

Whilst extolling the virtues of the Casino within the pages of that particular issue, Dave also looked at the 'rival' publications, mentioning that *"the outlook for existing soul mags is bleak at the moment, most of the mags that have been around for the last five years or so have either gone into semi-retirement or just disappeared. On the positive side, two new mags have appeared."*

SKM, however, strode onwards, and upwards, as issue No.21 (March 1995) saw a new contributor join the likes of Arthur Dudley, Dave Halsall, Rob Moss and Bill Randle, that new addition being akin to a football club signing a multi-million-pound superstar, as Dave Godin was certainly considered that by many within soul music circles. It is without doubt that the presence of Dave Godin within its pages would have seen the readership of *SKM* increase and do much to guarantee its future.

Whilst writing this particular piece I thought that to do *Soulful Kinda Music* justice a complete issue listing, akin to a discography, would be required, so I was surprised to find with the pages of issue No.26 (June 1996) that Stephen Copeman had penned an article entitled 'The Story So Far', which covered the first twenty-six issues. Perhaps his comment: *"Soulful Kinda Music is delivering the goods with a real passion, which is not easy with such a demanding insatiable and diverse public"* summed the magazine up perfectly.

Always looking to improve, the introduction of a full colour cover for issue fifty-six, with Maxine Brown taking the honour, took the magazine forward, but it was also to see the last of Dave Godin's articles. There was something that was unknown at the time, and it was four issues further on (No. 60 December 2004) that Dave's passing, two months previously, was recorded.

The 18th Anniversary edition of *SKM* appeared in March 2008 (No.72) and it was to be the last. In his editorial Dave wrote: *"This will be the last issue for a while because I'm starting a new job this month which will take more of my time, but the magazine will still appear sometime in the future."* The fingers were crossed, but that seventy-third issue never did materialise, leaving a huge void in the world of soul music publications. Later, on the Soul Source website, Dave was to elaborate a little more, saying: *"the mag has been part of my life for the last eighteen years, but sales have dropped to a quarter of what they were five years ago (and I don't think the quality of the contents has dropped), so it just became a question of whether it was worth spending all that time producing it, and the cost of getting it printed to sell less than 200 copies which is what happened with the last one. It's a decision I've been thinking about for nearly a year now."*

Obviously giving up something that you had nurtured from infancy was always going to be hard, but pressure of work and Dave's contributions to the bookshelves had to also come into the equation; but it must have been difficult and also disappointing to call it a day? *"It was a combination of things that eventually killed it off. When I started it was with a manual typewriter, there was no internet lol and most of the articles by contributors arrived in the post as hand written articles with photocopied labels that I cut out and stuck down with Pritt stick. I upgraded to an electric typewriter quite quickly, but it was only when PCs became commonplace, and meant people could email me, that things got easier.*

"However, this also led to the demise of the mag because once the internet really kicked in, people

WIGAN CASINO

Soulful Kinda Music
A Special Issue For Wigan Casino's 20th Anniversary

£2.50

LIMITED EDITION
20 years of memories

Issue Seventeen

stopped buying mags in anything like the number they used to. All the info was becoming available on the net anyway. It meant sales dropped to less than 200 copies per issue, and given the amount of time it took to produce, it just wasn't worth doing any longer. I was sorry to see the mag disappear, it had been part of my life for twenty years, but I'd started my own website, and wanted to concentrate on that. I wasn't sorry to see the workload go though. Producing forty pages every three months was hard work."

I did, however, wonder if Dave ever considered resurrecting *SKM* at any time down the line. *"No! lol. My wife died in 2010, and I lost a lot of interest in life in general for a long time. Restarting the mag came a long, long way down my list of priorities. I was still doing the odd discography mag though (I think there were twelve 'Special Issues' in total) and found that I was enjoying doing the detective work involved in compiling discographies. That's what led to the books.*

"I've now published nine books and have two more in progress; I think when they are published that will be enough."

Having mentioned the enjoyment in doing the 'detective work' for his discographies, as something of a finale, I wondered if there were any real 'stand-out' memories from those seventy-two issues of *SKM*? *"Without a doubt the interview with Don Mancha,*

when I found out who Jack Montgomery was for the first time would be the highlight"* came the quick reply. This was an interview that was to appear in issue No. 32 (December 1997).

As Dave mentioned, he also produced a number of 'special issues', off-shoots of *Soulful Kinda Music*, including *Rare Soul Labels Volumes 1 – 5*; Artists Discographies; Label Discographies; *The Collectors Guide to Detroit* in August 2006 and *The Collectors Guide to Chicago* in January 2008.

Sharing the same title as Richard Temple's huge northern floor-filler and the Manchester record shop, Pete Smith's BEATIN'RHYTHM made its initial appearance in July 1989 direct from the editor's St Leonards-on-Sea, East Sussex home. It kept to the same, now common, layout format of A4, although it was really A3 folded over, but was still side-stapled and for the first eight issues or so it concentrated more on UK releases than any of the other publications ever did.

" I've had some experience in running a fanzine (non- soul related) in the past" wrote Pete in his first editorial, *"and have been into the northern scene since 1974 so I know most of the complexities involved in a project like this. I've also contributed to magazines in the past, most recently the 'Owls Effort' fanzine, but thought it was about time I stopped lining other people's pockets and did something for myself."*

He also mentioned as to what sort of direction his own publication would take – *"The UK's top Northern Soul DJs were jetting out to the USA in the hope of uncovering the next 'monster' sound. What many people didn't realise was that many excellent Northern sounds had actually been released in the UK in the 60's, but due to lack of distribution and airplay they sold only a handful of copies. Not only that, but several excellent dance records had actually been produced in the UK itself and were just waiting to be discovered. It is these records and their labels that this magazine is going to be based around. It's not going to be about the artists and their careers, but simply a magazine about rare UK soul records."*

Having been involved with a fanzine before was obviously a huge help, being aware of all the pitfalls, but Pete mentioned that it wasn't soul related, so what was it? *"Missing Link - David Bowie fanzine,"* came the reply. *"It was all about bootlegs, live tapes, rare videos etc. It lasted for approximately fourteen issues from 1984 to 1988."*

Pete was certainly true to his word and those early, three dozen or so page issues of *Beatin' Rhythm* covered releases on the likes of Columbia, Parlophone, HMV, CBS, Fontana, Decca, Polydor and Sue among others. There were numerous reviews, backed up by interesting articles on subjects such as 'Collectable LP's and EP's from the Sixties', 'Whatever happened to…', 'UK bands who did cover versions of soul tunes', 'Shopping – the best shops for soul records' and 'Independent UK record labels'. There was also 'The Top 50 UK 45's', but can anyone guess what was considered to be number one? You would probably be wrong, as it was Chapter Five – 'You Can't Mean It'. Really! How could this be better than Frankie and Johnny or Timi Yuro? There was also an article in issue six which covered what other fanzines were out there, or had been, with Pete giving them marks out of five.

Included in that list were the following and their respective 'marks': *Collectors Soul* – *"an interesting magazine with a lot of historical content"* Rating **½; *Soul Cargo* – *"Rather too much of a hotch-pop for the northern fanatic, but still interesting reading."* Rating ***; *Soul Time* – *"In my opinion, one of the best, if not the best soul fanzine of the lot, not so much for the content which is nothing out of the ordinary, but because of Dave McCadden's brilliant sense of humour and fearless slagging off of people he thought should be slagged off."* Rating *****; *New Soul Time* – *"Lots of listings, reviews, venues and a few records for sale, but often less than twenty pages thick."* Rating ***; *Soul Symbol* – *"Maybe I would have appreciated this mag more if I'd attended Yate instead of the Casino, but this is one to give a miss I'm afraid."* Rating *½; *Talk of the North* – *"The mag does what it sets out to do and does it well."* Rating ***; *Soul Source* – *"The main content is venue reports but there's the occasional discography and a few letters etc. A bit of a ragbag really but chockfull o' memories."* Rating **; *Nite Life* – *"Takes over where Soul Time left off."* Rating ****; *It's The Beat* – *"Less entertaining than its predecessors, being rather brief and lacking in satire that can be found in Dave's [McCadden] other mags."* Rating **; *Northern Noise* – *"As with Wigan Casino's own record label, its magazine was also a crock of shit (now there's some objective journalism for you)."* Rating *; *Okeh Northern Soul* – *"Issue one has the dubious distinction of having the worst cover ever seen on a magazine, an A4 page with a drawing of a clenched fist, somebody doing a handstand and the title handwritten. Loads of wasted space and.uninformative articles."* Rating **; *Midnite Express* – *"Something for everyone here. A very good mag, highly recommended."* Rating ****½; *Shades of*

BEATIN' RHYTHM

NORTHERN SOUL FOR COLLECTORS

UK SUE LABEL DISCOGRAPHY...NORTHERN SOUL ON CD...1974 REVISITED plus Rare 45's galore in glorious monochrome, news, reviews etc.

BEATIN' 10
RHYTHM

IN THIS ISSUE....The TWISTED WHEEL Revisited....SOUL DOWN UNDER....
UK RCA & MGM Discographies....DARROW FLETCHER....Northern Soul CD's
Now featuring not only UK rarities but also USA Northern Soul 45's
42 SOUL PACKED PAGES....PAY NO MORE THAN £2.50p....SUPPORT THE 'ZINES!

Soul – *"Always a good read, but its popularity can be put down to the fact that there was little or no competition in the late 80's and a real dearth of northern soul reading material."* Rating ***; *The Owls Effort* – *"This could have been a great mag, but Richard's off-handedness tends to offend and half the time he probably doesn't realise he's doing it."* Rating ***½; *Detroit City Limits* – *"A must for all Detroit Collectors."* Rating ****; *Soulful Kinda Music* – *"Still going strong and improving all the time, SKM covers a broad spectrum of soul music but with the accent on northern."* Rating ****. Interesting thoughts!

Despite its standard A4 size, there were also a couple of issues published in A5, *"Simply to cut down the price of photocopying"* - a size I personally prefer, and then *Beatin' Rhythm* took on a more modern look when computers began to come to the fore and that slightly different look was to set in from issue number fourteen. But by now, there was little regularity between issues as that fourteenth issue (August 1995) was the first for the year. The following year, there were no issues forthcoming and most people thought that it had died a death, but like the boomerang, back it came with a fifteenth issue in January 1997; although by now the majority of the content was centred around cd reviews.

Beatin' Rhythm is still talked about today, something that Pete must be proud about, while he must have been ticking all the right boxes; but from a more personal point of view what did he think the magazine gave its readers that others didn't? *"Firstly, I think it filled a gap, as all the other fanzines were about American releases. It also introduced people to an awful lot of records they would otherwise never have heard – don't forget this is way pre- internet. For instance, if I had to do a label discography, I'd have to find a publication and then glean the info from that.*

"There were obviously high and low points along the way. The 'lows' were never being able to get enough copies made. I also deeply regret an editorial I did mentioning Dave Godin, totally uncalled for and embarrassing. I knew what I meant, but it came out the wrong way. [Prior to speaking with Pete, I was going to print part of that editorial relating to Dave Godin, as I thought it worth including, but as it was something that he now regrets I decided that to simply leave it at that]. *"Highs", were mainly discovering new records. The first mentions of things like Ketty Lester 'Some Things Are Better Left Unsaid', Leonard Whiting 'That's What Mamma Say' and countless others were in my magazine, found by me or the readers."*

Issue sixteen of *Beatin' Rhythm*, another A5 version, is dated Autumn 1997, and although Pete mentions in his editorial that the next issue would be out around February 1998, having found no other issues, I wondered if this indeed was the final issue of *Beatin' Rhythm* and why it suddenly stopped. *"Yes, it was,"* confirmed Pete. *"I had a new girlfriend (who I eventually married) and didn't have those long lonely nights to work on it like I used to have."*

As something of an add-on, I have an A4, twenty-two page *Collectors Guide To UK Label Northern Soul* that Pete published in 1992, covering records from eighty-five different labels. Bet no-one could name them all? I did wonder if there were any other 'supplements', but Pete confirmed that this was the only one and that as it was so expensive to produce, he just did a run of around one hundred.

I will finish the eighties as I did the seventies, by throwing in another two obscure publications that remain outwith my collection and knowledge. Firstly, there is one called *Right Tracks*, edited by Ian Stebbing. A note tells me that there were three issues of this, from around 1982, with the third of that trio being dated early 1983. The other title is *Okeh Soul Promotions*. Edited by Neil and Jackie Clewes, there are at least two issues of this one, with the second dated December 1988.

THE NINETIES

It is a highly debatable point that had it not been for Motown, then northern soul as we know it would never have materialised. Motown was the label above all others that filled those youth club dance floors, continuing through the decades as the vaults were opened and explored for those recorded but shunned and rejected tracks that still spring up today, countless years after having been put onto tape via the fabled Snakepit.

Back in the sixties, we had Dave Godin's *Hitsville* dedicated exclusively to the sound of the Motorcity, but it was to be another twenty years before another publication was dedicated to Motown and its artists.

MOTOWN INTERNATIONAL COLLECTORS CLUB spanned both sides of the Atlantic, with both UK and USA distribution and marketing, and had the man whose idea it was to put such a magazine together, Reg Bartlette of Winnipeg, Canada, at the helm. That name might not be a familiar one to many, but he not only wrote the excellent book *Off The Record: Motown By Master Number – 1959-1989* and owned Mel-O-Dy records, but at one time owned arguably the biggest Motown record collection in the world.

A number of copies of this publication had come my way, but a copy of the first issue of the *MICC* publication had failed to materialise. However, I managed to get in touch with Reg and a copy of the cover was forthcoming. He was also able to update me on when that first issue actually came out. *"It was January 1991. I had just sold my Motown record collection at this time to Berry Gordy, Jr. I knew the Gordy family, especially Esther. The entire 10,000 plus original collection, considered at that time to be the most complete in the world, with all the 45s from every label consisting of a commercial pressing and a white label promo of every record. Originally shipped to Los Angeles, the collection eventually went to Esther Gordy Edwards at The Motown Historical Museum on West Grand Boulevard where it all began!"* But was Frank Wilson's 'Do I Love You' amongst them I wondered? *"One disc I did not have was the Frank Wilson on Soul. That one was a toughie, and far too expensive for me even when I saw one for sale. The collection had been about 99% complete, with the odd evasive disc. NO acetates though. The mint copy I had of the Saundra Mallett on Tamla single, I sold separately for $1,500.00 to a UK collector (of which his name escapes me). The entire collection was sold to Berry Gordy through my friend and former Motown President Mr. Ewart Abner II. He originally saw the collection in my home when he visited with me on a few occasions. When I decided to sell the entire collection as a complete entity (not piecemeal), I called Abner, told him, and the next day it was sold to Berry."*

The cover of that first issue featured the Miracles, with artwork that was to become familiar as each issue appeared and as Reg was to reveal, *"the wonderful artwork impressions of Motown artists by the wonderful Motown impressionist artist Mr. Chuck Frazier. Each issue had its one-of-a-kind Motown artist impression cover."* For me personally, the cover that features The Marvelettes is a standout and can't be bettered.

M.I.C.C.
INTERNATIONAL COLLECTOR'S CLUB

The content of that first issue included MOTOWN FROM THE INSIDE... (A personal story from Mr. Joe Shillair - who worked for Motown during Motown's Golden Years), MOTOWN ON VIDEO (a select listing of Various Motown artists in video performances from the 60s, 70s and 80s), MOTOWN JUKE-BOX EPS (a complete listing), UK's NIGHTMARE record label (the complete story), MOTORCITY record releases to 1991 (12" singles and albums), MOTOWN MEMORIES (various clippings and early marketing advertisements from the 60s) and PICTURE THIS (a pictorial of rare labels from Motown's earliest 45 releases). Issue two was a Supremes Special, and issue three a Diana Ross Special, which Reg describes as *"without question, one of the best issues ever".* Issue four was a David Ruffin Memorial Issue, while five contained a special profile on The Marvelettes.

Issue six featured Rare Earth, seven saw Mary Wells remembered and eight was a memorial tribute to Eddie Kendricks.

I didn't have all of those issues, which could see each one weigh in at around fifty pages, but it is after issue eight that things become a little difficult to follow if you were trying to keep track of the publication. *"I started the fanzine because of my then passion for Motown history,"* continued Reg, *"but I also felt there was a need for such a thing, as there was nothing like it around at the time. After issuing the first eight issues of which I did all content myself - I believe them to be the very best of all that came out afterwards, it was also at this time that I had sold my Motown collection, so was really in the process of eliminating it from my life. It was a bit of a trauma. So, overall, I was getting a bit tired of the whole Motown thing anyway."* Was Mick Wilding involved on the UK side of things at this point, I asked? *"Yes,"* came the reply. *"I had designated Mick to be in charge of 'finding' more collectors to join the club in the UK. We'd known each other for a number of years prior, but he felt that HE ought to run the fanzine, at which point things went a bit overboard. Quite frankly, I didn't need the hassle from Mick. So, I said 'here, it's yours. It's only a fuckin' magazine'!! We haven't really communicated since, and it's now some 25 plus years. Mick also had amassed a large collection at one point, and I've heard that he lost EVERYTHING when his house went on fire."*

So, Mick Wilding took over with issue nine, but since issue five it had also had the additional heading of Yesterday-Today-Forever, so I wondered, did the name change with the new man at the helm? *"To the best of my recollection, the name of the magazine/fanzine happened at the discretion of Michael Wilding,"* replied Reg Bartlette. *"I had no involvement in this decision to change the name."*

On the whole, overall content was good, if perhaps basic at times, while adverts for Motown releases etc are of interest, although you obviously do get the likes of the Motown of the 1990s, which many simply ignored - myself included, unless it was unreleased material.

All in all, there were twenty-eight issues, the final one coming out in March 1998, and in his 'farewell speech', Mick Wilding said that many were already aware of his decision to stop producing a printed publication and concentrate on the internet site. That final issue was taken up with an exclusive interview with Brenda Holloway, spread over twenty pages. Also included were various record label scans and a promotional advert.

Getting in touch with Reg Bartlette produced something of a bonus in the form of a previously unknown publication – MOTORCITY BEAT. This is obviously related to Ian Levine's Motorcity recording venture and was produced by Mick Wilding in 1992 whilst he was running the Motorcity Information Service.

Reg Bartlette was to say that he thought only three issues were produced and they were *"used for informational purposes. Each was approximately four A4 double-sided pages folded in half. Only three were ever put out by Mick. I'm sure he's forgotten about these by now. Good information though if one is a collector of his output."*

Pete Lawson's THE GOSPEL ACCORDING TO DAVE GODIN was no ten-minute tea-break read, as its sixty plus A4 pages would take you considerably longer to digest, and sitting with your feet up and a cup of coffee it would pass a pleasant hour or so.

I have quoted more than a few editorials within the pages of this book, with most saying little more than what the aims of the publication were. Pete Lawson, however, appeared to take his just that one step further, writing: *"And of course although we must know our place on the Northern Soul scene, and remember whoever we are, we owe it all to the scene, to black America, and to people like Mr Godin.*
"And when everything is put into perspective we know where we stand, what we have done and those who have reaped more than they have sown, the mouth pieces, big heads, money men who do more moving of their mouths and more counting of money with their hands than any constructive contribution to the scene which goes hand in hand with their over-sized ego's and total lack of love for our scene."

But away from the dislike that Pete Lawson obviously had for a few people on the scene, and who

are still very much involved, the first two of the trio of issues that I have are full to the brim with the usual fanzine material.

From issue one, which came out in 1990, take your pick from 'Venture and Maverick Records'; 'Sixties Newies'; 'The State of the Northern Soul Scene' (four pages); 'Dave Godin interview' (ten pages); reproductions of the *Blues and Soul* articles from when Dave Godin visited the Twisted Wheel and the Highland Room at Blackpool Mecca; 'Al TNT Braggs'; 'The Apollas'; four pages of spoof letters; fourteen pages on Wand Records including discography and a Lou Courtney discography.

There was no controversy in issue two, which came out in 1991, just reviews, label listings and odd articles such as a look at 'Rare Motor City Sixties Soul'; 'The Quest For Soul Satisfaction at Allanton' and the 'Patti Austin Story'. Again, the content was spread over more than sixty pages.

I had always thought that there were only two issues of *The Gospel*, but there was a third, although this takes the form of a tribute edition to editor Pete Lawson, who had died in tragic circumstances in Manchester.

Pete had laid the groundwork for issue three and it was in this completely un-edited format that it was printed, with blank spaces for images and odd scribbles still intact. The content included 'The State of Northern Soul – The Final Episode', 'The Sixties Rare Soul Scene', 'Back to the Semi-Obscure Sounds', 'Those Lyric Turn On's', 'Head-to-Head with Butch - sixties and seventies newies DJ Mark 'Butch' Dobson' (eight pages), 'The Tempests', 'Live Act Reviews', 'R&B and the Long Hot Summer' and a few of Dave Godin's articles reproduced from *B&S*. Some fifty-one pages in total.

So, yes, it is out there, but trying to find a copy is as difficult as trying to find one of those rare sounds that you have had on your 'wants list' for a number of years. The money from its sale, by the way, went to Pete's mother.

The nineties were arguably to eclipse the sixties as the boom time for soul music. For those who were around, nothing could, or ever will, take away those sixties' years. It was a carefree time, an entirely different world altogether. Those who were around then had seen marriage, often divorce too, families grow up and mortgages paid. They had money and leisure time and many returned to their passion for music, replacing long gone record collections as best they could, whilst tentatively venturing to a nearby venue that had advertised a 'Soul Nite' to see if they still had what it took to strut their stuff on the dance floor to those all too familiar tunes. The nineties were also to see some quality reading matter appear.

One of those publications, however, took its readers right back to those halcyon sixties days, and nights; and with collecting in mind, it came as something of a pleasant surprise when I stumbled across copies of Keith Rylatt's contribution to the world of soul in print with COME AND GET THESE MEMORIES. I had recognised the title from my scribbled notes, but had simply taken it as being 'just another fanzine', but it was much more than that: it was a treasure trove of soul music memorabilia. The only down side was that Keith's publication was to last for a mere three issues.

It is also one of those publications that contains no clues as to the actual date that issue one appeared. Keith himself is uncertain, while a fellow collector puts issue three as being c.1993, and as Keith himself mentions in issue three that the publication title should be changed to the 'Come And Get These Memories Annual', we will simply say that issue one appeared in 1990.

"Well, after 25 years of buying R&B magazines, I've decided to have a go myself. Apologies in advance to anyone expecting an in-depth intellectual delve into the undiscovered world of R&B, this is, as billed, a scrapbook, concentrating on the more visual aspects of sixties soul and ephemera.

"Between the mid-sixties and eighties, I bought every R&B, Doo Woop, Blues and Soul publication I could lay my hands on. John Broven's 'Walking to New Orleans' for instance, really opened up a whole new area of black music for me. But towards the middle of the eighties, I began to become disillusioned with the mags. I was buying, mainly on the grounds that the same artists, label stories and discographies kept cropping up over and over again. The editorial quality and sincerity were never in question, but within the

goldfish bowl of sixties R&B there is only so much you can turn up, hence some of the dross discovered and played at Wigan." That was the opening of Keith's editorial in issue No.1, a spiral bound A4 thirty-four page 'Sixties Soul Scrapbook'.

There was little in the way of actual reading between those pages, an article on The Impressions with accompanying discography, one entitled 'Soul Punters' and another the 'Bright Star Story' was about it. But the rest of the content was vast and varied, everything from label scans featuring Motown 'back room boys', 'dance hall classics', R&B 'instrumentals' and 'vocals', adverts for Sue Records and numerous others, the music score for 'If You Ever Walk Out Of My Life', a couple of sheet music front pages and for some reason adverts for Levi jeans. The crowning glory, however, was the reproduction of front covers of almost a dozen publications, ranging from *R&B Scene* and *Soul Music Monthly* to *Time Barrier Express*, *Yesterday's Memories* and the French produced *Soul Bag*.

Numbers two and three, separated by some twelve months, were both side stapled and contained much of the same content as that initial issue, throwing club membership cards and fliers into the mix, but in number two, the magazine's illustrations had been replaced by books, amongst which were *Chicago Down* by Mike Rowe, *Walking to New Orleans* by John Broven, and

They All Sang On the Corner by Philip Groia. Number three, which was mainly printed on light blue paper, had no publications reproduced, but loads of fliers, Major Lance album scans and two interesting articles - 'The "King" Mojo club, Sheffield' and 'When Oldies Were Newies' amongst the hugely varied content.

But as with numerous other publications, there was no fore-warning that *Come And Get These Memories* was about to cease publication as Keith's editorial in issue No.3 promised "*to get straight on with issue 4 for the new year*", which would have been 1986; and it failed to appear.

As Keith was, or at least had been, a keen collector of soul music publications, I considered it worthwhile to ask him about collecting and his own personal involvement in pushing soul in print out to the masses.

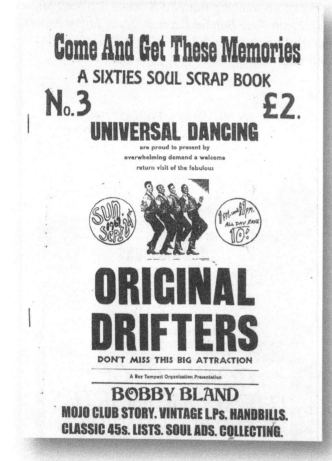

" *After mulling things over for a couple of days you have been mercifully saved from me launching into a lengthy diatribe regarding the word 'collecting'. Almost every artefact is collected by somebody, somewhere... milk bottles, silver tea spoons, fossils... and I've always been slightly irritated when I'm described as a 'record collector' as I can honestly say that every record I now own I like and play and have not purchased them for any other reason. But sadly, this hasn't always been the case; commencing in the early*

seventies I caught Detroit Disease and spent all of my waking moments and non- essential cash buying every record I could find that was vaguely Soul related and originated in that city. Many were very average, a few expensive and some, outright pop rubbish – have you ever listened to 'Only A Boy' by Spider, Snake & Eee on La Beat? I was addicted, a besotted Detroit record collector! Luckily after ten or so years I recovered and regained my sanity'

"*Unlike milk bottles, or records for that matter, Soul magazines are multi-dimensional; 45s have only an A and B side to deliver, whereas most magazines have at least twenty pages of fare. So, yes I do openly admit to collecting Soul magazines but their content was and still is satisfyingly diverse be it label listings, their history, artist discographies or stories, photographs, record reviews etc.*

"*Although I never even saw a Soul magazine until 1967, the first issue of Blues & Soul, I was sufficiently bitten and began buying it on a regular basis and eventually expanded to subscribing to Clive Richardson's Shout around 1970 and a couple of years later, Hot Buttered Soul, courtesy of the late Chris Savory of whom I will come onto shortly.*

"*Obtaining these various publications was not that easy; some emerging specialist record shops might stock them otherwise it would be word of mouth or a small ad in a national music paper. Although I spent three years in Manchester as the sixties ran into the seventies, Blues & Soul was the only Soul magazine I saw on open sale and that was in a newsagent. As soon as I moved south however and ventured into London most Saturdays I came across Compendium in Camden, Moon Dog's in Manor Park, Record Corner in Balham and a little later Black Wax in Streatham where other Soul and Blues mags were on the counter.*

"*This leads me onto my association with Chris Savory; Chris lived on the Isle of Sheppey, a rather windswept and desolate island off the north Kent coast where the rivers Medway and Thames converge and in 1973 I moved to nearby Sittingbourne, the last outpost before crossing onto Sheppey. As I was still subscribing to Hot Buttered Soul, I quickly made contact with Chris who, like myself, was a school teacher. Although Chris's wife Caroline drove, he did not and because the Island was only served by a single-track railway and one bus an hour, I soon became handy for lifts as I had bought a VW for £60, but unbeknown to Chris, a nervous passenger at the best of times, I had not passed my test! On my first visit to Chris's new detached house on Scrapsgate Road, Minster, I was made welcome and whisked off to his record room and the most 45s I'd ever seen in private hands and he proudly showed me his latest trophy, a single sided green demo of Darrell*

Banks's 'Our Love (is in the pocket)' but it was one of those blank green test pressing labels with very basic credits, very typical of all Decca group records, and so with hindsight it will almost certainly have been on the London label as I've never seen such a disc connected to EMI.

"HBS was different to its predecessors and counterparts in that it covered the North and Midlands Rare Soul scene along with contemporary releases. Also, it made no apologies about being a vehicle for record sales, initially Chris's own but soon many other sellers. Chris didn't waste any time in letting as many record companies as possible know about HBS and the commercial opportunities it offered and soon he was receiving dozens of review records every month, from Reggae through Soul to Disco. It is arguable that his approach to running a Soul magazine was slightly more money orientated than others but producing such a publication was not cheap and Chris's aim was to at least break even each month, usually only achieved by the proceeds of his record sales. Like some others on the record scene Chris was not secretive about his sources and during his time as a columnist for SMG magazine produced a guide to second hand record shopping in and around London.

"I soon became involved in helping out with HBS, sometimes in production or distribution and more enjoyably accompanying Chris to concerts to interview artists, and at the end of my apprenticeship I was presented with a RABINC press card (Rhythm & Blues Incorporated) that represented Black Wax, HBS, Shout and SMG and was even dispatched on solo missions! On the topic of distribution, one of my first assignments was lugging two, fifty count, bundles of HBS via National Express coach to the Queens Hall All Nighter in Leeds, the VW would not have made it. Towards the end of the decade Chris relocated to Newcastle-Under-Lyme, Staffordshire, HBS evolved into 'Soul Cargo' and he got involved in organising record fairs. Ironically, despite the distance now between us I was more involved in the new venture than HBS.

"About the same time I moved to Gravesend from where my next door neighbour Terry Waghorn ran 'Rock Pile' magazine and possibly since I was currently writing for Rod Dearlove's excellent 'Midnite Express' I decided to have a stab myself, launching 'Come & Get These Memories', a title based upon The Marvelettes hit and had a sub-title of 'A Sixties Soul Scrap Book'. It was intended to be more diverse than the usual issues covered in contemporary Soul magazines, I wanted it to be far more visual and incorporate other topics ranging from vintage Levi's to Real Ale but such notions didn't get beyond issue one which I'd christened 'The Young Mod's Forgotten Story'. Apart from postal sales it was

stocked by Vinyl Experience, Out On The Floor and Compendium in London and Goldmine in Manchester. Issue two followed a few months later but now with 100% Soul content, obviously not too many folk out there sat around in old inns discussing Soul in vintage jeans while supping Old Peculiar! A whole year then elapsed before issue three emerged and was in my view the best as I'd by then recruited a couple of scribes and sales hit the dizzy heights of forty. It did however also coincide with the birth of my daughter Lucy, a growing Soul club venture I was a partner in and my record sales enterprise called Premium Stuff and so the intended number four never materialised. The short-lived project did however have a silver lining as one of the subscribers, Stuart Russell of Bee Cool Publishing, contacted me some years later to invite me to write a book about the Twisted Wheel Club.

"The bulk of my quite extensive magazine collection went to Modus the House of Soul who specialise in such items including books and original posters; their website www.house-of-soul.co.uk is well worth a visit."

From rhythm and blues, the music, and publications, had drifted into what was simply defined as 'soul music', and from there it changed again to out and out 'northern soul'. But many grew tired of the 'stompers', some never even took to them in the first place, and then suddenly the tempo slackened, giving way to a more mellow, mid-tempo sound with softer vocals. This was 'modern soul', later to be joined with yet another new labelling, 'crossover soul'.

MODERNITY

ISSUE ONE.
JULY 1991.
£1.20.

A MODERN SOUL FANZINE.

The Talkin' Loud label, Jet Star Distribution, Max Rees laid bare, CD soul - a rip off ? The Real Deal in Cambridge, & all the usual fanzine page fillers.

Many of the publications began to feature 'modern soul' within their pages, but it wasn't until the arrival of **MODERNITY** in July 1991 that a publication appeared that was geared up 100% to the modern side of things.

It was edited by Newmarket based Peter Ferrie, and although it was modern in its musical outlook, there was nothing modern in its style and presentation, being the usual A4, photocopied, side-stapled reading matter. *"Any new fanzine has to have a reason for being written and a clear idea of what it wants to achieve"* penned Peter in his first editorial." *'Modernity' will never match the quality, nor the range of 'Blues and Soul' or 'Voices from The Shadows'. Both are excellent at what they do and both have their own corners of the market sewn up. What I hope to achieve is some sort of middle ground. Only time and future issues will decide if I've managed it.*

"As you look through this first issue, remember it's only the start. This is mainly a trial run to prove to myself and others that I CAN actually put together a fanzine. I tried once before in the Spring of 1989 and it all ended in tears, disappointing a lot of people."

Within the twenty pages of that first issue there were reviews, both record and venue, an interview with a guy who ran a second-hand record shop in Cambridge and another who was based in Chapel Market, North London. There was also a page on 'CD Soul – A Rip Off' which made an interesting read.

Modernity would certainly have had a niche in the fanzine market, but it appears to be something of an elusive publication. I have no idea how many issues there were (it is so annoying not being able to confirm what is what), although I am sure I did see an issue five for sale at one point. At least Peter Ferrie achieved his ambition.

Oh, how I dislike those publications that are undated, especially those first issues, whilst the irregularity of the majority of them does little to help when attempting to work out some sort of time scale as to their lifespan.

Dave Halsall's **BUZZ** is a prime example, but thankfully I knew Dave, so was able to ask the question as to when that first issue made an appearance. *"It was started in mid-1991, if I remember correctly, as an idea, while the first issue came out January/February 1992,"* came the reply.

For many, that first issue is out there on its own, an award winner, not for its content unfortunately, but for its cover, as it is considered to be the 'worst ever cover' on a soul fanzine! The black and yellow design does nothing to grab your attention and certainly gives you no clue whatsoever as to its soulful content.

Despite this, it isn't the worst in my eyes (and I don't say that because I know Dave), as there is another within these pages that takes the award. In issue two, Dave was to comment: *"I will say, that I more than anyone was disappointed with the cover* [of issue one]. *I wanted something different. Bloody hell, it certainly was!"*

Once you get past the cover, it is like opening a dirty, rusted door and finding yourself in a bright, airy and comfortable room. Dave was also quick to inform everyone who bought that first issue what they could expect to find, writing: *"Buzz is here with the intention of enriching, enlightening and hopefully educating us all, both in musical forms we adore and those that we*

may have a slight bias opinion against."

Dave didn't care if it was acid-jazz, Motown, oldies, modern soul or Ian Levine's Motorcity label, he covered them all, giving his publication a wide and varied look at the ever-growing soul scene. But why did he consider the idea of starting a magazine? *"Basically, most of the mainstream publications like Blues and Soul, Echoes etc did not cover what was happening at ground level, at small clubs, venues etc, and the Northern Scene had its own fanzines,"* he began, *"and I and others believed there was a huge gap in the new indie Soul records and real soul club's playlists. I think a group of us were just chin wagging somewhere and I said we need a magazine to fill the gap, so the idea went from there."*

Issue one consisted of twenty-eight pages (not counting the cover), while issue two stretched to forty-four, plus it had a glossy cover with a much better design.

It was a massive improvement, with a more quality look, and you would have been hard pushed not to find something to your taste.

Turning the pages, I only wish I had drifted back into the music around the time of this issue (early 1992), as I   would certainly have gone to Pontins, Prestatyn Sands for their 4th Magic of Motown event which featured The Four Tops, Edwin Starr, Jimmy Ruffin, The Marvelettes and The Supremes. A bargain at £79 per person for the weekend.

Sadly, *Buzz* was not to last, with issue three being the final one, due to Dave finding contributors' copy failing to appear on time, messing up a planned schedule, so he simply decided to call it a day.

Speaking about the magazine in general, Dave was to say: "*I managed to get some great DJs and collectors (all friends) involved and gave them a free hand in what they wanted to write about. Two main problems like all editors will tell you in their labour of love is getting unpaid writers to meet deadlines and sales.*

"Perhaps I did it at the wrong time during that recession, but I won't know, everybody had their own problems and it was a learning curve for me.

"It was an eye opener, as I found it was very time consuming, from compiling, getting the print shop to deliver on time and then getting the mags out to shops etc. My job didn't really give me that

time to spare."

But was he disappointed to call it a day? "*I was disappointed to stop doing it, as it had begun to take shape and people commented on it growing into something even though it was only three issues. But it wasn't done on a computer like now, just an electronic typewriter and photocopier and it may have got better. Sadly time, money and other commitments meant that was it.*

"If I had the time now, it would be a digital magazine I suppose, as I don't go to as many venues as I used to, but with the internet, YouTube and other media outlets a magazine review would be out of date before it hit the screen!!"

1991 also saw the appearance of **NORTHERN NITELIFE**, another A5 sized issue which during its lifetime would span anything from twenty-four to forty pages.

Issue one, undated, was given away free, with second and third issues selling at 95p and all subsequent ones at £1.50. It also had an initial dual editorship, with Pete Hollander and Dave Carne at the helm.

Initial plans were, if the irregularity of the other publications were anything to go by, perhaps a little presumptuous, as Pete mentions in his 'Introduction' that this was hoped to be a successful fortnightly magazine. Dave on the other hand used his 'Introduction' to say "*I feel for a long time there has been an important gap in the northern soul scene – a publication whose primary focus is on venues which*

£2.00.

BUZZ 3 issue

Black music review

Kae laDrae

Reneé Knott

Elizabeth Withers

Jonathan "Pony" Scales
ScaleSoft Records International
Chicago, Illinois 60657

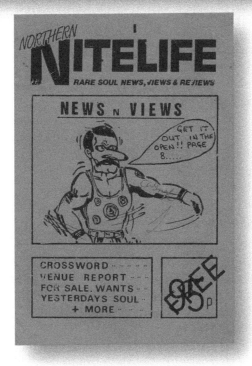

NORTHERN NITELIFE
RARE SOUL NEWS, VIEWS & REVIEWS

NEWS N VIEWS

GET IT OUT IN THE OPEN!! PAGE 8.....

CROSSWORD
VENUE REPORT
FOR SALE, WANTS
YESTERDAYS SOUL
+ MORE

FREE p

keep everything ticking over. There have been magazines dealing with the vinyl – some extremely good from a collector's point of view, with many stunningly studious articles on labels and artists. However, these are primarily for collectors and where there is reference to nighters etc. it is sadly of secondary importance. (I would like to emphasise that I'm not slagging the likes of 'Shades of Soul' or collectors – I'm a rabid vinyl junkie myself)."

Wanting to know a bit more about *Northern Nitelife* I got in touch with Pete and found we had a mutual interest, but it was the magazine that I wanted to quiz him about. Why did he start it? *"I fell in love with the Stafford Sound and the mid-tempo tunes coming out through the 90s, although I missed Stafford altogether as I finished with northern after seeing Wigan go too commercial, it was no longer an underground scene which I fell in love with in 1972.*

"Much later in the late 80s I was working nights and the company was playing Signal Radio. Dave Evison was on and was going on about this all-nighter here then another and another!

"That was my roll call... within a couple of months I was a regular at Bradford Queens Hall and the 100 Club. So as a regular I was getting to know quite a few DJs as I requested tunes I liked, for instance Gary Spencer, Carl Fortnum, DJs at Bradford then Ady Croasdell and Butch at 100 Club also many from Shotts all-nighters Wilton DJs like Dean Anderson, Kitch, Guy Hennigan etc.

"At that time, I had my first go at promoting along with Mark Bicknell in running Droylsden then after that Hyde Town Hall both all-nighters were based on a mainly upfront northern that I loved with some good oldies DJs to mix it up a bit.

"I started Northern Nitelife while running those all- nighters more as a light hearted view of the scene.

"There were a lot of fanzines covering collecting and the history of the scene, plenty of buying and selling of records, so Dave Carne and myself thought it would be a bit of a laugh and had fun doing it.

"Very old school to make. A load of flyers, a photocopier with cut and paste meaning cutting out of other information and glueing it all on cardboard."

Obviously, a magazine could not live on venue reviews and adverts alone, and although they often reproduced articles from the likes of *Black Music* and

The Face, there would be a number of well written pieces on various subject matters – 'Whatever Happened to Modern Soul', 'On The Downbeat', 'Save Our Scene' and 'An Insight Of The Scene In The year 2000' with Mark Sargeant's regular contribution always well worth a read. It took *Northern Nitelife* a handful of issues to find its feet and as Pete was to admit in his editorial of issue four *"there have been a few teething problems in the first few issues, but things seem to be going a lot smoother."* They certainly were, as the issues that followed certainly gave you plenty of reading matter, which saw the publication last for sixteen issues, the final one coming out in 1993.

Glancing through the first issues of many publications, they give little idea as to how, and if, they will progress. Will the second issue be better than the seemingly average first, or will there actually be a second issue? Such questions were asked by the appearance of **VINTAGE SOUL** in the summer of 1992.

The cover gave little away. A 1968 Detroit Radio Chart from July 1968 and a bottle of 'Vintage 60's & 70's Soul'. Neither did the style – typical fanzine – A4 and side-stapled – as per normal. Inside, on page three, under the heading 'WHAT WE ARE ABOUT', you were left in no doubt as to what it was all about and what you had in your hands. *"Vintage wine is produced in those years from which the best examples emerged. So, it is with 'Vintage Soul' ....and the years in question run from the early 60's to the mid-70's: post-rock 'n' roll to pre-disco. If you prefer, Soul as it was the first time around."*

Editor Pete Nickols was to continue; *"Fanzines come and fanzines go and sadly, few covering essentially 60's and 70's soul music remain. Canada's 'Soul Survivor' was superb, but ultimately, was not aptly named and is badly missed. 'Voices From The Shadows' continues, thankfully, but seems more interested in 'contemporary sounds' these days; 'Sweet Soul Music' has departed for that soul-graveyard in the sky to join with the artist who provided its original raison d'etre, the late, great, Otis Redding; Steve Bryant's wonderful 'Souled Out' was soon 'bowled out', and so it goes on.*

"Any fanzine's continued existence depends upon

an ability to overcome an almost constantly precarious financial situation, to write consistently interesting 'copy', to publish as regularly as indicated so as not to let its readers down, and to stick strictly to the kind of music which it purports to specialise. A failure on any one of these counts spells almost certain doom. VINTAGE SOUL has set out its store and intends to stick to its guns. We believe good, interesting 'copy' is more important than any going 'glossy'. If and when we can afford to do both, well and good – until then I'm afraid it's A4 and staples (with no disrespect to Pop or Mavis).

"We believe too in making as much good vintage soul music generally available as is possible. While many existing fans (like ourselves) will have their own cherished original recordings, this should not stop them applauding the reissue of such previously hard-to-find material. A reissue hardly ever devalues an original and at least others, possibly too young to catch the track the first time around, can then enjoy previously rare and hidden gems."

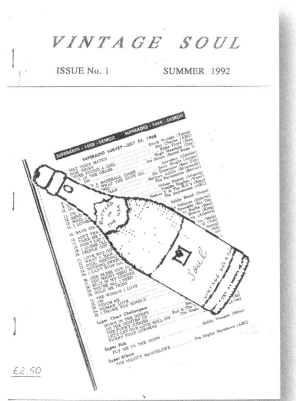

Wow! Quite a speech and quite a promise, considering that for many, the face of soul music was changing, fed up with those tried, trusted and often overplayed tunes. But there were others who liked to be caught up in that 'time warp' and didn't want to change, and there must have been plenty who warmed to *Vintage Soul*, its policy and its contents, as it was to stretch to a more than creditable thirty issues, finally coming to an end in autumn 2000.

You could have a good calculated guess as to what some of the content would be within the customary three dozen pages. A complete issue listing would well be in order for this fanzine, not just because I like it, but because it deserves it and, like the odd other publication, as I have mentioned before, forms something of an encyclopaedia of soul music from the period.

Catching up with Pete just as the book was heading towards its final proofing, I asked him about putting his excellent publication together. "*I home-published my Vintage Soul fanzine from Summer 1992 to Autumn 2000, thirty issues in total published quarterly, and I still retain the 'masters'. They were created on A4*

sheets, photocopied and stapled together, with the graphics often incorporated by simple cut-outs glued to the paper. The circulation was not great (in the hundreds) but nonetheless was widespread throughout the world."

Why start a fanzine? "*I started the fanzine after my local radio R&B/soul show 'A Shot of Rhythm 'n' Blues' - Two-Counties Radio FM – 2CR – broadcasting 2 hours weekly from Bournemouth,*" replied Pete. This came to an end after some five or six years when the station was sold and the format changed.

"*For years prior to this I had been a big collector and fan of what I would term 'classic' soul music, chiefly from the 60s and early 70s, although I started collecting records as a young teenager way back in the rock 'n' roll era.*

"*Although never employed full-time in musical pursuits, I have written articles and contributed to books on the subject for many years, starting way back as a part-time writer for Record Mirror, then magazines and fanzines like Record Collector, Now Dig This and Voices From the Shadows. I provided many entries for the Guinness Who's Who of Soul Music and the Virgin Encyclopaedia of R&B and Soul. In the era of the worldwide web I became a major contributor to John Ridley's Sir Shambling Deep Soul website and produced for that site many articles on soul performers, CD reviews and the first ever 'history' of the Quinvy Studio in Sheffield, Alabama.*

"*I have also regularly compiled and annotated many reissue CDs of soul material for Demon, Charly and Ace record companies. These included Excello-Abet label compilations, Chess artist compilations including the first-ever CD of Irma Thomas' Chess material, the first- ever CD of Jean Wells' output created directly from tapes supplied by her producer Clyde Otis, a 3-CD book set of Ann Peebles' work and possibly my main achievement, a 4-CD boxset of Hi Records soul material called Royal Memphis Soul which still fetches good money on auction sites today.*

"*The main reason I started Vintage Soul was (a) because the ending of my radio show freed up some*

CLASSIC
SOUL AS
IT WAS

Vintage

THE FIRST
TIME
AROUND

Issue No.19 - Spring 1997

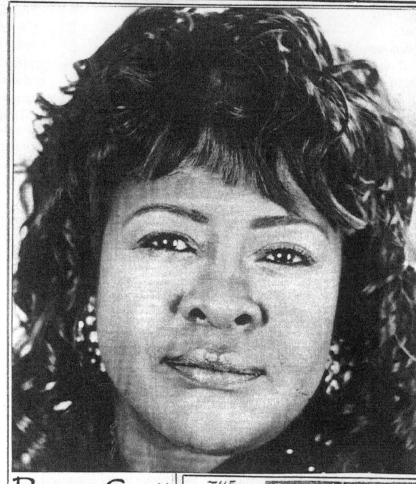

Peggy Scott

debut album, HELP YOURSELF

THE COMPLETE Oscar Toney Jr

DEEP SOUL Part One

If a tick appears here ☐

your subscription should be renewed before 1st June 1997 please to ensure a copy of the next Issue.

UK Subscription rates: £3 per Issue (inc P & P) or £11 for 4 Issues (a £1 saving).
EU rates: £3 per issue only.
Elsewhere: 4 Issues only for £15.

All cheques to be in £ sterling and payable to PORTMAN (not Vintage Soul) and addressed to:
Vintage Soul, 31 Strathmore Drive, Verwood, Dorset BH31 7BJ, U.K.

60's &
70's

SOUL

FROM THE
USA

All back numbers currently available at £4 EACH

the way fanzines like *Voices From The Shadows* were moving away from 'classic-era' soul and concentrating more and more on contemporary styles. I wanted to retain a focus on the original material which created the genre in the first place, although I also wanted to concentrate on emotive often gospel-based soul rather than crossover pop-soul like most of Motown's output or the fast-tempo dance-soul as championed by the northern soul fraternity (to which I never belonged, even though I lived and worked in Greater Manchester from 1967 to 1976)."

For a very brief run through the issues we have: 'Jerry Ragovoy' - four parts; 'The Muscle Shoals Story' - twelve parts; countless artist profiles from the likes of Little Willie John, Otis Clay and Jackie Wilson to Candi Staton, Kim Toliver and Betty Harris; reviews aplenty.

To maintain such an interesting publication over the course of thirty issues, keeping to the promised time scale - it appeared on a 'seasonal basis' - was a very creditable achievement and also, unlike many, Pete Nickols actually announced the end of his publication when the time came. Leaving his editorial to the end of that thirtieth issue, he wrote: "*Sadly, this issue will be the last issue of 'Vintage Soul'. When I started the 'zine nearly eight years ago, I remember saying that the history of popular music was littered with the remnants of failed fanzines and that this was chiefly due to the inability by their editors to produce each edition regularly and on time – people (and that would include me) quite understandably don't like parting with forward subscriptions only to have to wait years before the magazines they've paid for in advance out of their hard-earned cash usually appear! Well, I'm glad to say I've managed to publish 'Vintage Soul' pretty much 'on the dot' each quarter and 'irregularity' (unlike the tale of the badly constipated man) is not the reason that the death-knell bell is now sounding.*

"Frankly, it's just that I simply want MORE TIME and if it takes more time to do other things in life that I want to do then the 'zine will suffer both in quality and regularity of appearance and I don't want that to happen! I still hold down a pretty responsible 9 to 5

Candi at Sweet 16

job, but I'm beginning to plan for my retirement and I also want to spend more time with my wife, more time motor caravanning, more time actually listening to my thousands of LP's and CD's and more time reading my vast library of music related books."

He went on to add: "*Any fanzine which survives has my undying admiration because for sure I know how hard it can be to keep it going! Long may all present stalwarts survive – more power to their soul elbows.*"

I imagined that Pete enjoyed his time at the helm of such a prestigious publication and made lots of friends? "*I had some great subscribers to Vintage Soul who regularly commented, corrected and updated my articles but the actual work of creating the magazine was wholly down to me – with my wife (who has no great knowledge of and no interest in soul) nonetheless providing invaluable help with the subscription, photocopying and mailing duties. One subscriber was David Cole and I like to think it was his interest in Vintage Soul which prompted him to start his own much more glossy and (for a time) highly successful soul magazine In The Basement (sadly now no more).*"

Many are still of the opinion that *Vintage Soul* is one of the best to appear, but what did Pete think was a stand-out publication? "*The best soul fanzine of all time? I would pick the fairly short-lived Canadian-produced Soul Survivor, followed by Trevor Swaine's Souled Out. The best current fanzine is my friend Heikki Suosalo's Soul Express.*"

Vintage Soul was gone, but certainly not forgotten.

Had I seen it on the shelves of the local WH Smith's I would have more than likely just given **SOUL CD** little more than a courtesy glance, as the George Benson cover shot (not that I have anything against George Benson and I do like some of his recordings) and the sub-headings of 'Brit Funk – A historic ride on the Caister Express' and 'Neneh Cherry – I'm not afraid to say what I think' on the front of that first issue would have done little to tingle the taste buds, never mind encourage me to part with £3.95 to buy a copy, even if there was a free cd. Anyway, in 1992 I was still quite a distance from making my return to the northern soul arena. I still had my records, but they were seldom played, and as for reading matter on the subject of soul music, it never really entered my head. It was therefore a few years later that this publication was bought in a nice cheap lot on eBay, complete with the free CDs. Anyway, they were never exactly free as you had to buy the magazine to get them.

Published by Northern and Shell, who were London based, and edited by Stuart Kirkham, there were only a couple of contributors whose names mean anything to me - Paolo Hewitt and Roger St Pierre. This is, as you would expect, a first-class publication to look at and is a nice easy read, but in comparison to the photocopied fanzines it cannot hold a candle to them despite the gloss.

'The only guide to soul and dance on compact disc' it declared and I suppose it was, but by the time issue six had come along it had decided that it was now 'The Funky Magazine For Funky People'. I suppose it was simply moving with the times, if indeed there were 'funky people' around.

There was the odd attraction for the old-school 'soulie'. Issue one had The Four Tops and The Temptations; issue two, Otis, Edwin and Smokey; issue three gave you Stax, Aretha Franklin, Marv Johnson, Patti Austin and Fifty Great Motown Songs. The latter

thankfully was not in any kind of numerical order and besides the likes of 'Beechwood 4-5789' and 'Heaven Must Have Sent You', they included Rare Earth's 'Get Ready'. Ah well!

Sadly, after issue three the magazine sort of lost its way. There were still the likes of Marlena Shaw, Harold Melvin and Dionne Warwick to be found within the pages, but they were completely devoured by Jamiroquai, Mica Paris, M-People, Incognito, New Jill Swing and many more. It was not just the magazine content that drifted in a different direction, the 'free' CDs did as well, going from the likes of Gladys Knight, Fontella Bass and Norman Connors supplying the goods in issue one, followed by Jackie Wilson, The Moments and Lee Dorsey, to in latter issues drifting towards Incognito, Al Jarreau and The Salsoul Orchestra.

As well as the far from in-depth features, there were also record - sorry, cd - reviews, a few sales ads and a look at equipment, but by issue ten, the soul fraternity would have left this publication sitting on the shelf. That tenth issue carried the title – Volume 1 No.10, but I don't think a Volume 2, or a No.11 for that matter, ever materialised. But, somewhat surprisingly, what did materialise was another similar publication, unknown to me until fairly recently, entitled **SOUL & BLUES ON CD**, which has an issue one publication date again of 1992.

This particular magazine was published by Brockland Publishing with Nicola Shepherd as editorial director and the esteemed Sharon Davis amongst its contributors, and there is a possibility that this one actually appeared first, as its editorial claims that it is *"the only magazine to offer free cover mounted music containing classic soul & blues tracks"*. But then again.

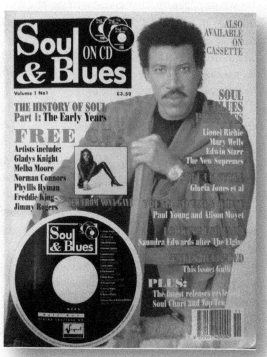

Once again, the first cd oozed quality in the artists – Gladys Knight, Norman Connors (again), Melba Moore and Phyllis Hyman, while the magazine, consisting of eighty-two pages, slightly less than the previous publication, presented more of the same, with features on Mary Wells, Edwin Starr, The New Supremes and Saundra Edwards, with others on 'Young Gifted and White' - Paul Young and Alison Moyet, 'Soul UK Style' and 'The History of Soul'. This was a far better read, with better photographs than its opposition. It was also forty- five pence cheaper!

But it is there the story of *Soul & Blues on CD* has to end as I have never seen another issue, and this one only appeared in a job lot on eBay, which earned me an email from the company after I enquired if the seller would sell me that one issue if the lot didn't sell. It didn't, I said sorry, and got the magazine for a couple of pounds. Another one was added to the growing list.

GENE CHANDLER

Howard Earnshaw had decided to go into the world of soulful reading production with *Out On The Floor*, back in 1981, but unlike many, he didn't give up the ghost following the demise of his first journey into the world of soul music publications, although it was to take him a dozen years before his fingers would once again flow across the keys and bring us something to read on the music we all love. So, we fast forward through time to 1993 and we find Howard having decided that he

wanted to get back into the nitty gritty game of producing a fanzine with the first issue of SOUL UP NORTH making an appearance.

But before venturing any further, and you utter the words "I've got that first issue," there is something that has to be revealed – *Soul Up North* issue No.0. Yes, prior to that very first issue, Howard published a 'dummy'.

It wasn't so much a 'dummy' issue, but a handful of pages telling the world that *Soul Up North* was coming – *"Hello, and welcome to the preview issue of what I hope will be a welcome addition to the Northern Soul scene"* being the opening two lines of that initial editorial. But as well as using issue zero to spread the word as regards to its imminent arrival, Howard also used it as a plea for help, asking would-be scribes to send in articles, promoters to publicise their venues and the general soul public to write with their news and views. He also laid out his plans for that forthcoming first issue.

The rest of that 'dummy' issue has nothing more than a list of content, not that there was much: a Groovesville label listing and a page detailing what the future of *Soul Up North* would entail. The back page had an illustration of a spaceman firing a ray-gun under the heading of 'Look Out For The First Issue'.

That first issue of *Soul Up North* made its appearance in the early months of 1993, and I think Howard would agree that this initial issue was basic, but it was a case of finding your feet as many others

had trodden a similar path with look-alike publications and went on to bigger and better things. But was *Soul Up North* a better title than *Out On The Floor*, I had to ask, and why change? *"I decided on a fresh start,"* replied Howard. "Soul Up North was a pun/play on the words 'it's grim up north'. I'm not sure exactly how long after 'Out On The Floor' I started it, but it was probably three of four years at least, maybe longer."

Why start a fanzine in the first place? *"I'd always fancied producing a magazine after reading 'Hot Buttered Soul' and then 'Shades Of Soul' and 'Black Beat' and others. I was talking about maybe starting my own with 'Soulful Kinda Music' editor Dave Rimmer at an all-nighter and he convinced me to give it a go.*

"I kicked off with the a free/giveaway promotional issue, cleverly numbered zero. I think I still have one somewhere up in the loft and I think it had six pages and I wrote everything in it."
It was a fanzine for the 'Fans of Northern Soul' and that first twenty-four-page issue included a history of Soul City, the Neptune label, venue guide and report, cd review and an article on record buying in the States. As I said, it was basic, and the following half dozen issues contained more of the same, but there was a notable difference when issue No.8 (Dec/Jan/Feb 94/95) came out. This issue was more compact and consisted of thirty-four pages, although the index on page two simply numbered the articles and not the actual pages.

By the time it reached its teens, the layout had been developed and taken on a format that would remain through the course of time, as would contributors such as Dave Halsall, and I wondered if back in those early days Howard ever gave it any thought that *Soul Up North* would be not simply a successful and respected name on the scene, but still be going strong today, soaring off into more than one hundred editions? *"I had a goal, a dream, that I would get to issue 100, and then call it a day. But as the magazine got bigger and I stated to get (IMHO) better and more interesting articles, we still go on!!*

Issue 80   Autumn 2013
THE FAN'S FANZINE
Soul Up North
£3   5 EuroS
6 DollarS

Debbie Taylor

"Never did I imagine it would still be going after I retired. Hopefully it will last a few more years, depending how it is received out there in Soul Land." I imagined that a lot of the readers have been with *Soul Up North* for years, maybe even from the start, but did he still get new ones? *"Of course, there are still subscribers from the very beginning. A lot have dropped out, but fortunately, there seem to be lots of new ones, which more than compensates for those who have left."*

Having produced a football memorabilia collectors 'magazine for over thirty years, there were times when I felt that I had done enough, reached the end of the line and considered that it was time to blow that full-time whistle. Had Howard ever felt like calling it a day? *"I always get stressed as the next issue nears completion, but the relief of picking the finished issue from the printers and the positive feedback from those who read it makes it all worthwhile."* But what actually keeps you going? *"Two main reasons. One, I have made so many friends in the years I have been involved in producing it and meeting them when I go out with the mags under my arms and two, I love reading the informative articles written by the fans who never fail to astound me with their knowledge of the soul scene. It's got to a point now that it might be my death that causes the mag to stop!!"*

As I have said, *Soul Up North* has maintained a similar format throughout its entirety, and there is not too much of a difference between issue twenty-six and one hundred and six. Obviously more pages, and far better copying, but the standard remains the same, as does the wide array of articles. Not only that, there has only been a £2 increase in the cover price as I type between that first issue and the current one.

Many other fanzines tried different formats, went glossy, shifted from side stapling to centre stapling, and added colour, but Howard remained true to the old saying that 'if it ain't broke don't fix it', with his only concession being adopting a card cover. He obviously has a considerable way to go to surpass the likes of

Blues and Soul and *Manifesto*, but they are/were in a different field. As I write, he is only an odd issue or two off the one hundred and twelve figure that *Shout* reached, and will soon surpass it, but *Soul Up North* is a number of steps up the ladder to its distant cousin and it is a publication of which its editor should be, and undoubtedly will be, extremely proud.

I have no recollection as to what the summer of 1993 was like, or for that matter where I went on holiday. Neither was I aware of the emergence on the soul music scene of what was to become one of the best publications dedicated to the music – SOUL UNDERGROUND. Yes, perhaps I have said that about quite a few of the publications, but this one is more than worthy of the praise.

Edited by Mark Bicknell, this was a publication that certainly gave you value for money, often drifting into sixty-odd pages, with a list of contributors (along with the man at the helm) that would have given you a more than decent 'Northern Soul Five-a-Side team' Pete Lowrie, Ady Croasdell, Brian Rae and Roger Banks – not that I have any knowledge of any of them being able to play football!

As well as the first-class content, another big plus point was the fact that looking through those back issues today, there are no rusty staples; but that is of little concern to the multitude, it is what is in those stapled pages that matter, and as I rate this publication ahead of one or two of the others, it is worth a closer inspection than most.

It was £3 for that Summer of 1993 issue. A4 in size, side stapled as per norm and forty-six pages of a very easy to read font size, with a content that catered for all tastes – Tony Clarke, Little Milton, Jerry Williams and Jimmy McCracklin are all featured, along with Pete Lowrie's 'The Other Side of Motown Part 1', 'Gig Guide', 'Sellers Guide', 'DJ Profile' - Ian Clark, reviews and so much more.

Four issues per year was Mark's aim, but he was also quick to state: *"The survival of this publication all depends on how well it's supported. I will work my arse off twelve months of the year to put it together, the rest is up to you folks."*

Issues two and three appeared in Autumn and Winter of 1993, although the latter is dated Winter 1994, and as time passed, three issues, rather than the hoped for four, became the norm. Many would have preferred it to be more regular, but the quality on offer helped suffice. In any case, issues number six and seven contained over sixty pages each.

'Modern Soul – A Case For The Defence' by Mark Sargeant; 'Bootlegs' by Mark Bicknell; 'Collecting Rare Soul Albums'; 'Beach Music Stateside' by Mick Howard; 'Looking Back at the Twisted Wheel' - John Smith; 'Who Wants to Be A DJ' - Mark Bicknell; an in- depth look at Pete McKenna's *Nightshift* book and 'Groovesville Master Tapes – The Untold Story' by Martin Koppel all continue to make interesting reading today, while the popularity of this magazine is clearly identified in issue No.9 with a mention that there were now no back-issues available.

Issue No.11 saw a drop down to forty-four pages - perhaps the arrival of a new addition to the Bicknell household being the reason behind this, but it sprung back to sixty for No.12. Two issues later a considerable number of publications that had gone before, and indeed that were to follow, were put in the shade when No.14 appeared, as this was a glossy covered, centre- stapled issue, and it was still only a very reasonable £3.

Alas, as Mark was to write in his editorial of issue fifteen, a massive seventy-two pager, going glossy was *"perhaps something of a mistake as the printers being rather busy cannot always meet my deadlines. Plus, the cost of production have almost cleared out the Soul Underground Bank Account – indeed it has! The situation has left me with two choices, either shut down* publication completely or revert back to our old format which to be honest is almost the same as the new look apart from a bit of red ink! Otherwise, content will have to be cut dramatically to offset the huge costs of printing, rather than our original method of production and sixty plus page content. To be honest with you all, I'm really quite sad with almost going back on my word and promise of bigger and better things for 'Soul Underground'. However, I would rather maintain our strength as an informative, factual, 'soulful' publication, than lose it in terms of content or worse fold the operation."

Mark added: "Now we are an established magazine there will be no stopping us with 14 issues behind us which may not seem a lot in four years I know, but you would not believe the amount of work that goes into producing a sixty plus page magazine and without the contributors I would still be on Issue One."
Sadly, there was no number fifteen.

By 1993 some had drifted away from the 'northern' side of the music, moving towards neo-soul, jazz, funk, fusion, Latin and the like, and it is only right that there were publications that edged towards those genres. *Blues and Soul* would certainly have encompassed such sounds, albeit on a limited basis, but for a totally independent feel, many would turn to the Birmingham produced **VIBE**. This is another publication that, although 'on the list', was unknown with regard to content, before it was offered in a 'job-lot', when a part collection was offered to me (great things these job-lots), and although my musical tastes can vary it took me down an avenue that I was quite unfamiliar with.

Again, only a few copies came my way, so the exact date of *Vibe* first appearing in the marketplace is unknown, but the first issue I have is number five and inside there is a mention of an open day, three-day event at Stratford-upon-Avon, entitled 'The Phoenix 1993'. But not only do I not know when that first issue appeared, neither do I know how many issues there actually were. I have a number sixteen from the Winter of 1995, so at least we know that much.

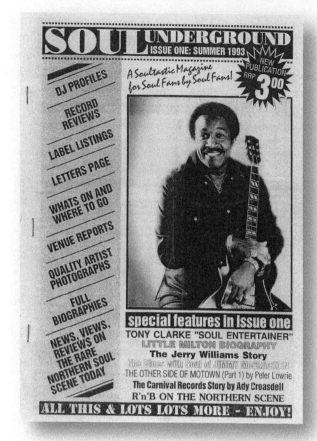

Going back to that issue number five, it is card covered, A5 size, with twenty inner pages of reading – an article on funk; 'Searching for the Right Vibe', which is a venue review of a visit to Dingwalls in Camden Town; 'The Quest' - another visit to London, but to Soul Jazz record shop. There was a review of a Wynton Marsalis Septet concert in Birmingham, an article on the 70s albums of Roy Ayers, Jazz Orientations, a Jazz profile, 'On The Cusp', which was also jazz linked, plus a number of adverts. Told you it was different!

Edited by Graham Radley and Steven Williams, the magazine must have proved popular, as by issue eleven, it had stretched to fifty-two inner pages and by issue sixteen to fifty-six, so there was plenty of reading. An 'A- Z of Jazz', Jon Lucien, D-Influence, reviews, an article entitled 'The Trouble With Soul Nowadays' by Andrew Allen which begins – "For the nineties soul connoisseur times are hard", adding "The fact that 'major label' record companies are increasingly failing to give albums a UK release and, even more so, a vinyl release only increases the problems for the nineties soul collector. It makes it all the more frustrating when in his monthly 'Soul Sauce' column for 'Blues and Soul',

Richard Searling gives excellent reviews of tracks which are either, [a] promotional only and not available for at least another year. Or; [b] only imported in quantities of '1' – I kid you not! Such information is enough to push a soul addict over the edge."

Goucher entitled – 'So You Think You Are A Soul Boy', with part one giving you a whistle stop trip through the 70s and 80s and the plagiarism of white acts of black American music. Part two sees Brian say that his first article caused *"quite a stir"* and he goes on to list twenty 'soul drenched tunes' from the last few years, which included Lyn White 'Stranger in the Street', Ruby Andrews 'Casanova', Bert Robinson 'I Can't Let You Go' and Sweet Obsession 'Give Me All My Love Back'. Despite its jazz leanings, this is a well-produced magazine and a credit to its editors, and if I were to find a few of the missing copies, I would certainly buy them.

There have been a number of 'one-off' publications over the years, but perhaps none bore the quality of **TRACKS TO YOUR MIND**, which was published in 1994 by well-known DJ and record collector Tim Ashibende. A4 size, card cover, thirty-six pages, printed in an exceptionally large font size; perhaps he realised that in later years many of those who took to re-reading his publication would not have the same level of eyesight as they did when they handed over their £2.50 for that first issue.

'The fanzine for the discerning "Rare Soul" collector' proclaimed the cover, adding that it was a 'New Jersey "Rare Soul" Special', with Tim writing in his introduction that he hoped, over time, to illustrate with various stories and biographies that many of the assumptions surrounding many of the artists were *"more than dubious"*. He went on to add: *"One other motivating factor for me, in putting together this magazine, is quite literally, the inaccuracies I've read over the years about different aspects of the scene and its music"*, before going on to mention a trio of examples.

Tim was not, however, having a pot-shot at all those publications that had gone before as he was more than complimentary to many in his editorial. *"Over the years there have been many fanzines dedicated, almost exclusively, in most cases, to Rare Soul. Their names are legion: 'Souled Out', 'Yesterday's Memories', 'Blackbeat', 'Soul Music', 'Collectors Soul', 'Hot Buttered Soul', 'Soul Symbol', 'Sounds of Soul', 'That Beatin Rhythm', 'Soul Source', 'Soul Up North', 'The Owls Effort', 'Soulful Kinda Music', 'Shades of Soul', 'Manifesto'. There are also many more, and some like the latter three are still current; in fact, Derek Pearson's 'Shades' is perhaps the longest running of the amateur fanzines. I use the word amateur to distinguish them from the more professional magazines like 'Blues and Soul', 'Voices From The Shadows' and 'Soul Survivor' which are long running but which, overall, have tended to cover more generic soul, though they do touch on Rare Soul, but to a lesser extent."*

He continued: *'Some of these magazines have been excellent, and all have had time, money, and a genuine love for soul music invested in them: perhaps more importantly they have served as the only means by which fans of Rare Soul could read about the records which have motivated them to dance, collect and listen for almost 30 years. For this at least, they deserve our respect."*

Tim's publication was intended to add that extra dimension to the world of soul publications, giving *'Rare Soul some more meaningful and historical perspective, and be remembered for something more than baggy trousers, idiosyncratic record-collecting, Pye Disco-Demand, and all night-discos"*, as he had a wealth of information and interviews with *"enough material 'in the can' for another 15 or 20 magazines at least"*.

ISSUE No. 1   £2.50

1967 - Jersey City, N. J.

BURNING SENSATION
(Paul Kyser, Jr.)

KYSER RECORDS

Covington Music
(BMI)
TKT Production

JP-2122-B

ROBBY LAWSON
Under J. Covington, Jr &
N. Adamson, Supervision

TRACKS TO YOUR MIND

The fanzine for the discerning
'Rare Soul' collector.
includes
NEW JERSEY 'RARE SOUL' Special:
PAUL KYSER
ROBBY LAWSON
SUPERLATIVES
SHALIMARS
SUPERBS
RONNIE GOODSON

DANSETTE

Centering around Robbie Lawson's 'Burning Sensation' recording, it contained in-depth interviews with Earl Morgan and Paul Kyser, who wrote the song, and certainly laid the foundations for a publication that could well have become an excellent archive of soul music, but unfortunately the hoped for sales figures were never reached and due to the disappointment of those initial sales, no number two, which was to be a 'Detroit Special', was forthcoming, with that first issue becoming something of a collector's item in the years to come.

I found *Tracks* totally different from any other fanzine/magazine of the time, and wondered if that had been Tim's intention? "*Yes absolutely*" he replied. "*I knew what else was out there in terms of other soul fanzines and magazines, because I'd religiously and consistently bought and supported them all over the years. With absolutely no disrespect to other fanzines or their producers, I felt a lot of what was out there (though not all) was about records, not music, and there's a big difference in my view. Many of the fanzines were about label scans and discographies etc. There's absolutely a place for those, and I too enjoyed looking at and reading that stuff. But equally sometimes I felt I was reading opinions and assumptions about the backgrounds, origins, people etc behind records, and not facts or substance. I felt there was a gap and a niche which I could attempt to at least partially fill. Without meaning to sound intellectually superior, I wanted to set the bar high for my fanzines, just for my own personal standards. I wanted the fanzines to be the Rare Soul equivalent of the 'Guardian' not the 'Sun'. My view was that the two could quite happily sit side by side, appealing to different readerships or demographics.*"

Personally, I think if you are going to write about something then you have to search for that different angle as it gives you some individuality, but did Tim think by concentrating more or less on the one subject matter it failed to grasp the attention of some? "*Ha ha ha. Yes, it absolutely and it definitely failed to 'grasp the attention' of many many, not just some lol. I always suspected it would be that way, and I expected it not to appeal to the majority, and was prepared for that. But I think I was genuinely shocked (and hurt) that so so few collectors were willing to pay the measly amount of £3 to find out the story behind some of the best records to come out of New Jersey; records they owned (or wanted to) or lusted after.*

"*I can tell you now, that quite a few of the key collectors, DJs, etc on our scene definitely did NOT buy my fanzine. These are key people who profess to love the music, collect it, live for it. Yet still they couldn't be bothered to just delve a little underneath and find out a little more about the background to records they love.*

"*My hurt is my fault; I was naive back then, about the level of real deep interest in our music. I confused serious interest in vinyl with serious interest in the music holistically. I'm wiser about it all now, I hope, and have understood and accepted that there are many levels of interest from zero or superficial to really deep etc.*"

The magazine is still talked about today, but did Tim find at the time that sales were less than expected? "*I only did a run of 500 copies and unfortunately it's taken me the last thirty years to sell about 300 to 350 of them. I have about 100 left, and probably gave fifty away to friends, family, etc. Hugely hugely disappointing, but I think it says more about our collecting scene than it says about me or my fanzine. I didn't expect huge sales, but equally I didn't think it would take me so long to sell so few. I'm sure by the end of the first year after production I'd still sold less than fifty!*

"*I'm an avid reader so I read all the time, but some people aren't and that may be why my fanzine doesn't hit their interest area or concentration span. Photos and scans are easier to look at and absorb if you're not a reader. I understand and accept that, and accept that it probably contributed to poor sales. Having said all that, any commodity has to reconcile with there first of all being a market, and secondly also reconcile with what the market wants. If my fanzine did neither, then that's a business or marketing failure of mine; I can't blame consumers for that.*"

You had a load more material to use in what were hoped to be future issues. What made you decide not to proceed with a second issue, as I am sure the publication would have gone on to be quite successful? "*I don't mind admitting that I was hugely hurt and wounded by not only the lack of sales but the apathy too. I (wrongly) took it personally. I remember hurriedly trying to get the run printed in time, so I could take them with me to sell at that summer's annual Cleethorpes Weekender. I felt sure there would be love, enthusiasm, and support, translating into good sales there, so I was very excited about unveiling it there. I couldn't have been more wrong. If I sold twenty over that weekend of two all-nighters and two all-dayers, I'd be amazed; probably ten to fifteen copies!*

"*The reaction was lukewarm and it hurt me. People I knew well and respected would pick it up, flick through it and put it back down without buying it. They'd then go and spend more than that amount on a pint or five!*

"*I also endured ridiculous criticisms about there not being 'enough pictures' in there. I got used to responding by saying two things: 1) 'If you want pictures buy the Beano!' 2) 'Don't you think if I'd had photos of The Shalimars, Superlatives, Robbie Lawson etc I would have included them?' I still think those critics deserved those responses, because they are such petty and superficial criticisms. However, those comments do tell us a lot about where the real 'interest' is, and actually confirms the reason I felt there was room for something different. Clearly, I was wrong.*

"It hurt, but I've moved on from that and still believe in what I did.

"Sometimes to turn the tide you have to swim against it. As a collector of many things, I also appreciate that sometimes, something not appreciated contemporaneously can be sought after years later, so who knows, maybe in a few years there will be more support and recognition for my fanzine than there has been historically. However, I can't forget those who did and always have supported it, and to them I say a huge 'Thank You'.

"All I was trying to do was to shine a light on some background to the fabulous music we love. If others don't or didn't want that, that's fine; each to his own. Just as long as they also understand that paying huge amounts of money for records, without also having any interest in the human beings who were behind them (and their story) means there's no connection between them and this collecting hobby. To me that's selfish, narrow minded and unacceptable. That attitude just renders a record to be a trophy, rather than a work of 'art' someone invested time money and hope in. It's a complete disconnect between product consumer and its producer."

Obviously knocked back by that lack of interest and perhaps more so by lack of sales, I wondered if Tim ever thought about resurrecting *Tracks* at any time later on, or doing another magazine? *"I've never stopped thinking about it really, to be honest, but common sense has always held me back, plus the many ups and downs of life got in the way; as they do. I'm not sure whether I can label the fanzine a failure or not; maybe it was in terms of sales, and my own hopes and aspirations for it. I had hoped it might be the springboard for a book, but I know now never to be foolhardy enough to do that now lol. It definitely didn't pan out as I'd hoped. A lot of time and money went into it, and I'm very mindful of not repeating the same situation all over again.*

"However, there are two big considerations. One is that I told these people I was gonna tell their stories in published form, and I'm mindful about keeping that promise. In that respect I've already partly failed some of them. Dena Barnes passed away in 2008 without ever seeing her story in print from me. I'll always feel ashamed about that, and likewise, the same situation with Joe Hunter, Mike Terry and others.

"The other consideration is that just possibly with Facebook and the Internet generally, there 'seems' to be a bigger audience and a greater appetite for information and background now than there was before. But I'm still not entirely sure.

"I'll expand on why I say that. I've noticed for example that in Facebook's Rare Soul Talk, at best there will be between 100 and 300 people who will comment or give support to an interesting intelligent, informative, post of background information. That sounds ok 'til you realise it's almost the same low amount of people who have so far bought my fanzine, over a thirty-year period, and also that it's actually a very very small proportion of the total amount of 'members' of that group.

"My point is that clearly there seems to be still only a very small proportion of collectors or Rare Soul enthusiasts who are moved enough by such a post to comment or signal their interest. How much lower a percentage would then be motivated enough to pay for such information via a fanzine? For me the jury is still out on that question, but in the interests of my promises to those I met and interviewed I may well once again try with another publication or two, and see what happens. I have enough taped interviews and letters and other memorabilia for possibly another ten to twenty fanzines, that's for sure, and they're all digitised now."

Summer had been and gone and the leaves were beginning to fall off the trees when the first issue of **MANIFESTO** appeared in September 1994. Subtitled 'A Magazine For the Nocturnal', it could have been just the thing to pass an hour or so during those dark winter nights that were just round the corner. Or was it?

To be completely honest, issue one, twenty glossy pages for £1.50, was nothing special. A few lines on the Ritz, slightly more on eleven years of Porthcawl and a couple of pages on Stafford and The Catacombs, two pages of what's on and a top-ten of chewing gum. Honest! Unlike a number of the featured publications, it did nothing to grab you and make you think 'Wow, I must buy this every month or whenever it comes out.'

But it was early days for the Ian Palmer and Dennis Lee edited magazine, who proclaimed that their aim was *"to provide a magazine that covers the great social scene that has always been the bonding force of the northern soul scene."*

Issue two appeared two months later, with an additional four pages, taking it up to twenty-four, while two issues further on, which featured the first part of the Wigan Casino Story, it had increased again to twenty-eight pages. Another two months down the line (No. 6 – Winter 95/96) and it expanded again in pages to thirty-two and in price to £2.50. It had improved, not just in the number of pages, but in content, and was beginning to drift away from the sometimes 'laddish' behaviour which simply didn't fit.

Interviews with a number of the scene's 'faces' - Chris King, Bob Hinsley, Pat Brady, Ginger Taylor, Richard Searling, Ady Croasdell, Brian Rae and the like aided the noticeable improvement, with those additional pages also being a notable factor. It did, however, have something of an irregular tendency, as it would appear every couple of months and then not been seen or heard of for four. For those who collect fanzines/magazines, it is also worth noting that when it comes to *Manifesto*, there is no number twenty-one. After number twenty comes twenty-two, then it is twenty- two(b), then twenty-three. Every little bit of info helps.

August 2001 (No.31) saw the last editorial from Ian Palmer – "*I wanted to start a magazine that conveyed that spirit, that showed the scene for what it was, a good night out with your mates listening and dancing to some of the greatest dance tracks ever recorded and having a bloody good laugh while you're at it. And I like to think that's what 'Manifesto' has done.*" From then on it saw Stuart Russell and Mike Ritson of Bee Cool publishing at the helm, with issue No.32 taking on a new cover design, as the magazine continuing to move forward.

It was now something of a 'must read', with contributions from the likes of Soul Sam, Neil Rushton, Tim Brown, Mark Bicknell,

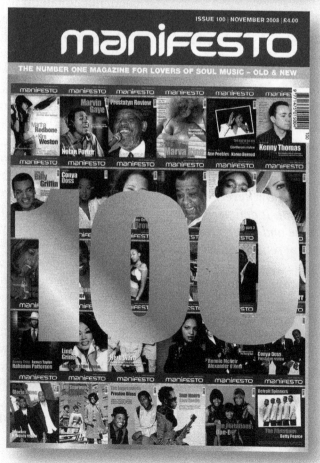

Steve Handbury and Steve Guarnori, all names of note on the scene. The centre spread of photographs taken at various soul nights/all-nighters would always help sales from those who wanted to see themselves within the pages. Reviews were plentiful within what could certainly be described as a 'quality' publication and more often than not, they would, for me anyway, throw light onto previously unknown sides.

Whilst enjoying the discovery of those new tunes to my ears, I found just as much pleasure, perhaps more, in issue No.54 (September 2004) and a two-page article by Keith Rylatt, the first of a series of five articles covering soul magazines and fanzines. Subsequent articles covered books relating to the music. Needless to say, those copies have been thumbed a bit more than others.

It was of no surprise that *Manifesto* flourished and managed to hit issue No.100 in November 2008. The sub-heading of 'The Number One Magazine For Lovers Of Soul Music – Old & New' would certainly not fall foul of the Trade Descriptions Act. In the editorial of that iconic issue, Mike Ritson mentioned that they were still there thanks to the support of the readers, the advertisers and those who had contributed. But it wasn't all smiles and back slaps in the 100th issue as it also carried an obituary of Levi Stubbs, the distinctive lead voice of The Four Tops who had recently passed away.

As time went on issues became somewhat irregular, but it still maintained a high level of written content thanks to the regular contributors such as Keith Rylatt, Soul Sam, Simon White and Tim Brown; although as time passed, many were to forget about its existence and as I write this, the last issue I have seen was No.156 (March 2019).

Because of the time gap, longer than normal, I decided to get in touch with Mike Ritson, not simply to find out if I had missed any issues - I hadn't - but to see what was what. But before asking about the next issue, or even if there was going to be one, I decided to go back to the start and find out how the association with *Manifesto* came about. *"Bee Cool, the company I was involved in with Stuart, simply fancied having a magazine as part of our portfolio and so we bought 'Manifesto' for what was a lot of money. Perhaps too much! We wanted to be like 'Blues and Soul' but covering the Northern Soul scene. But with living in the south, it had its problems and it was soon discovered that things were going to take a bit more than we had originally realised."*
Having mentioned *Blues and Soul*, I asked Mike why *Manifesto* never sat alongside it on the shelves of WH Smith and the like? *"Money. To get on the shelves of WH Smith you had to buy a licence, or at least you did have to back then. It was very expensive. You would have needed to sell something like 10,000 copies. It was also a case of sale or return and we certainly didn't want unsold copies lying around gathering dust.*

"We did manage to get it into Borders, who although an American company had shops here in the

UK, so that was something.

"Oh yes, I also remember that Ian Palmer managed to get a copy on a shelf in the 'Cabin' on Coronation Street."

But what of the future? Will *Manifesto* appear again? *"I want to say yes,"* replied Mike. *"I would certainly want to do one other at least, but we are in an extremely difficult period. Bee Cool are still trading and are still a limited company, but the printers we used are no longer there. I do it for the love of the music, but you simply cannot lose money. It costs around £4000/£5000 per issue to produce, so you have to take in quite a bit on advertising. If it is to come out again, perhaps even only once a year, it would have to be done to coincide with the likes of the Blackpool Soul Festival when there would be a lot of interest and something that could generate sales. I have to add that the quality of the last few issues was far from what we wanted, so this is something that we would want to improve on, plus the need to find a new printer, before another issue can appear."*

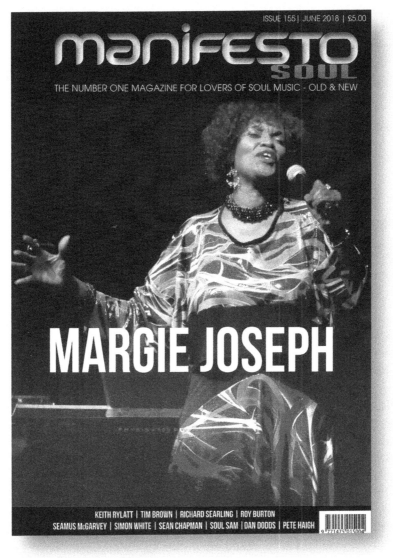

I have spoken highly of all the publications within these pages; some I liked more than others, but having spent thirty years putting together a twenty- page newsletter on football memorabilia every couple of months relating to a certain club (I'm not going to mention the name in case it offends!), I know only too well how much time and effort goes into putting such things together.
Having a subscription service made things that little bit easier and you knew what sort of print run you required.

I know that the people who subscribed to my newsletter enjoyed it, as I was told how much it was liked and appreciated often enough.

Because of having, let's say, inside knowledge of what it takes to produce a publication, that is one of the reasons why I have spent so many hours reading hundreds of soul fanzines/magazines and enjoying the majority of them. However, not every fanzine brought enjoyment, hours of reading and a gateway to previously unknown sounds. There was one, bought blind as part of a collection, which, even at the 50p or whatever it cost, was a complete waste of money. But I had it on my extensive list of publications, so it was purchased and another was stroked off the list. They say that hindsight is a good thing and had I known what this particular publication was like, I would simply have left the box beside the name blank, or with an asterisk and a noted comment.

R SOUL was, and is, unlike any other soul fanzine, either before it made its appearance or after. It is undated, but as there was an advertising four pager for the 1995 Cleethorpes Weekender in it, I will take that as a clue and say it appeared that year. Neither have I any idea who the editor(s) was/were.

There are a few record reviews scattered through the eight issues I have, along with an odd venue report, but the majority of each twenty-page issue is made up of articles, cartoons and loads more, which make fun of countless names on the scene. One issue was actually re- named 'Hamsters Monthly'! Some of it might be deemed funny, but sadly it wasn't for me and those eight issues are down at the bottom of a box and certainly won't be re- read.

Finding a copy of the first issue of many of the publications featured within the pages of this book is akin to finding a first-edition of some classic book, although the price tag on the latter way exceeds that of any mere soul music fanzine. They do, however, have

their similarities in the fact that many first issues would have something of a limited print run and also be seen as a tester/taster, with our fanzines more than likely being lesser in numbers than any leather-bound work of fiction or non-fiction.

Such is the case with **WHISPERS GETTIN' LOUDER** as issue No.2 of the late Steve Jackson's publication finds a mention in the editorial that there were no copies left of that inaugural issue and that he was delighted and amazed at the response and feedback he had received. That second issue, despite having an increased print run, was also noted as having sold out in the editorial of number three.

It took Steve those first couple of issues to really find his feet and the direction he wanted to go in, and from issue three (November 1995), it was up there with the best, and had increased from thirty-two pages in number two to forty in number three; hence the price increase from £2 to £3. Issue two, by the way, is a strange one, as the cover has been glued on to what is page two. It must have been a printing error which was to leave the backs of both those first two pages blank. Personally, I would just have left it as it was.

With the likes of Andy Davies, Brian Goucher, Fish and Peter Burns amongst the contributors, you knew you were going to get a decent read and what perhaps

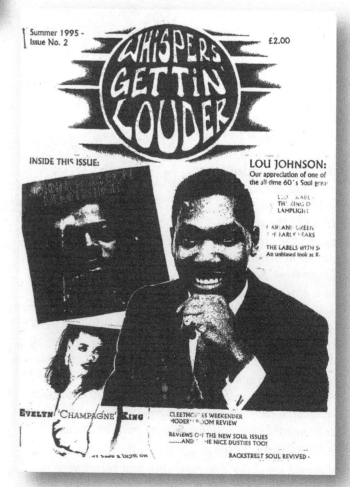

attracted many to this publication was the distinct lack of discographies. Any that did find their way onto the pages were minimal and blended well into the actual text rather than taking over page upon page. Perhaps the connoisseurs and the anoraks might have bemoaned the lack of such information, but other publications catered for their needs and the lack of them in *Whispers* freed up the space for interesting and informative reading matter.

One huge plus point of this magazine was emphasised in the editorial of No.4 (January 1996). A letter had been received complimenting the publication, adding: *"The various contributors wrote intelligent and non-political pieces on the music we love."* In reply, Steve wrote: *"Thank you – but the day we have to start having a pop at people who don't share our taste or opinion, then I'm packing it in."*

What perhaps gave *Whispers* an edge was its mixture of 'old' and 'new'. Contents within the often forty-odd pages included the likes of venue reports, readers charts, DJ play lists, 'Soulology' - an article on different record labels such as Ko Ko, Hi and Kayvette, 'The Pedigree Hall of Fame' - which included the likes of Laura Lee, Willie Hutch, Wilson Pickett and David Ruffin, 'Down at the Club', all more or less regular features, while issue No.10 listed the

Top Fifty records of 1997. What was number one, I hear you ask? Adriana Evans 'Looking For Your Love', with Jeffree's 'Love Loan' at number two.

There were three issues per year throughout 1996 and 1997, taking you up to issue No.9. These were followed in February 1998 with No.10 and Summer [?] 1998 - No.11, but as far as I can make out, none followed, and in common with others, there was no advance warning as regards to its eventual disappearance. It was certainly missed.

'A Magazine For Real Soul Lovers – Full Of Soul Old And New With No Boundaries' was what the cover of LOVE MUSIC REVIEW proclaimed to be when that first issue appeared in December 1995. Not only that, it was the first and the only soul related fanzine/ magazine to be named after the man at the helm!

Edited by Warrington based Andrew Love, you had two options when buying this forty-page, A4 publication. One was to pay £5 and receive a ninety-minute tape featuring the tunes reviewed within the pages, or you could simply obtain a tapeless copy for £3. The choice was yours.

Although having announced that it covered soul 'old and new', Andrew admitted in his editorial that he felt there was a void that could be filled by something a little different, as most magazines had a strong northern soul bias, and whilst he was a product of that

LOVE MUSIC REVIEW

A Magazine for **Real Soul** Lovers

Issue 3
July '96

£3.00

(£5.00 with review tape)

The Spectrum of Soul old and new – with no boundaries:

- Deep
- Northern
- Modern
- Sixties
- Seventies
- Eighties
- Nineties

Rodney Mannsfield and Bobby Thurston classic albums reviewed

Yarmouth & Southport Weekenders

Vinyl/CD Reviews

Cotswold Comments · Reflections

Goucher's Corner

A Night On The Soultown

Cooking With Crossover

Jazz Fusion Reviews

bobby thurston

scene, he felt there was so much being missed that didn't fit the Wigan stereotype that he resolved to produce something that featured everything. *"There were actually two reasons behind the publishing of 'Love Music Review',"* said Andrew. *"One was that I'd always loved reading soul related magazines and particularly Rod Dearlove's. There always seemed to be an eternity between issues, now I know why, so I thought I would give it a go.*

"The second reason was I'd be talking to people about records and was amazed at how limited their exposure to loads of great music was, so I thought why not spread the faith. I would ignore the very obvious stuff that was well known and share the cheaper, the less well known and the un-played, or indeed unreleased.

"I needed to find a way to let people hear what I was writing about so came up with the review tape. Well, one wouldn't work without the other really.

"I then realised I needed more opinions than just my own and grabbed some friends who thought like me, all local at first but I soon found some from further afield."

Most of the publications that lasted beyond less than a handful of issues took their time in progressing through various stages of change and improvement, but *Love Music Review* was different from the rest as it bounced from its incarnation as just another A4, side-stapled look-a-like to a card- covered, digital print job by its second issue in April 1996. Although eight pages fewer, there would have been no complaints from those who bought this second issue if they had also purchased number one, as it was properly designed and printed, giving it a real quality look, complemented by an impressive array of contributors, names like Steve Plumb, Brian Goucher, Pete Thorpe, and Barry Maleedy.

I put it to Andrew that it was something of a big step to take so soon. *"Yes, the first issue was very trial and*

error, with a second-hand pc, a hand-held scanner and a stapler. The software was all new to me, although I did have an art background from the seventies.

" After it came out, via selling in clubs and a couple of record shops, I started getting letters and phone calls with kind words and from one, Roger Williams, who worked for a printing firm, he said 'great mag, I can make it look better'. So, he did!

"I consider myself as a fanatical collector of records, but my wallet wasn't as bulging as some, Steve Guarnori's for instance, so the revenue from the mag helped pay for more records to review, sometimes I sold them later. Bit of a looping conveyor belt really. The big money records didn't interest me if they were well known and often overplayed to the detriment of often better tracks."

But were the 'free tapes', which had a hint of exclusiveness about them, an important part of this fledgling publication? *"Regarding the exclusive tracks, Steve Plumb, John Smith and a couple of others offered me some of these and I agreed as long as I could put them on the tape for everyone to hear."*

This format continued for another three issues before the card cover was dropped, but the layout and everything else remained the same.

Although mainly reviews, records, CDs and concerts, you did get the odd artist article within the pages, featuring the likes of Jackie Ross, Sonny Charles and Jimmy Burns; but one thing you did not get was regularity. 1996 saw everything go to plan with three issues in April, July and October, but issue five did not appear until March 1997. Number six followed in June of that year, but it was April 1998 before number seven came out and Spring 2000 before you saw number eight.

"Like all of us, I aimed to get four issues out a year for the foreseeable future," Andrew responded, *"or until I had nothing new to say.*

"The problem has always been getting contributors

135

to contribute and do it to a deadline. I could've done it all myself, but who wants one person's views and picks over a whole magazine?"

In his editorial for that eighth issue Andrew finished with a *"solemn promise that it won't be even half as long as this issue for LMR 9."* As I had never seen issue number nine, I presumed that it had never materialised, but in conversation with Andrew, he revealed that a ninth issue certainly did materialise, but not until April 2015. As Andrew still had a spare copy of that elusive ninth issue, I received my copy a mere five years and a few months late! However, I have got to say that it was well worth the wait.

I was expecting nothing more than a follow-on to issue eight, but I was pleasantly surprised to open an envelope and find a full colour A5 publication of forty-four pages. Not only that, I have to go on record here and say that taking this magazine as simply a 'one-off', it is without doubt the best publication I have seen relating to the soul music scene. And I do not say that simply because Andrew has connections with my local area - plus I must state here and now that I have never met him - it was simply a magazine that had a bit of everything and at the same time looked really good.

So, what makes *Love Music Review* No.9 so special? Excellent layout and a selection of first-class articles – 'Slow to Mid-Tempo', 'Dancing Delight', 'The Deeper Side Of Soul', 'A Hitch-hikers Guide Through the Rare Soul Clubs of Northern England', an interview with John Manship, 'Soul Essence Weekender Review', 'Ten Years of Soulful Dance Music At Lytham', 'Collecting Vinyl, A Female Perspective' and articles from Steve Plum, Brian Goucher and Peter and Cath Mason. Oh, and a couple of excellent colour photographs.

Apparently, there are still *"a good few articles in the can"*, so there might even be an issue ten one day. The fingers are crossed.

With Christmas 1995 just around the corner, it was certainly the season of goodwill for those who attended soul events in the Midlands, as not only did the area suddenly have its own publication in **SOUL TIMES**, but it was also FREE!

Ok, it certainly wouldn't have helped you pass an hour or so waiting for Father Christmas to arrive, as the A4, eight-page publication was full of adverts, with the only actual reading being a 'Welcome' and a couple of paragraphs or so on the cover artists – The Soul Survivors, an eight-piece Midlands-based band.

With the advertising rates more than likely covering the printing costs, it would have been good to have a little reading tucked in between its pages, but it wasn't to be. Those adverts were a mixture of soul events at countless different venues in the Midlands and some records for sale.

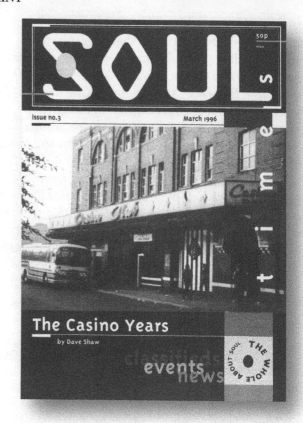

Issue two (February 1996) was, again, what was to be the standard eight pages; however, there was now a page, or near enough, of reading - 'The Philadelphia Sound' took the honours in this issue, and so it continued. In the issues that followed, there was a small article on the Wigan Casino and another on the Harvey, Tri-Phi and Miracle labels, but all the others were to be Motown based.

April/May 1997 (issue 11) was a double issue and had stretched to twelve pages, as did issue twelve, which covered July and August of that same year. As well as Thelma and Ge Ge record label listings, there was also a feature on Barbara Carr, so were things finally looking up? Sadly no, as issue twelve appears to be the last.

If ever a soul music magazine should have appeared on the shelves of the High Street newsagents then it was **IN THE BASEMENT**, as it would not only have filled a void, but also have put those soul music publications that did - *Blues and Soul*, *Black Music* and *Echoes* - to shame. From the pen, typewriter or whatever of Brighton based David Cole, *In The Basement* first appeared in February 1996. " *'Oh no, not another fanzine' was the immediate reaction I received from those nearest and dearest to me when I announced my intention to start 'In The Basement'.*

" *'But', I protested, 'soul fans can never get enough reading material about their subject. After all, look at all the magazines that pour through my letter-box and the fact that I'm constantly wishing either they came out more often or there were more of them'"* were David's opening comments in that first editorial.

David Cole had first put pen to paper in regards to soul music when he was as a contributor to Rod Dearlove's *Voices From The Shadows*, and in that opening editorial he was to add that this new magazine would be *"dedicated to 'real' soul"* and that the readership at which it was aimed would agree that there was *"precious little soul as we understand it in the rap, hip-hop and associated styles currently coming out of America."*

IN THE BASEMENT

ISSUE No:1   FEBRUARY 1996

Jr Walker
Don Covay
Marva Wright
Rhythm & Blues Foundation
36 pages of reviews.....and more!

dedicated to 'real' soul   £2.50

Was that 'precious little soul' comment a dig at the likes of *Blues and Soul*, I wondered? *"I'm not sure I remember when I said that - or even, if - but I certainly lost it. I think Blues and Soul lost its way when it allowed its content to be dictated by advertisers, as its coverage changed from proper soul music to whatever was popular at the time. As for soul from America - it seemed any black artist from the South over fifty was dubbed 'blues' and the crap that came out on labels like Ecko and Carl Marshall's productions were so poor they must have been scribbled down on the back of a fag packet and the 'musicianship' - performed on some sort of cheap computer - just totally demeaned soul music. As for rap... don't get me started!"*

Few, if any, who produce fanzines/magazines have any idea as to how long their journey through the world of publications will be, and when David Cole

joined that happy band of editors across the country, he had no idea as to what lay ahead. *"No, I didn't"* replied David. *"As I think you know, I used to write for 'Voices' but, when that started to only be printed very sporadically, I asked Rod if he would mind me doing something for myself. He gave me nothing but full encouragement so, having recently taken voluntary redundancy, I decided it would be something to do while I found other activities to keep the wolf from the door. Thanks to support from a number of UK indie record companies, like Topsy, it just grew. My first face-to-face interview was Trudy Lynn who was absolutely magnificent and, again, so encouraging and made me feel: You can do this!"*

As I said, it should have been available on the High Street, perhaps establishing an even wider readership; so why did David not pursue this avenue? *"Being of such niche market interest, I had to do my own distribution as to use a national distributor meant surrendering circa 50% of the cover price. Some chains, such as Borders and HMV, allowed me to deal directly with shop managers and negotiate terms but others, Smith's being the prime example, would do nothing without a go-between."*

It wasn't until issue number thirty (May-July 2003) that I discovered the magazine, when a chance meeting with someone I knew simply to say hello to in passing led to a new friendship and he pushed a copy of *ITB* my way. As I was just getting back into the music at this particular time, the magazine was like a breath of fresh air and I was immediately hooked.

But twenty-nine issues of this progressive new magazine had already been issued, with each one continuing to show an improvement on the last. Each issue would also conjure up a new name amongst the featured artists, while the review section was studied closely and I was soon to learn that if David Cole recommended something within that section of the magazine, then it was a 'must buy'.

Having digested that issue number thirty, probably re- read a couple of times at least, I became a subscriber, and continued to be throughout the years that followed until that final issue fell through the letter box in the spring of 2012, sixty-four issues after that first one appeared sixteen years previously. By then, however, I had found all those missing issues, with the collector within me insisting that I had to have nothing less than the full set.

During its lifetime, the magazine never progressed to colour within its pages; it wasn't needed, as the majority of images used would have been in black and white anyway, but it did see colour used on the front and back covers, inside and out, from issue number twenty. *"This may be a one-off or it may become a*

DEDICATED TO REAL SOUL

In The Basement

ISSUE No: 30
MAY-JULY 2003

£4.00 (U.K.)

WILLIE HUTCH
THELMA HOUSTON
CALVIN SCOTT
CHARLES WALKER
JOHNNY MOORE of the Drifters

NEWS*VIEWS*REVIEWS...
and much more...

regular feature" said David in his editorial, adding that the magazine had also *"broken the sixty-page barrier with four extra pages"*, although even this wasn't enough to include everything he wanted to.

In The Basement was arguably more in-depth than any other publication, and the work that went into each issue must have been rather time consuming, so I asked David about how long it took to put each issue together. *"Pretty much the full three-month interval,"* came the reply. *"I used to try to leave writing the reviews until close to deadline dates in order to keep them as up-to-date as possible, but the features I would put together across the period, not least because of the time required for getting pictures together, setting the pages, etc. At the end, I tried to limit the pages to seventy-two as to go over that figure meant a different postage price bracket. Also, I tried not to have more than twelve pages of adverts."*

Let's drift back to the subject of the cover for a minute. This, for me at least, was another of the magazine's plus points. Many editors were more than happy to put a few label scans on their front pages, but this was not for *In The Basement*, as although artist photos were often used, more so in the later issues, more often than not David would use some random photo taken from an album cover or elsewhere, something that gave the magazine that distinct look of quality, not to mention difference from the rest of the pack. *"I tried to find pictures that reflected the 'settings' for black music and/or something I thought atmospheric"*, he replied. *"I usually adapted LP covers that I particularly liked and which did not scream 'copyright'. Initially, I did not want to use specific artists from that issue's features as I thought, if I featured one, I would offend the rest. That's why, when I first started to use artists, I put them all on the cover. The first 'solo' artist front cover was The Dells as I thought I could justify that as their feature was a ten-pager. It proved popular and was an incentive to continue. I should add that I was often asked by outlets why I did not use artists as they felt they would be more eye-catching sales-wise, but it took*

a long while for me to realise they were right!"

But what about the actual content, I hear you ask? News Round Up; Soul Bites; Readers Forum; Reviews – albums, CDs, DVDs and books; gig reports; general articles and events were what regularly filled the pages. Sadly, obituaries were also a much too regular feature. It was, however, the artist 'mini-biographies' with an accompanying US discography that was the stand out feature of this quite superb magazine. By the time you turned the last page of that final issue in the spring of 2012 you would have read about the lives of a total of 309 featured artists, from the likes of Jackie Moore, Viola Wills, Nella Dodds and Willie Hutch to Linda Clifford, Jackie Ross, Tobi Lark and Wilson Williams. A complete listing of every artist featured in-depth, as well as a listing of the editor's 'Star Pick' CD releases and the 'Vinyl Spotlight' albums were all included in that final sixty-fifth issue.

So, issue sixty-five and the end of the journey, but although David stopped *In The Basement* in its printed format he continued to compile reviews and the like on his basement-group website. The magazine was sorely missed. An encyclopaedia of soul music.

I had one final question for David, and that was did he ever regret stopping the magazine when he did? He replied: *"Not really. Had I kept it going any longer I would be bankrupt. I felt I had reached the optimum cover price and I was ploughing too much of my own money into it. Also, delivering mags around the country by public transport - I don't drive - was not easy as I had deteriorating health. Wandering city streets from station to outlet dragging a wheel-case of mags was becoming rather a chore so, with the mag birthday, I thought that it was the appropriate retirement age for both of us."*

From sixty-five issues of *In The Basement*, to no idea how many issues of **LADIES OF SOUL**, as I only have two issues. Indeed, when I started writing this book, I only had the one.

Ladies Of Soul

★ doris troy ★

Fan Club Magazine

Edited by Chris Williams from Northampton, that first issue stemmed from July 1996 and saw Ortheia Barnes, Thelma Houston and Linda Lewis make up the content which was to fill a mere sixteen pages, with no added extras. Unfortunately, there is nothing within the pages, or on the cover, to indicate if this was issue number one or twenty-one.

I think the second issue that I obtained could well be an earlier one, as there are a couple of reproduced articles within the pages regarding a performance by 'The Supremes', who in fact had nothing at all to do with the Motown trio, and they are dated February/March/April 1995. The cover is also slightly different from that other issue as it carries the sub-heading 'Fan Club Magazine'.

Heavenly harmonies

Featuring Doris Troy on the cover, this second issue I obtained also contains articles on Jackie Moore and a three-page interview with the voluptuous Miss Lyn Roman. Pity the quality of the scanned photos do not do her full justice!

Eighteen pages in total, but three of those are blank, and both this and the other issue I have can be perhaps described as primitive, although the Lyn Roman interview is an interesting read.

Ladies of Soul is an excellent subject matter for a fanzine/magazine and could have enjoyed untold issues and years in existence, while being worthy of a more,

let's say, professional format, but I don't think it would have lasted too long. Hopefully one or two more copies will surface at some point.

It's October 1996 and that man Dave McCadden is back with yet another joust at the soul music market place, bringing SOUL GALORE, a forty page, A5 publication and his first for the best part of nine years, to the multitudes.

What I really enjoy about purchasing those old, long forgotten publications, is not just reading them - that is of course the main reason - but occasionally finding letters or other printed matter tucked within the pages. In issue one of *Soul Galore* I was to find a letter that Dave McCadden had written to a new subscriber named Alan, who had just purchased the first five issues.

In it, Dave wrote: "*All subs run out with issue 7. This is a deliberate policy so I don't get mixed up or find myself with financial difficulties in the event of packing it in. I return to Uni in September, so I need to assess the situation and decide whether to continue.*

"*However, the strength of the support has been so good that I am 99% certain it will continue.*"

It did indeed continue and Dave produced nine issues (up to August 1998), and it has to be said that there is a difference about *Soul Galore* compared to his other 'tongue in cheek' publications, as he drifts away from any jovial digs at the masses and concentrates solely on reviewing records, many with a label scan, coupled with a few record sales, plus the offer of a *Soul Galore* tape. It has to be added, however, that one of two of the reviews are a little unconventional, but they certainly made for the usual McCaddenesque interesting reading.

The majority of the records reviewed were not hard to get rarities, although there were a few, but a decent mix of sounds which might have tweaked a few ears with a forgotten favourite, or nudged a mere novice to go searching for that never previously heard title. All in all, I found all the issues of *Soul Galore* highly enjoyable, and they are worth searching for it you don't already have them.

NB. Dave McCadden passed away in a Manchester Hospital in February 2006, two years after having been diagnosed with a brain tumour. The man and his publications are certainly not forgotten and are an integral part of northern soul scene.

Having lived all my life north of Hadrian's Wall, in a small rural town, alongside people who had no or little love for soul music, I did try to solve that problem when it came to disco nights at the local youth club and made a couple of long-lasting converts. Many years later one girl I hadn't seen for some considerable time turned up at a local soul night and when I told her I was DJing she said that I had introduced her to the likes of soul and Motown, and was later quick to say that I hadn't lost my touch since those teenage days. Anyway, if the local soul scene was confined to my

house, there were other areas in Scotland that could boast of a reasonably healthy soul crowd, with the likes of Edinburgh, Dundee and Aberdeen well to the fore. Glasgow was never really, and still isn't, considered as having leant to the sounds of black America, although I seem to recall mid-week soul nights in the city centre in the late sixties.

It was not, however, uncommon for broad Scottish accents to be heard at numerous venues south of the border back in the day and even more so now, and not simply at the bar, in the record sales area or at the side of the dance floor; they could also be heard introducing the tunes from behind the decks as many of those Scottish disc-spinners gained a positive reputation.

One of those who embraced the soul scene on both sides of the border was David Miller, who got caught up in the enthusiasm of it all and decided that it was time that Scotland had its own publication covering the Scottish soul scene. This was only Scotland's second contribution to the scene as it was preceded by the previously mentioned *Jock's View of Soul*, although you might care to throw in the double-sided A4 sheet produced under the banner of the *Scottish Soul Circular*, which was nothing more than a "*newsletter aimed at informing people in Scotland where and when forthcoming local soul events are taking place.*" (I've only seen number two, which is dated June-September 1990.)

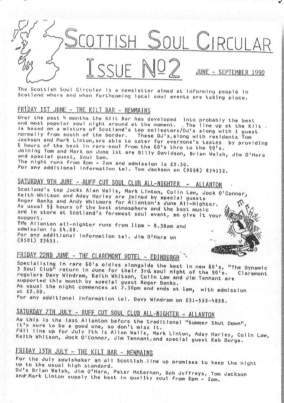

With Father Christmas preparing for his annual sojourn around the world, SOUL VIEW made its bow, and if you weren't a DJ or a promoter on the scene north of the border then you would not have been one of the fortunate few who were sent a copy of the first issue.

That initial twelve-page issue, produced with the usual typewriter and glue format, received a positive response, but according to its editor was *"bad typing and poor layout and not exactly a basis for success, but the aim was to write about the Scottish soul scene."*

Looking back, David was to say: *"I had written several reviews on soul nights I had been to and felt very disillusioned with all that was going on. My intention was to send some of them to other magazines but I thought it better not to do this as I had written some pretty damming stuff. I showed the reviews/articles to some friends and they thought they were good, so I decided to put them all together and print them up. So, with my trusty typewriter and my scribblings 'Soul View' No.1 emerged.*

"I decided to be more diplomatic and changed the reviews somewhat, which is something I now regret. I printed twelve copies and handed them out to people who I regarded as the 'main players' on the Scottish soul scene and it was very well received."

One well known face on the Scottish scene, Kenny

Burrell, was to write to David and say: *"Once again thanks for the surprise [issue 1], I'm saving it as doubtless it'll become a collector's item."*

David continued: *"I had many promises of contributions and stuff and could really see 'Soul View' take off, after all this was Scotland's first ever magazine dedicated to rare/northern soul. I must admit that at this point I began to wonder if I was the person to be doing such a mag as I was a novice on the scene and my knowledge was far less than most. However, I carried on, 'Soul View' No.2 was released soon after, much the same as issue No.1 with poor layout and bad typing, but it was beginning to take shape."*

Issues one and two, that second issue not appearing until fourteen months after the first, were certainly basic, but when issue three materialised, around the spring of 1997, there had been a noticeable improvement and copies of this third issue were sent south of the border in an attempt to broaden the readership. One of those who was sent a copy was Dave McCadden, who, although complimentary, suggested to David that he should drop the 'Scottish angle' in an attempt to give the publication a much wider appeal. Although he respected Dave's experience and advice, David Miller decided to ignore it for three reasons – *"1. It was Scotland's first ever rare/northern soul magazine and I was extremely proud of that. 2. I thought that most of the southern based magazines tended to ignore the Scottish soul scene (you only have to look at Manifesto's map to know what I'm on about) and 3. Southern based magazines had long been established and it wouldn't seem right to thrust 'Soul View' upon them, after all, what could 'Soul View' provide that the others couldn't."*

Like a good wine, *Soul View* matured through time and by issue ten (December 1998), its second anniversary, it was certainly something that David Miller could be proud of, and now boasted of thirty-four pages. Three issues later it had bounced to a more than creditable sixty pages. Long gone was the *"bad typing and poor lay-out"*. That excellent thirteenth issue should have been a landmark one, propelling *Soul View* forward, but unfortunately there were to be only two more to follow as number fifteen brought down the curtain on a publication that showed what could be done with dedication, perseverance and, above all, time.

"Well, here it is, the last ever issue of Soul View Magazine, reality kicks in and I must admit to feeling a little sad, not just personally but for all the people involved with the magazine, however, this is it and no point dwelling on it" were the opening couple of lines in David Miller's editorial in that fifteenth issue in autumn 2000.

David continued to say that he would be writing for a few other magazines and he closed by saying: *"That's it from me, it's been a hoot most of the time and a very enjoyable experience although I have to admit that celebrity status on the scene isn't all it's cracked up to be, now I can fade in and out as I did before without being hounded for autographs – seriously, I owe a huge debt to all who have made Soul View Magazine possible, see you around."*

Having mentioned autographs, whilst reading issue eight of *Soul View* I got to pages eight and nine and noticed that someone had been writing with a marker pen on page ten, as whatever had been written could be seen through the page. Writing found within back issues is certainly not uncommon, as you can find the odd tick beside certain tracks, or on occasion a blank in a discography having been filled in. Anyway, having read pages eight and nine I turned over and was surprised to see, at the top of what was a copied press release referring to Al Wilson and his record 'The Snake' gliding into the American Top 100, was written in black pen – 'Best Wishes, Sincerely, Al Wilson'. To be honest, I wasn't impressed, overjoyed or in seventh heaven, as 'The Snake' is a record I care little for, but upon reading issue nine it was pleasing to be able to add a little story to the signature.

Apparently, in June 1998 (issue No.9 was dated Autumn 1998), Al Wilson had appeared at the Cleethorpes Weekender and David Miller wrote the following in his review of the event. "*I had the good fortune of meeting the man himself after queueing for almost two hours, but it was worth it, he took time out for a chat and to sign a photograph and a copy of S.V. which will be treasured.*" At some point, the issue must have been sold, as it was 2019 when I purchased it, along a few other issues the magazine.

Some six years after its curtain call, shouts for an encore were audible and in 2006, following a request to help raise funds for a charity, *Soul View 2* made an appearance. Following in the footsteps of the original publication, it was more of the same for six issues between February 2006 and May 2009. It retained that tartan edge and in that final, thirty-four-page issue the 'Soul Scotland' page displays a wealth of events across the country from Kilmarnock to Fort William and Dumfries to Aberdeen, along with record and gig reviews, the story behind 'Do I Love You' and more.

To his credit, David Miller never charged for advertising space and that final sixth issue was also given out free to a 'select few'. David repeated the old mantra of being let down by people who promised articles and at one point had decided not to produce the sixth issue. He went on to say that there would only be a limited number printed and each one would be numbered - the one I have is No.8 - whilst adding that despite having been let down, he would continue to

produce *Soul View*.

Sadly, issue seven was never to appear. An editor's lot is not a happy one.

If I were to compile a top ten of the vast array of soul music publications featured within the pages of this book it would be a difficult task, although having said that, I know what numbers one and two would be without giving it too much thought, although I will perhaps leave such matters to the end. However, what I do know is that the next fanzine to make an appearance - SOUL RENAISSANCE - would without a shadow of doubt feature within that listing.

Martyn Bradley's excellent publication did not get off to the best of starts as the front cover of issue No.1 (April 1997) saw 'Renaissance' spelt wrongly! Some might have noticed, but few, if any, would have cared, as here was quality with a capital Q. This was no toilet seat read and if it was, you had a problem. This was a couple of cans or a pot of tea read as it contained a previously unmatched 117 pages, and a price tag of £3. 'For Lovers Of Quality Soul Music' proclaimed the cover sub-title and the publication would certainly turn out to be that, over the course of the next three years.

As co-promoter of the Dudley and the Albrighton soul nights, Martyn had his finger on the pulse, but he was more than aware of the pitfalls in producing a fanzine, writing: "*This magazine is not intended to become a regular fanzine, I don't even know whether issue two will see the light of day, but like all the fanzines it is meant to be interesting and informative.*

144

In parts, it may look a little amateurish as regards layout, but it is all part of the learning process." He continued: *"If we only produce 100 copies of 'Soul Renaissance' it does not matter, for me it will not determine whether or not issue two is produced, money is not the goal. I go to work to earn money."* He added: *"Bringing all the factions of the scene together is one of the goals that I pursue, unity is strength."*

So, what was in that initial tome? Part one of an interesting interview with noted DJ Guy Hennigan, venue reports, record reviews, 'Why So Many Chemist Shops Were Turned Over In The Sixties' - a six page article by Dave Price, and Soul Sam asking 'Where Has All the Vinyl Gone?' were only part of it all.

Issue No.2 did make an appearance, although not until June 1998, as feedback on issue one had been positive and encouraging and no-one would have begrudged the 50p increase in cover price despite this latest issue being only a mere 113 pages – four less than issue one. Two was much of the same plus 'LA Soul Trip '98', four pages covering the DJ play lists from a Yarmouth Weekender, 'Detroit Trip' - twenty-two pages including photos - and an article on Stafford.

It was March 1999 before the ninety-six-page issue number three appeared with a much better font and size, with those improvements continuing right through to the tenth and final issue in March 2007, by which time photo reproductions and label scans were excellent.

Excellent too were the articles that continued to be published – 'The State Of The 60's Newies Scene' (eighteen pages over two issues); 'Obsession With Obscurities'; 'The Current State Of The Scene'; 'Rare Soul Bites Back'; 'R&B For Beginners'; 'Who Would Be A Promoter' and 'eBay Tales' being amongst them. A sub-editorial in issue No.8 – 'Is The Northern Scene Approaching Meltdown?' produced numerous letters, enough to fill seven pages.

If you haven't seen this publication, seek it out. It doesn't appear for sale too often, which is no surprise really, but it is worth the search.

Content for a soul related fanzine was not a problem, as there were countless artists and labels along a countless number of other avenues that could be ventured down in order to make a publication of interest, as well as being different from the norm. What wasn't so easy was finding a name; more so if you wanted to include the word 'soul'; and as a fanzine proved to be a collection of articles and other bits and pieces, then perhaps SOUL NOTES was as good a name as any.

This was the fanzine for those who attended the Penrhyn Old Hall venue in Llandudno, edited by 'Paul and Lynda' and given away free. The first issue that I have is dated May 1997, but there was at least one prior to this as a letter states *"thanks for your letter, tape and fanzine. Soul Notes was brill ..."*

That May issue consisted of twenty-six pages, containing the usual mix of reviews and articles, while a second issue I have from July 1997 contained four pages less. Unfortunately, I have no further info as regards the frequency of this publication except for a note that there were further issues in September and November 1997 and January and March 1998. No matter what, credit must be given where due, for taking the time to produce something of interest on a regular basis and giving it away free.

Another undated first issue is HEART FULL OF SOUL, which was something of a rarity as it came from the north- east of England where, although there was a thriving northern soul scene, publications were certainly not commonplace.

Edited by Allan Coney, who was based in Newton Aycliffe, with contributors such as Dean Anderson, Pete Lowrie and Roger Banks, this twenty-eight-page, A4, side-stapled publication, although perhaps a little spacious in places, was on par with the majority of other similar offerings out there.

'Written by collectors for collectors and people who take their music seriously' was the *Heart Full Of Soul* subtitle and that first issue included articles such as

'What Is Soul?', 'Were venues like Stafford, Mexboro, Shotts and several others in vain?', 'Fifty-one Amazing Facts', 'Soul in Doncaster', 'The current soul scene', 'The Van Dykes', alongside book reviews, a couple of small label listings. 'Bishop Auckland Biggies', 'Collectors Corner'and a soul night review – the Border City Soul Club in Carlisle, giving it the makings of a good read.

As I mentioned, that first issue was undated, but issue two is – Autumn 1997, so let's assume that that inaugural one materialised in the spring or summer of that same year. The second issue, while giving the readers more of the same, consisted of forty pages, but again could have seen costs cut a little as there was a fair amount of empty space.

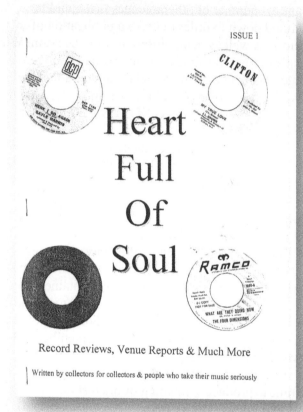

Issue four saw a similar number of pages, but printed only on one side. Well, at least my copy is, and there is no sign of the staples having been removed and it having been copied from an original. What had been recently removed, however, was a driving licence and credit card from a wallet at the Wilton Ballroom and some records from a sales box at a Musselburgh all-nighter, according to a letter in this particular issue. Not things you want to experience on a night out in the usually friendly surroundings at a soul event.

With a fifty pence increase in cover price, issue five saw the magazine having had something of a makeover, hence the increase, and it was certainly worth it as it had now taken on a more professional look. The 'Las Vegas Soul Convention', 'What is

Northern Soul' and a good article on The Marvelettes made up the bulk of the reading, with venue and record reviews and more helping to pad out the thirty-six pages.

The undated issue number six saw *Heart Full Of Soul* end up in hot water as it published an eleven line 'Ode to Kev Roberts' which brought a writ from the subject matter's solicitors. It didn't, however, bring about an end to the magazine as it carried on for another three issuesat least, issue number nine, the last one I have, being published towards the end of 1999.

1997 was quite an exceptional year for soul fanzines, with **NORTHERN ESSENCE** getting in on the act in what must have been around the autumn of that year. Edited by Pete Coulson from Failsworth, Bolton, a look though issue one of the standard A4, side stapled twenty-page publication makes it difficult to guess as to what direction this one would actually go. There were no clues to be found within its pages – a brief feature on The O'Jays with discography, a look at the Chess label, venue reports, three pages of cd reviews, 'Dance Fads' part one and four pages of adverts was what you got for your £3. Perhaps a bit steep for what it was.

Issue two was much better value with thirty-two pages for the same cover price, even though seven of those covered an interview with Tommy Hunt, which in itself was an interesting read. An increase of six pages for number three and *Northern Essence* was now

heading in the right direction. Of this there was no doubt, as issue five hit a massive sixty-four pages and included interviews with Jerry Williams and Brenda Holloway, plus a four-and-a-bit-page biography of Lou Johnson. It was of little surprise that this proved to be the most popular issue, with sales increasing by 50%.

As sales increased, page numbers decreased, with issue six having forty-six and issue seven a mere forty. Issue eight saw them drop again to thirty-four. Was this the beginning of the end?

The reading material remained strong, although it had a particular leaning to venue reports, not a bad thing really as it perhaps encouraged people to give a new venue a try, but there were always plenty of reviews, articles on the likes of Sammy Campbell and The Del-Larks, Millie Jackson, The Masqueraders and an eight-page interview with Barbara Lynn, part of which was carried out by Dave Godin.

That issue eight appeared late in 1999, while an issue nine came out early the following year. I don't think a tenth made an appearance.

Way back in time, *R'NB Scene* was only fractionally more than an advertising outlet for the Twisted Wheel in Manchester, while *Northern Noise* was unashamedly a promotional tool, as if they needed one, for the Wigan Casino. However, along came 'The Official 1998 Northern Soul Review', the first, and only real promotional publication for a company. Entitled **TOGETHERNESS** and edited by former Wigan Casino DJ Kev Roberts, it was unfairly shunned by some due to its close ties with Goldsoul as many were to consider them as simply 'cashing in' on the ever-growing northern soul scene.

So, I put it to Kev, did you launch the magazine as, let's say, an advertising outlet for what was to become Goldsoul? The reply was straight and to the point, *"Yes, but*

there was also the sense that there was going to be something of a revival on the scene and that revival needed a publication to go with it." Around this time, the fanzine culture had perhaps died a little and personally I thought that there was a space ready to be filled; was this also something that Kev had picked up on? *"Yes certainly, that was another reason."*

With the fanzine culture in its final throes and grinding to a halt, it was welcomed by those seeking their soul reading fix, whether or not they attended Goldsoul events.

The first issue was a forty-page affair, with the only colour on the front and back cover, and it could possibly be considered as being awash with adverts for events, CDs, clothing and magazines. But there was still plenty to read – Richard Searling's 'Reflections'; Neil Rushton's 'The Future is Modern'; 'Do I Love You – The Truth'; Chris Conroy exploring 'The Renaissance of Northern Soul'; Tim Brown with his 'Top Twenty Northern Soul Rarities'; Dave McAleer wrote about the Pye Disco Demand label; Terry Jones penned a piece on the London Soul Scene, while there were also contributions from Greg Tormo, Dave Rimmer and Kenny Burrell. Who could really complain about that lot?

It was originally planned to be nothing more than a once-a-year publication, but in his editorial for issue two (March 1999) Kev wrote:
"We have been so outweighed by demand that we will now be publishing on a twice-yearly basis, so make sure you get your copy and exclusive FREE CD with each issue by subscribing today."

That second issue had increased to sixty pages, Dave Godin was n board and the magazine went from strength to strength, and perhaps most notably it showed no bias as there was equal coverage, or near enough, to both the northern and modern scene. The list of contributors surpassed any previous publication as alongside Messrs Roberts, Searling, Godin and the aforementioned names, you could find Ralph Tee, Glyn Thornhill, Soul Sam, Bob Hinsley, Pete Smith, Pete Haigh and Ian Levine with his 'Rarest of the Rare'.

Issue No.8 (Spring 2002) brought another milestone as *Togetherness* became a thrice yearly publication, increasing to sixty-eight pages with issue nine. Two years further down the line it was quarterly and a massive ninety-two pages. But the first of those quarterly issues (No.14) saw the end of *Togetherness* and the reign of Kev Roberts as editor, with the role, whilst not exactly seeing a first, producing something of a rarity with a female steering the ship.

After fourteen issues it changed to *N.Soul*, and although the numbering sequence continued, as did layout etc, I wondered if Kev considered *N.Soul* to be a completely different magazine? "*No, not at all, it was only a very slight diversion.*" But change was to come.

"*I have been charged with the task of broadening the content and scope of the magazine, commissioning informative articles, attracting new contributors and continuing to give fair and accurate exposure to events and promotions under the banner of Northern and Modern soul*" wrote incoming editor Alison Holden, and she certainly came in with a bang as not only did the magazine have a new name, but it had also increased to 140 pages. Her reign, however, was short lived, as four issues on Kev Roberts was back at the helm and remained in charge until the final issue in the winter of 2006 (No.24), by which time it was back down to fifty odd pages, but still an enjoyable read. Perhaps somewhat surprisingly, sales declined and this was the sole reason behind its disappearance. I imagine that time was another consideration, as with the Goldsoul empire increasing,

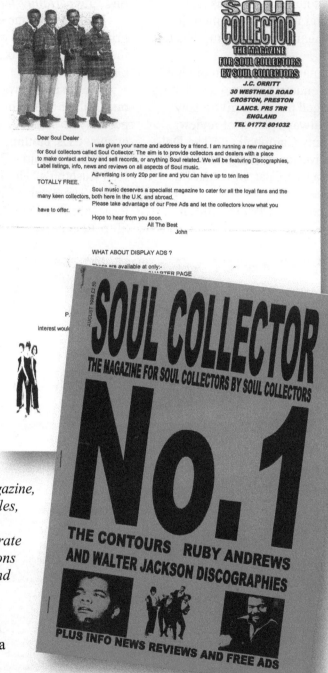

with events across the country on a regular basis, producing a magazine was far from being a priority.

There can, however, be little doubt that *Togetherness/N'Soul* had played a part in reviving the soul scene as a whole, creating events like the Whitby and Blackpool Tower weekenders, amongst others, which continue to thrive today.

'The Magazine For Soul Collectors By Soul Collectors' was the sub heading of SOUL COLLECTOR, which made its initial appearance in August 1998. It was edited by J. C. Orritt, the guy who, a decade earlier, had brought us *Soul File*. His latest offering could be considered a typical desktop production job, and to be quite honest, I find *Soul File* to be a much better all-round publication. *Soul Collector* was the standard A4, side stapled production with that first issue consisting of thirty pages. The main articles centre around The Contours, Ruby Andrews and Walter Jackson, supported by club events and news, cd reviews, a couple of vinyl reviews, record fair diary and small ads. All for a cover price of £2.50.

Two months later, issue two saw an increase of four pages, with the content being much of the same, with 'Wigan Casino – 25 Years On' and 'The Great CD Debate' being the main reading.

There was no issue three as far as I can gather and whether *Soul Collector* could have gone on to challenge the others around at the time we will never know.

A computer certainly made a difference and this had become obvious with the appearance of each new title. One that clearly showed the difference made its debut in the first month of that final year of the nineties, when Tony Horn issued No.1 of SOULIN'. Thirty A4, side stapled pages, priced at £3, this oozed computerisation right from page one, making it easy on the eye and a first- class publication.

As always, a look at the editorial gives you an idea as to what the man at the helm hoped to achieve and what his labour of love was going to provide. Tony wrote: "*What began as something of a fantasy many years ago, long before PCs became as commonplace as sliced bread, has turned into a monster I certainly hadn't envisaged. I'm sure other fanzine Editors will bare* [sic] *me out when I say, that you decide that because you love the music so much, you feel like you'll be giving something back, by writing, to the best of your ability, about the artists, labels, producers and entrepreneurs who have inadvertently given us so much pleasure over the years.*"

He continued:" *You begin with a few ideas about some of your favourite artists or labels. Then you fill out with loads of reviews, and club reports, and topical matter, and it presents a really fresh approach compared to all those other fanzines from where you drew your inspiration. Then you realise you can't do the whole thing alone, so you badger your mates and acquaintances to do some articles. 'Yeah, great idea' they say. Months down the line, you're still waiting for the promised copy. And, since you are not paying them, you don't want to be a pain in the*

arse with persistent phone calls. After all, it's not their baby. And you begin to question everything you have put together so far. You become overwhelmingly self-critical. Almost every article of my own in this first issue has been written several times. And what will the serious Soul heads make of it?" He ended by saying: "*Having finally got this first issue out, I of course wait with baited breadth for response from you the readers.*"

Under the "Soul Heads" microscope went a profile and discography of The Independents, 'Street Corner

Symphonies', 'Club Call', 'The Two-Step Story', profile and discography on The Montclairs, 'Desert Island Books essential soul reading'; 'The Anatomy of a Soul Collector'; 'Detroit Revisited'; DJ Tony Parker's current faves; 'Album Trackin'' and 'Net Some Soul – a guide to soul on the internet'.

It was summer 1999 before issue two appeared with more of the same, but the reality of producing a fanzine/magazine had by then well and truly hit home. "*I had naively assumed that having devised layouts and formats for issue one, I would sail through the preparation of number two*" penned Tony in his second editorial. "*Harsh reality lesson number one!*" he continued. "*Having now learned how very time consuming this hobby is, I will have to be realistic and commit myself to an issue every six months. I'm sure you will all understand, and I'm equally sure that you would rather have a quality magazine twice a year, than a poor one four times?*"
And so it continued twice yearly until issue No.7 – November 2002 and what was the final issue.

That *Soulin'* had to fall by the wayside like so many others was, I consider, unfortunate, as issue six had seen an improvement in the quality of illustrations. Tony had been unhappy with what looked like alright photos on his master copy, turning out much darker when photocopied, so he had gone for digital printing. Also, unlike the majority of publications, *Soulin'* could be regarded as edging more to the modern side of things rather than full-on northern, thus giving the readers something different and away from the norm. First class and up there with the best in my opinion.

If *Soulin'* did have a fault, it was one that befell countless other publications and it was that during the course of time the staples would become rusty, giving them a far from perfect look. I suppose I could remove and replace, but with so many in the collection it would take an absolute age, along with a few different sizes of staples depending on the thickness of each one. It's not a task I would want to take on despite having the time to do so.

With the new millennium edging closer September 1999 saw a new publication evolve in the south of England: **SOUL TRAIN**, edited by Malcolm Collins from Brighton, who, writing in his editorial, was completely unaware that the excellent *In The Basement* also stemmed from that locality – "*As luck would have it that magazine is a glossy and is far more produced, and I am told is generally concerned with modern soul only and does not report on the scene and the music as a whole.*" Ah well, whatever!

The thirty-six page *Soul Train* would have been another excellent addition to the soul in print market place, even though Malcolm appeared to have his sights set on a readership in the south. Despite this, it would certainly have appealed to anyone with an interest in the music as, like most publications of a similar vein, the content was interesting and varied.

'The Southern Soul Scene', The Astors, Jimmy Radcliffe, singles and cd reviews, Port Records, 70s Soul, Modern reviews, Album Tracking, a review of the film *The Strange World of Northern Soul*, a two-page reproduced article on northern soul taken from the *Guardian* newspaper and the editor's view on the current state of the scene formed the majority of the content. The latter was an interesting read, particularly today, as Malcolm felt that, having hated his first few nighters, the northern soul legacy "*can be really hard to live up to until you find your feet socially and musically on the scene, and is sometimes an element which has lost a lot of people who would otherwise have stuck around.*

"*As an example, who the hell would want to go to a 'Northern Soul Convention'? Sounds like those attending are going to a Stationary Conference at the Brighton Centre. No! I for one have always preferred to do my clubbing Friday night style, dancing, drinking, and running about talking nonsense! Couple all this with a generation who have come back after ten or fifteen years and you have a strange cocktail of people all pulling in different directions. Some clinging to the past, some only looking forward, with a loony like Ian Levine at the helm!*"

He added: "*Don't get me wrong, the music should include Northern Soul records and Modern ones alike, but getting rid of those narrow-minded promotors and venues in favour of progressive ones that appeal to all is the only way forward.*"

Certainly, an interesting and thought-provoking piece and something that gave the magazine an added edge.

Sadly, I have no further issues of *Soul Train* so have no idea if Malcolm got any response to his hard-hitting article.

Just to wind up the 1990s, another couple of those 'still to come my way' publications. From late 1992, or so I believe, came *Soul Trade* edited by Karen Joy Langley. Content wise, I have no idea, but I am led to believe that there were at least twenty-five issues published up until 1995.

How many issues of *The Soul Divided* appeared, I have no idea, but it was edited by Paul Davies and I am told that there was one issue in 1999 and another in October 2002.

THE NEW MILLENNIUM

As the new millennium dawned, northern soul was arguably about to enter a new period in its long and eventful history, with the music as popular as ever, and events every weekend of the year spread across the country – over saturation according to some. The devotees never had it so good.

The nineties were arguably to eclipse the sixties as the boom time for soul music. For those who were around, nothing could, or ever will, take away those sixties years: it was a carefree time, an entirely different world altogether. The venues were also different, often verging on depleted and grotty, but for those who had never ventured through its doors before, many were to gaze in awe as they entered the grandeur of the Blackpool Tower Ballroom for the first time, to spin and backdrop on that vast polished floor that had been trodden on by thousands of feet, millions even, to a vast array of music – who would ever have thought it would play host to northern soul? I certainly didn't when I first set foot on it back in the sixties, never for one minute thinking that countless years later I would be back, with the sound of a live showband replaced by those ageless northern tracks, many of which I had first heard at the opposite end of the promenade at the Blackpool Casino. That same feeling must have swept over those who had walked off the Whitworth Street pavement in Manchester in a different era and ventured down those steps into the cellar that was the Twisted Wheel.

Blackpool, for me, is a special place, a town full of memories; or at least the Golden Mile and a few streets running off that promenade on the Lancashire Riviera certainly are. In the late sixties, I used to go camping when a member of the local Boys Club at Peel Corner, a couple of miles or so from the town centre, and on the first night of what was a ten-day holiday, I discovered the Casino, at the entrance to the Pleasure Beach. There was music and there were girls, what more did you need? Little did I know as I climbed those winding stairs, akin to a helter-skelter, what lay ahead.

Never mind the two go-go girls dancing at either side of the stage, it was the tunes that DJ Gary Wilde played that captivated my attention. I was already into soul, but this was something else.

The Casino became a regular haunt over the course of three years, as did visits to the Mecca, and after a lengthy gap of nothing but memories, along came Togetherness at the Tower and the Soul Festival at the Winter Gardens. Blackpool was once again the place to be, creating even more soulful memories. But Blackpool had always enjoyed a soulful reputation and it is from there that we add another publication to the ever-growing list –
IN THE NEIGHBOURHOOD.

Set up in the mid-1980s, the Neighbourhood Soul Club held events in various venues around the town, such as the Wainwright Conservative Club and the Savoy Hotel, and it was at the latter in July 2000 that the Soul Club held their first Northern Soul All-Dayer And Black Music Record Fair. Available at the event and priced at £1 was the *In The Neighbourhood* magazine, a publication of real quality. I believe at their 'normal' events, a newsletter or whatever was given away to the first 100 or so through the door.

For that July 2000 event, the magazine was issue No.5, but unfortunately, I have no idea as to when issue one came out, or indeed if it was of a similar style and content to that fifth issue that I have here. Perhaps issues number one to four were the previously mentioned newsletters. That seems more than likely.

IN THE NEIGHBOURHOOD

Issue No.19   Saturday 27th April 2002

BETTYE LAVETTE

OFFICIAL MATCHDAY PROGRAMME £2

Anyway, as I said, the magazine was quality – A4, all glossy, forty pages and what makes my issue even better is that it contains a separate sheet listing the DJ times, a four-page mini-programme and two tickets. On the cover, it states that it is the 'Official Matchday Programme' and in the centre pages DJs names are set out on a football pitch and listed as 'Rare Soul R&B' v 'Classic Oldies'. Turning the pages, it is indeed like a football programme, with pen pictures and features on all the DJs, and for something that was given away free it was a credit to all involved.

Unfortunately, issues of this publication are few and far between, but a handful have found their way north from Lancashire. Issue number fourteen is more identical in format to issue five, but I have no idea what came in between, as this one covers the Club's second all-dayer in June 2001. Again, I think the 'missing' ones were perhaps nothing more than general 'newsletters 's handed out at the regular events.

Fast forward a year to April 2002 and it is issue number nineteen, with the Neighbourhood Soul Club having taken a step up in the world and commandeered the Winter Gardens to showcase their first live act - Miss Bettye LaVette. The magazine was now priced at £2, but you got a sixty-four-page publication that had not simply features on the DJs, but record reviews.

Issue number twenty-three covered the fourth all- dayer in February 2003, a thirty-six-page issue, but two months down the line, for their Easter Weekender, it was back up to fifty-six pages. This Weekender, like the February one, was not simply confined to the Winter Gardens, but also took in the Savoy Hotel and The Station Hotel. None of the times overlapped.

In all, I believe that issue twenty-three was the last one published, but I could be wrong. In any case, it seems that only the Weekender publications have survived the strength of time.

It is somewhat surprising that given the popularity of the Motown sound and all the unearthed treasures that continue to appear, and indeed are still to be discovered, that there have not been more publications dedicated to the Hitsville studios. Berry Gordy's empire has obviously received countless column inches in the majority of the publications that have come and gone, but only an odd one has concentrated solely on that particular label. One that was designed to glorify the label was MOTOWN CHATBUSTERS, which first appeared at the dawn of the new millennium. Many will be familiar with this

particular title, but from a collecting point of view, how many will have what was titled the 'Inaugural Issue'? This 'tester', with a sub-heading of 'Interviews, reviews and news of Tamla Motown music in the 60's and 70's', contained David Ruffin's last ever interview prior to his untimely death, another with former band-mate Eddie Kendricks, some album reviews (well, CDs really), a listing of four readers' various 'Motown Likes' and 'Motown's Top 50 Dance Tunes' compiled by Richard Searling and Chris King. No prizes for guessing what was No.1 – yes it was that Wilson guy, but I was surprised to see The Temptations 'Come On Back To Me Baby' at No.7 and Stevie Wonder's 'Nothing's Too Good For My

Baby' at No. 11, sitting above the likes of Barbara Randolph's 'I Got A Feeling', which was No.19 and Kim Weston's 'Helpless' at No. 42. The Isley Brothers 'My Love Is Your Love' just sneaks in at No. 47! It is interesting, however, to note what ones you would still expect to hear at an 'oldies' night some twenty years later. Following that tester, issue No.1 came out in August 2000, and given the volume of talent that came out of 2648 West Grand Boulevard Detroit, it is perhaps surprising to find a builder from

Todmorden in Lancashire grace the cover of that initial issue. I mean no offence to my friend 'Ginger' Taylor, DJ supreme (excuse the pun), but not only does a photograph of Ginger grace the cover, he takes over five of the inner pages, recalling his thirty-three-year Motown love-affair.

Early issues of *Motown Chatbusters* were A4, two dozen pages, and printed in black and white, and they were an excellent read, with interviews, like Ginger's lengthy story. Issue two saw one with Edwin Starr take up seven pages, and another with Carlisle Motown collector Pete Lowrie took up five pages in issue four, while the following month, one with Brenda Holloway filled a lengthy sixteen pages.

Over the next four years it appeared on a regular basis, turning glossy but with the only colour appearing on the cover and sometimes in the centre pages. It was, however, forced to change its name to simply *Chatbusters* to avoid a clash with the *Motown Chartbusters* albums.

To be honest, I found the earlier issues better than the latter ones, although the photographic content in these later issues was far superior. All in all, if you are into Motown, then this magazine is a really good read and copies are still considerably easy to find, although one or two of those early issues sold out back in the day.

Content in those early issues contained enough to satisfy the most passionate lover

of the Detroit Sound, with articles and countless photographs, both old and new. It wasn't averse, however, to odd mentions of non-Motown acts and in issue seven, a seven and a half page 'Soul Book Guide', listing countless titles (omitting the majority of autobiographies) and also naming a handful of shops where the more difficult to find titles that might be out of print could perhaps be found.

In issue No.28 (Autumn 2005) there was an announcement saying that the new editor of the magazine, David Parker of Kingsley House Publishing, had taken a positive look at things along with the previous editor, Rik Williams, and sought *"guidance from subscribers and casual readers on the future of the magazine."* They also listed a couple of options – publishing it monthly at an increased cost, or combining it with a publication that the new owners already had – *The Beat*, and again, making it monthly, but covering rock and roll, soul and Motown.

After issue thirty, it did indeed change its name and was to be called *Soul Stars*, something that did not please many. I think it is safe to say that circulation dropped and although I have No.31 from February 2006, I somehow don't think there would have been too many more, if indeed there were any at all.

153

2001 saw well known record dealer Tim Brown dip his toes into the world of soul music publications with his RARE SOUL REVIEW. He was no newcomer to the fanzine and magazine pages as a contributor, a regular on the pages of *Manifesto* and *Soul Up North*, but this was something totally different.

Tim's knowledge of soul music is equalled by his knowledge of the world's zoos (honest) and through a friendship with a lad called Sam Whitbread they produced a magazine entitled *Zoo*. Having seen what Sam could do for this small glossy publication, Tim being also impressed with Japanese soul music publications, decided to dip his toes into the water and produce his own soul related magazine.

"Why another soul fanzine?" he was to ask in his editorial of issue No.1, replying to his own question with: *"Well, a number of circumstances have set me thinking over the past few months. Firstly, it has become increasingly apparent to me that as a leading collector and dealer in rare soul, I tend to overlook the fact that most people have not been exposed to the amount of music that I have. In fact, we could say that the majority of fans are not aware of the almost-infinite amount of good soul that exists. So, we are here to tell you about obscure and not-so-obscure, but over looked soul sides (anything beyond the well-known actually).*

"Secondly, I do feel there is a niche in terms of the style and calibre of reviews. It is not unusual to see a review elsewhere that explains little about the record other than where and how the reviewer bought it. It is also our intention to let the reader know about availability (or otherwise) and price. I am unabashed in my view that if I have a record for sale that is under review, then I will say so, althoughthere is little point in doing this on those rarities that fly out the door."

'Northern, Modern, Funk, Deep and More' was the by-line on the cover of *Rare Soul Review* and the

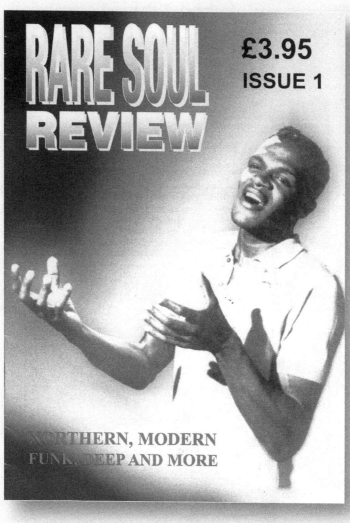

content was what it said on the tin, nothing but record reviews and the odd in-house advert, over the forty, glossy, A4 pages. These pages were broken down into a couple of different categories – 'A Gallimaufry of Soul'; 'A Funk Showdown' - contributed by Adam Leaver; 'Unissued Motown', plus 'CDs'.

Issues two (February 2002) and three (un-dated) were forty-four-page issues bringing much of the same, with issue two featuring 'un-issued northern'; 'recommended recent cd's' and 'crossover to the modern side', while the third issue saw Mark Bicknell and Rod Dearlove come on board, plus a few more cds than usual being reviewed, something that must have annoyed the purists and soul police!

The future looked promising for the publication, but having taken on the bulk of the writing himself, Tim realised that he had taken on a major task and it was *"a writing job too far"* and so *Rare Soul Review* was no more, leaving Tim to concentrate on his business, contributing to *Manifesto* and *Soul Up North* three or four times a year and visiting a few more zoos.

Before moving into 2002, I am going to sneak something in that turned up whilst in the process of writing this book. It is not a fanzine nor a magazine, but a newsletter, and as a newsletter can be considered a publication of sorts, I thought I would give it a couple of paragraphs.

Published, I think, by the 'North Manchester Soul Club', this four-page A4 size newsletter is dated February 2001 and is issue sixteen. The front page is something of an update, but it does mention the *"newly re-activated Twisted Wheel Club"* and that *"the hallowed walls of the original Whitworth Street club, are once again, breathing to the beat of pure 6t's rhythm, Soul, blues, blue-beat and even a taste of Ska."*

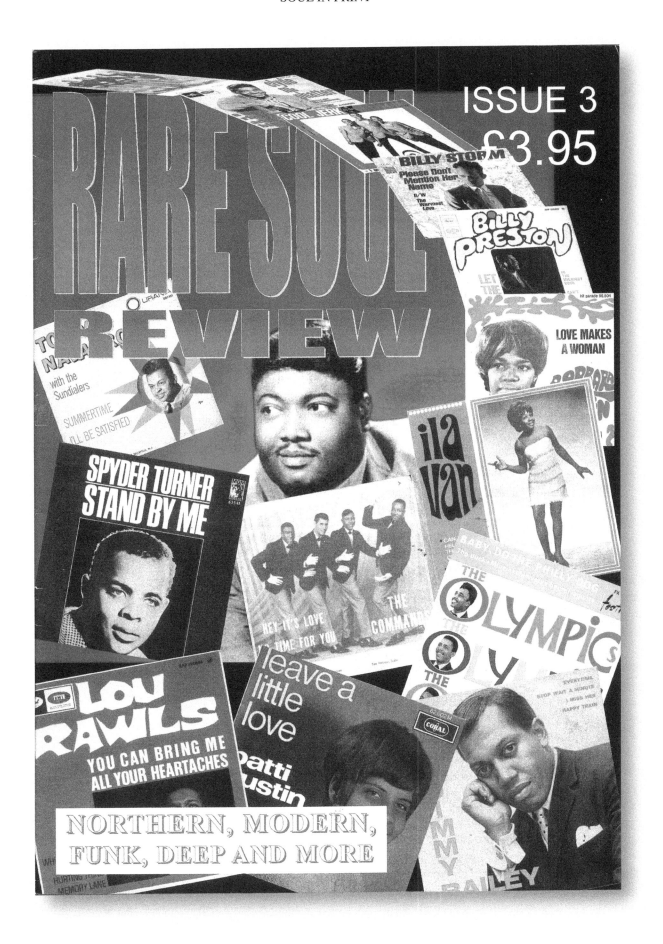

Pages two and three are a review of various events from 'Around the Region', while page four carries a 'What's On' for February and March 2001, and there was certainly plenty – twenty-nine events in total.

Basic, but a nice little read, and I wonder how many of these newsletters are still in existence today?

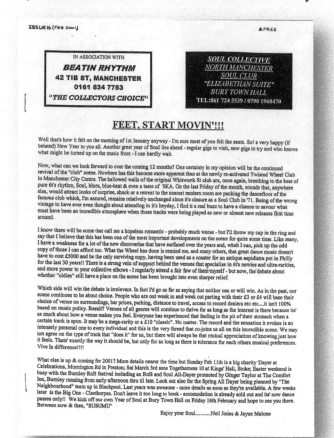

LIFE & SOUL was something of a continuation of *Soul View*, the Edinburgh based publication from David Miller, and it first saw the light of day in June 2002. It was a typical soul fanzine – A4, side-stapled, containing record and venue reviews, current top-tens, intermixed with the odd article.

February 2002 saw a veer away from the norm in the presentation of a northern soul publication. A4 side-stapling was indeed the normal way of things, but SOLD ON SOUL used desktop publishing to the full, plus it came with double punch-holes and inserted into a plastic cover. Perhaps I should say, that is what the copy I have looks like, as I have no idea if every copy was the same, as I imagine that it wouldn't have been cheap to produce this way. There was also, according to the cover, a free tape.

Edited by Steve Eckersley, with 'AKA: The Northern Soul Report' on the cover, it consisted of thirty-two, printed on one side, A4 pages. Content was a mix of the serious and tongue-in-cheek, with interviews with Ritchie Conn and Ali Duff; some label scans; four collectors' Living Room top fives; gig review; some snippets of info and a few photos.

There was to be no second issue, most probably due to costs, and it remains confined to the cupboards, storage boxes or wherever those who collect the printed word keep their treasures.

With the early years of the new millennium being short of soulful reading, the appearance of this thirty-six-page, well produced fanzine was most welcome. Unfortunately, it was to be a year before issue two was to surface - forty-eight pages, and it was never to be seen or heard of again. Like many others, committing the time to the publication was the reason behind its failure to re- appear.

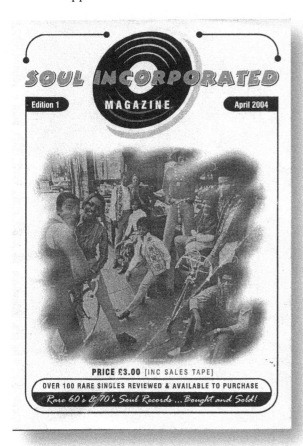

As I have a copy, I am going to throw edition one of **SOUL INCORPORATED** from April 2004 into the mix, even although it cannot really be regarded as a soul fanzine or magazine.

A5 in size, priced at £3, including a sales tape, this twenty-pager by Des Parker was little more than a sales brochure, *"over 100 rare singles reviewed and available to purchase"* being mentioned on the cover.

The records available for sale are reviewed in their different categories and are priced from £10 to £200, with 'Stop Breaking My Heart' on Parrot by Tom Jones – *"absolutely corking Northern Soul"* says the review, being at the cheap end, while Fredrick Hymes – 'Time Aint Gonna Do Me Any Favours' on Fab Vegas – *"an utterly awesome crossover winner"* is at the high end.

There may have been more issues, but even if there were, I would most probably give them a miss, but on the other hand...

THE SOUL SURVIVORS magazine could well be an issue that you have picked up at a major soul event, finding it lying amongst the countless fliers spread out over tables near to the entrance. I have certainly picked up one or two like that, but where I first set eyes on this publication escapes me.

Many who haven't seen a copy could well be surprised that it first materialised way back in July/August 2006 and was the brainchild of Anna Marshall and Fitzroy, with that initial sixteen-page issue considered to be something of a 'test run'. All I can say is that it must have passed with flying colours, as fourteen years later it is still going strong, but obviously much improved. The December 2020 – January 2021 was issue No.89.

Initially, it was decided to be a 'free' publication, published bi-monthly, with little reading matter other than record reviews and adverts and it was at places such as Blackpool and Southport that many would be introduced to this compact A5 size magazine.

Only having an odd copy of *The Soul Survivors,* I thought that in order to get a better picture of what it was all about and how it came into being I would speak to Fitzroy, the man at the helm.

So, *The Soul Survivors*, why did you and Anna start the magazine? *"Anna Marshall was an ardent follower of soul music from her teenage years who became a disciple of a predominantly white audience from Kent and the southeast on the UK jazz, funk and soul circuit. Anna had an idea that she felt would mutually benefit businesses through the social network and synergy of the soul community of fellow music lovers. The idea was to create an A5 printed magazine where those who loved the music, and frequented the various 'soul scene' events, could advertise their profession or business to like-minded soul and jazz funk enthusiasts.*

"Anna had already established locally an A5 mini 'Yellow Pages' business concept publication namely 'The Local Oracle'. Her thinking was that the soul, jazz, funk community and their familiarity with each other, via their mutual love of music, could profit by engaging with each other in business. In contrast, my experience from my teenage years in a multicultural and integrated London circuit, had developed from dancing in the clubs to deejaying, leading to twenty years of documented professional club and radio experience.

"So, when Anna shared her idea with me, my contribution was to bring my varied industry networking connections to the table, as I was active and established in the various London and surrounding counties arenas. This culminated in both Anna and I incorporating a classified section within

the magazine so that deejays and promoters could showcase their events to attract the wider range of club enthusiasts. Anna suggested the name and I came up with the tag line 'The info provider for the soul survivor.'"

Having laid the basic foundations, what were your aims? *"Being candid and honest, we were both editorial virgins within the music publication industry amongst the already well-established and iconic long standing white owned soul magazines. As a joint collaboration of black and white cultures, making a contribution as opposed to being competitive, we saw a gap in the market to create a 'people's' magazine rather than an industry led one.*

"Initially, as previously stated, the 'soulcial' networking of business was a leading factor but as time progressed the music industry side became more prevalent in uniting the jazz, funk and soul community. The magazine was given out free to the various fractions of the soul and jazz funk community and it became apparent that the advertised events,

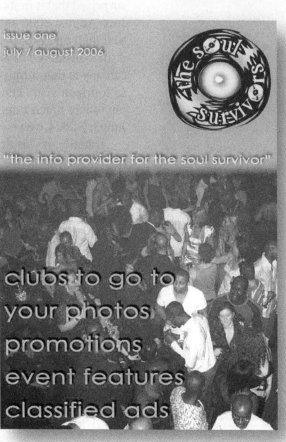

record/event reviews and the interview features were the popular topics for our increasing readership. We travelled to various events distributing the magazine in the London and surrounding counties and much further out to areas beyond the Midlands and the north of the UK, including the bitterly cold Welsh province of Prestatyn. Subsequently between us both we were able to create a respected platform where music was the nucleus and then were able to attract the musicians, artists, deejays, promoters and the club audience to communicate in one central place, The Soul Survivors Magazine. In addition, it was paramount that our aim was to unite the divided racial camps within the scene as well as the north and south of the UK disparity amongst the deejays, promoters and club attendees."

As southern based, I wondered if I was safe in saying that the magazine was geared maybe more towards the London modern scene, or was it aimed at the modern scene in general? *"Due to the initial southern Kent, and in the last five years London based location of the magazine, our southern audience have*

always had an easier access to getting the magazine. Pre the Covid pandemic, we were distributing roughly one thousand copies bi-monthly to various areas around the country including Birmingham, Manchester, Oxfordshire, Liverpool and Scotland. Our distribution via our annual paid subscribers reaches soul music enthusiasts in various European countries and the USA. I don't personally like the moniker of 'modern music' as it derives, from my understanding, as a north of the UK term in differentiating the 'Northern Soul' genre from forever evolving contemporary and progressive forms thereafter of black music. There were, when we started the magazine in 2006, an array of established 'Northern Soul/Modern' magazines in circulation like 'On The Scene' (from memory) so as a publication with little familiarity of that scene at that moment in time, we concentrated on what we knew. After travelling to various weekenders and getting a sense of the 'Northern Soul' phenomenon, we started to incorporate various editorial pieces and attract some advertising from those more experienced in that arena."*

I would, however, imagine that most of your sales down are south? *"We are a free publication but you can get it via the paid yearly subscription or purchasing back issues via our website www.thesoulsurvivorsmagazine.co.uk. I would say that our subscribers are spread around the country and beyond so in terms of sales it is not necessarily sold more in the south, but I would say due to our locality it is distributed there more so."*

Obviously, a number of the featured artists who have appeared within the pages of the magazine have had, let's say, success on the northern soul scene, but have you featured much 'northern' or ever considered featuring a 'northern' type section? *"As you have stated, yes we have over our fourteen-year duration featured artists and icons who have championed the 'Northern Soul' scene. I have personally interviewed deejays Colin Curtis, Richard Searling, Ian Levine, Neil Rushton, Ian Dewhurst, film maker Elaine Constantine, dancer Steve Caesar and the celebrated* and iconic singer Kiki Dee. I will categorically state this, that without question as well as there being a territorial north and south of the UK divide, there is noticeably a huge and on-going racial inequality. Yes, the genre celebrates the black artists and the music as the soundtrack to their lives. However, amongst the deejays, promoters, audiences and events it is hugely white dominated. There is a massive lack of acknowledgement or explanation as to why there is hardly any, if any, black representation.

"Yes, in those regions it's mainly the white working-class youngsters that embraced the music, but when I have spoken with some of the 'Northern Soul' interviewees, they claim that black people were only into reggae as a definitive response to the lack of representation. I refute that ethos as it's obvious that the black and white demographics and the racial tension in the late 1960s to mid- 1970s played a part in how this unfolded, and continued to manifest even when the Northern and progressive modern jazz, funk, soul and disco crossed over which formulated opposing camps. I have written many challenging reviews and articles regarding the 'Northern Soul' scene. This includes disgusting racial comments made by so called die hard 'Northern Soul' and mod/scooter fans calling black people 'animals' and that they should never have been let out of slavery chains, to consigning the adopted 'Northern Soul' black power fist emblem to the bin, because the 'Black Lives Matter' idiots are championing it. I won't apologise as an African Diaspora descendent in challenging such derogatory and bigoted rhetoric.

"As an honest observation from both a racial and territorial, cultural divide point of view, I did critique the much publicised Elaine Constantine 'Northern Soul' film. Initially Elaine Constantine was furious of my depiction and refused to speak with me when it was suggested that she showed a balance to my review. However, after some interaction Elaine invited me round for lunch at her office in Islington and we shared and documented our mutual differences and eventual understanding in an amicable and very friendly

manner, in our Jan/Feb 2015 edition of The Soul Survivors Magazine. We also, in recent years, were approached by Les Csonge and Ann Taylor of Soul Galore, both die-hards from the Blackpool Mecca and Wigan Casino eras in 2017, with an idea of doing a regular 'Northern Soul' feature which subsequently became known as the 'Northern Soul Survivors' article. This ran for the best part of three years to 2020 and it did give us a wider berth in reaching many of the 'Northern/modern' crossover audience. As much as we have tried to embrace many not so familiar branches of the soul tree including 'Northern Soul' we have found that with 'Northern Soul' it already has its audience and its authorities who do not support our publication in abundance despite our efforts to accommodate such a feature."

I have a copy of a 2008 issue that mentions that distribution of the magazine was 10,000. Was this a peak or do you still hit such figures? "I would say that was the peak, but we reduced that down to five thousand up until the pandemic struck. When we were covering the larger events like festivals and weekenders, we printed more magazines to accommodate the increased audiences. We are, due to the pandemic, currently printing a limited two hundred print run mainly for our loyal paid subscribers. Subject to the outcome of the pandemic we will naturally review increasing our print run."

Credit is certainly due to the magazine's longevity and the standard that it maintains, so how has it managed to survive since 2006? Did you ever think it would still be going after so long, and how long do you hope to continue? "Great question. Considering there were some who thought, and stated to my face, that we would only last six months, sometimes I ask myself that same question after running the magazine for almost fifteen years come this July 2021, as a bi-monthly printed and digital magazine. As an answer to that conundrum, I would surmise that the longevity of the magazine is down to the integrity of its content and to our ethos of being the 'info provider for the soul survivor'.

"From a previous survey our record reviews and interview features proved to be very popular. I am passionate about the music and its evolvement before, during and after my life time and its importance universally as an integral line of communication that comes from my African Diaspora lineage, which is open for everyone on the planet regardless of ethnicity or human status. My enthusiasm and encyclopaedic digital memory seem to have served me well in speaking with the many artists featured in the so far eighty- nine issues. As a music fan first, I think that many relate to the questions I've asked the interviewees and answers that they respond with and appreciate the documentation that appears to correct some previously very biased accounts and misinter- pretations of previous statements and opinions of the soul world. When we've interviewed some of the most celebrated and unsung heroes in their own words, you can get a broader vision of the plethora and tapestry that are secreted in the black music arena.

"After nine years, Anna Marshall left the magazine, so as the co-founder, I run with the baton not knowing where the finishing line is. The success of the magazine has been enhanced with the inclusion of 'Roll Call Of Fame' and record review articles, our 'Soul Survivor Awards', co-promoting and being sponsors for various events and having compiled by myself two compilations released on Expansion Records in 2013 and 2016. The brand is established and I have my fingers in a few pies and ideas that will come to fruition in the near future that will expand The Soul Survivors to infinity and beyond, hopefully!"

Having interviewed so many people over the course of the magazine life, is there anything or anyone that you have not included within the pages that you would like, or would have liked to? *"Yes, the well of soul musical libation is deep. Not landing icons like James Brown, Aretha Franklin, Prince and Maurice White of EW&F before they sadly passed. I'd like to feature Stevie Wonder, Quincy Jones and Diana Ross at some point.*

"Thank you, Iain, for asking me to do this, it's quite something recalling the history of something that kind of fell into my lap but that I was clearly ordained to do. Take care. Peace Fitzroy."

If you have not seen a copy of *The Soul Survivors* magazine, check out their website; as I write, the magazine offers a 'membership' service whereby you can receive six issues per year at a price of £40.

It was in the autumn of 2006 and in the Tib Street premises of Beatin' Rhythm, a regular haunt when in Manchester city centre as the other half decided to stroll, I saw the colourful cover of **THERE'S THAT BEAT!**, a Florida based publication produced by Dave Moore and Jason Thornton. As it was encased in a plastic bag, there was no chance of a sneak look through the pages, but for once I did think I could judge the contents by the cover so I bought a copy, and my thoughts were definitely proved correct.

If the cover looked good, then the thirty-eight heavily illustrated pages were something else. I had still to be introduced to the countless fanzines that had appeared over the years, but it was simply going to be a case of the Toussaint McCall track – 'Nothing Takes The Place Of You'. This magazine had it all.

With some magazines, a look at the page is enough, a quick scan over the content and you move on, but with this publication, there was something on every page to catch your eye. Each one was devoured slowly so as to gain full enjoyment from it and learn a bit more about an artist or a label.

"Carnival Records – Solid Soul Sounds From New Jersey'; 'The Story of Revilot Records'; Jackie Wilson and 'Golden World Is Falling Down' made up the bulk of that first issue, with the odd, briefer article tucked in here and there for good measure. Not much content there, I can hear some of you say. But alongside those articles were label scans, album covers, photos and memorabilia, enough to satisfy everyone.

Although in Manchester every other week, or sometimes more frequently, I didn't have the time to venture into the city centre and dash to Tib Street, so when each new issue of *There's That Beat* arrived, I got it posted up to me. No way was I missing out on a copy of this publication and regretting its loss in years to come.

All fanzines and magazines are produced as a labour of love, or at least the majority are; few are seen as a money-making venture. If a pound or two is made along the way, then well and good, but as long as it doesn't make a huge loss, then personal satisfaction is certainly the name of the game. Was this the case with *There's That Beat!*?

"When Jason, who is also a dedicated record collector, and I first met, we clicked right away," recalled Dave Moore. *"We both had an ambition to see our heroes' stories updated and produced with the same production values that their music was. That wasn't easy, as although it was a vanity project, neither of us could afford to lose too much money on it. The magazine never made a profit as the production costs were so high, but that was never the driving force behind what we did. "It was a complete labour of love. Jason Thornton, the graphic designer and my equal partner on both the magazine and the book (The There's That Beat Guide To The Philly Sound) did a fantastic job. We were a great team. In the main, I wrote and he designed the layouts."*

Obviously the layout and overall design of this stand-out publication could not have been achieved back in those early days of fanzine production and modern-day technology certainly helped produce something of such quality, but had Dave ever thought about going into the publishing side of things prior to this, when it was a more laborious job to put a publication together?

"I did a few newsletters back in the seventies when I was running soul clubs in Burnley," he replied, *"but really it was the catalyst of meeting Jason, appreciating*

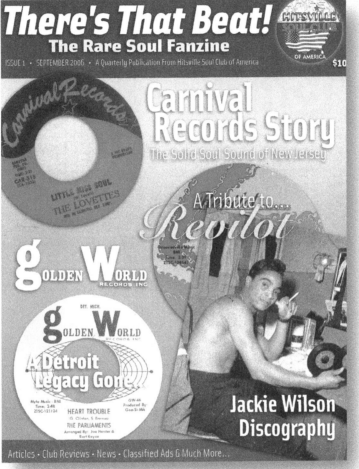

that he was a kindred spirit and seeing the skills he had that lit the touch paper. Without Jason it wouldn't have happened. My graphic skills have improved over the years but he is 'The Man'. To find someone with those skills who also has the same record/music interests and especially the same empathy for the people who created it all was very special."

Issue number two was simply a continuation of one, albeit with fifty-two pages, a previously unheard of fourteen-page increase. And so it continued – 'Impact Records', Van McCoy, 'Pied Piper Productions', 'The Motown Pinks Series', 'UK Issues – Classics and Rarities', 'Harthon Records', 'Motown Collectors Items', 'Mike Terry – Original Funk Brother', 'Loma Records', 'Gordy Grooves', 'Wille Tee Remembered', 'Motown Cardboard Records', Jimmy Radcliffe, the Soul Label, 'Soul Picture Sleeves', Bobby Patterson, 'Australian issued 45s and Eps' and the list goes on. It is little wonder that I have read them all countless times and it is sad that the magazine was to last for only eleven issues. I asked Dave if he was disappointed not to keep the magazine going, and if he was prepared to say why it failed to continue?

"Unfortunately, although we had much more material to utilise, I decided to leave the United States due to the economic tsunami in 2007," he was to say. *"The move completely disrupted my life for a couple of years, whilst Jason also moved from Florida up North just after, and neither of us were in a position to continue to dedicate the time to maintain the standard we wanted, so we made a decision to postpone any future work until we were better positioned. A few years later we decided to accept the task of creating the history of Philadelphia's musical legacy and hence 'The Philly Sound' book was born. A mammoth task that we are both extremely proud of."* [For anyone who has not

bought and read this book, it is a highly recommended read.]

Although it had a relatively short lifespan, the final issue of *There's That Beat!* appearing in June 2009, the number of topics covered and the subject matter as a whole must have created one or two stand-out highlights for both Dave and Jason, so I put this to them.

Dave; "*A few for me were... 1. We brought the three record producers who created the Dyno/Dynamics/Harthon records together for the first time in many years when we did the Hitsville Rare Soul Weekender in Florida. To spend a whole weekend with them was fantastic. When they saw young American fans dancing to their records it got pretty emotional. Weldon A McDougall III, Johnny Stiles and Luther Randolph were long time heroes of mine and became close friends. All three have since passed on and I'm so pleased that their musical lives have been preserved in the magazine and the book.*

"*2. I returned home once from a UK trip and had to drop my suitcase at the door as the phone was ringing. On picking it up a voice said 'Can I please speak to Dave Moore?' I answered 'Speaking' and the caller said. 'Hey Dave, it's Mike Terry here from Detroit, I just wanna say what a great job you and your guys (Eddie Hubbard and Jason) did on the Pied Piper article in your mag.' I was blown away and spent the next hour engrossed in conversation with one of the most humble 'musical geniuses' I ever had the pleasure to meet.*

"*3. I located Matt Lucas 'You Better Go Go' (Karen Records) in Northern Florida whilst researching the productions of Ollie McLaughlin. He invited me up to his place and I duly turned up there. He and his wife were the most genial hosts you could imagine and spending the day with Matt in his music room, eating loose meat sandwiches whilst trawling*

his memorabilia is a cherished memory. Matt was a world class drummer whose hero was Ry Cooder. He'd been married eight times and had recovered from addiction demons. He was a bit of a wild man of rock 'n' roll when younger and his face lit up when he was recounting some of his escapades which involved being run out of town in Arkansas by both the KKK and the local police!
A top man!

"*4. The American Soul era broadly ran concurrently with the Civil Rights timeline and as I discovered the role played by key people in using the music to improve the lives of people, I decided the subject was too ingrained in the story to simply gloss over. Meeting Wynne Alexander, the grand-daughter of WDAS radio station owner Max Leon, proved invaluable in my research and the access she kindly granted me to rare photographs and accurate information meant that the story could be told properly and all the people behind it could be given their due props.*"

From Jason came the following...
"*1. Having complete control over the art direction of 'There's That Beat!' was really enjoyable because it allowed me to break all sorts of graphic design rules and have fun with very conceptual layouts that had a retro feel, echoing the look and feel of the records themselves, using bold colours and fonts. The idea with each issue was to really draw you in so you couldn't put it down. Each article was unique and self-contained in its style, which could be a nightmare for most publications, but it meant total freedom for us. Like true anoraks, Dave and I have always had a philosophy of striving to be completely thorough, so it often led to our pages being overloaded with a multitude of labels, photos and artefacts that we felt needed to be shown.*

"*2. Being able to interview your biggest soul hero is an amazing feeling, so covering the life and career*

of Mike Terry (which was nearly impossible in just one article) was a massive highlight for me. His interview was the first one I ever did and each phone call brought forth new information that really surprised me, like coming to the rescue on the Shades of Blue 'Oh How Happy' session, as well as consulting people like Gamble and Huff on 'Cowboys to Girls' and working with Jesse James on 'The Horse'.

"3. Another memorable moment was spending the afternoon with Little Anthony in his hotel room, having him tell story after story to me, while handling all of his original 45s as we went along. He's like a stand-up comedian who can do great impressions of anyone from Jimmy Reed to Frank Sinatra. We even sang 'Better Use Your Head' as a duet!

"4. Also, since this was a magazine completely controlled by Dave and myself, it meant indulging any soul-related interest we wanted. It gave me tremendous satisfaction to cover The Unifics and Al Johnson's career and present it all in full-colour. I had a vision of the Al Johnson spread in my mind and being able to make it a reality was so satisfying.

"There's That Beat! was a small but mighty operation with a small circulation but those who do remember are still talking about our work eleven years later, so I guess we did something right."

There has never been, or I imagine ever will be, a soul music publication (in my humble opinion anyway) to compare with *There's That Beat!*, but I wondered if Dave's publishing days were over? "*I still research and write,*" he replied, "*but I do it at my own pace now, without the pressure of deadlines. I think I will always write about music and the people who made it but whether those scribblings will see the light of day, who knows?*"

There's That Beat! was a publication that many missed at the time and finding a complete set today can prove difficult.

So, we are now into the 2000s and we are down to only two or three regular publications, but the book is not finished yet, not by a long shot, as I continued to search whilst typing, not simply for those missing issues in order to try and complete a run of certain titles, but for anything I might have missed along the way. There were also one or two other publications which fitted the title 'Soul in Print' tucked away in boxes, so out they came as they also deserved their place within the pages of this book.

The majority of them could be dated and could also have been fitted into the 'sequence', but most of them do not fit the description of a fanzine, or a magazine, but they are, as I mentioned above, 'Soul In Print', as they are about artists and the music, so I decided to add them all together as something of a postscript.

P.S. AND THERE'S MORE...

Firstly, let's look at what could be called 'northern soul programmes'. I don't mean concert programmes, although that is certainly another add-on (one, however, that won't be covered here), but let's instead look at programmes issued to cover Weekenders. I must be honest and say that they are not something that I really bother about, but some I was given, while others I decided to buy as they were signed by a number of the acts who performed. Also, compared to some of the actual fanzines and magazines, they were cheap.

From the Cleethorpes weekenders run by Ady Croasdell come A5 size 'programmes', which as you would expect list the running order for the weekend, with an editorial, a piece on the acts that would be appearing, numerous photos from the previous year and adverts for Kent records who sponsored the events.

Of slightly more interest are the publications produced for the Prestatyn Weekenders and I have a handful dating between 2005 and 2017. These are all, bar one, A4 publications and due to the number of artists appearing contain considerably more than the previously mentioned Cleethorpes ones. Page numbers can range from a dozen to over thirty.

Content is what you would expect it to be. A listing of who was playing/performing where and when, a preview of the various rooms, a few articles and features on the artists who ranged from Lorraine

Chandler, Melvin Davis, Gwen Owens and Bobby Patterson to The Vibrations, The Dynamics, Tavares and The Velvelettes. Nothing overly exciting, but nice to have with the signatures on the relevant pages.

One other that has come my way covers the Bridlington Northern Soul Weekender in 2010. Another A4 job, but this is far better than any of the other two mentioned as within the thirty-two pages there are articles by Dave Moore on Chess records, Rod Allsworth on 'A Blackpool Phenomenon', Malc Burton on 'Soul in Yorkshire', Rob Wicks on 'Dreaming the Dream – the Punters View' and Carl Dixon on 'One Man's Dream or a Poison Chalis [sic]'.

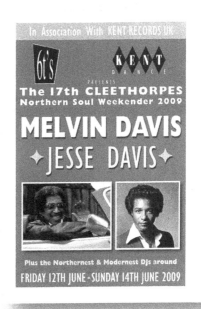

But let's move on.

It wasn't simply the UK that produced fanzines and magazines over the years, with a couple of overseas issues having been featured earlier in the book. The featured duo - *Soul Survivor* and *There's That Beat!*, however, were both readily available here in the UK from various outlets, but there were others, mainly from the United States, but not exclusively, that would find their way to these shores.

Let's first journey to the far east and Japan where we have **SOUND OFF** and **SOUL ON**, both being simply one-offs amongst the other publications that I have.

I have two issues of *Sound Off*; one is Volume 7 from 2003, and the other is Volume 4 from 1993, so it is difficult, no sorry, impossible, to even hazard a guess as to when this one first appeared or how many issues were actually produced. What I can tell you, however, other than I can't read a word of either publication - that's not true really as all the featured records have both artist and track written in English and there are countless label scans - is that if it was a UK publication it would be well received as it consists of more or less 116 pages of record reviews. Only six of those are full-page adverts, with one being for wigs! But I think that is simply a dated

reproduction from an American magazine. It is also impossible to say if Vol. 7 was larger than normal, as Vol. 4 consisted of only 72 pages.

As you can imagine there are a huge number of tracks reviewed and they are all divided into categories – 'Dancing to the Beat', 'Deep Soul 100', 'The Price Is Too Much To Pay', and 'Tom's Honeys' being amongst them. Although not being a record collector, I was quite taken in by the number of labels featured and the scans with more than a few that I had not seen previously. The issue of *Soul On* that I have is, like the previous two issues, slightly smaller than A4 and seems to be more of a review of current releases within its forty-four pages. The issue I have is volume 21 number 5, from May 1992, and is actually issue 232 of this publication. Any adverts are for records. Again, it is impossible to tell when it started, if this issue is its normal format, or how long it existed. It is quite possible that this, and the other publication, are still in existence today.

Both magazines are well produced and had they been in English and UK produced, then I am quite sure that they would have been well received.

From Japan, we go Stateside to New York and from 1975 we have **YESTERDAY'S MEMORIES**. For anyone interested in the early years of R&B music this publication is a must have. The editorial in Volume 1 Number 1 states: *"We are most concerned with having a publication that those serious about the history of R&B and R&R music will turn to.*

"To this end the majority of our articles will be about the vocal groups of the 1940s and 1950s.

THE SOUL MAGAZINE
VOL. 4   1993. 10
¥800

VOL.21   NO.232 MAY   1992

¥600

This will include R&B groups, R&R groups and some pop groups. There will also be general articles about certain types of music, as well as the roots of R&B in Gospel and Blues.

"A unique feature will be a column in each issue written by the men who made the music – the singers themselves. Some columnists you've followed over the years will be with us as well as many new hands at the writing game."

I have no real idea why I purchased a complete set of Volumes 1-3, with four issues in each, but they were an interesting and informative read, covering groups such as The Velours, The Olympics and The Ink Spots and countless others, some of whom had familiar names within their line-ups. Volume 1 No.3 for example features The Gladiators, who were to become The Zodiacs, who of course included Maurice Williams, who told his story within the pages.

The magazines, edited by Marv Goldberg (a New York R&B DJ), were professionally produced, with a page count of between thirty-two and forty-eight, and contained a number of excellent photos, as well as record sales, with the first issue appearing in March 1975. It was to come to an end in December 1977 after twelve issues.

Volume 3 number 4 was the final issue and the editorial announced that the magazine would no longer appear and that cheques covering all outstanding

subscriptions 'were in the post'.

Again, if you like your history, this one is a must, and forget about the mention of the content including "R&R and pop groups".

March 1979 saw the first issue of **THE ROCK 'N' ROLL BULLETIN**, a small 14 x 21.5cm publication, consisting of sixteen pages.

YESTERDAY'S MEMORIES

Vol. 1   No. 1   Issue 1 $1.00

THE FOUR TUNES

MAY 79 no. 3 $1

the ROCK n' ROLL BULLETIN

FOR THE R & R/R & B ENTHUSIAST

FIVE KEYS

Time Barrier Express

Vol 2 No 6   April 1976 $1.00

The 5 Swans
The Heartspinners
Checker Discog & more

By issue three it had increased to double the size and had record reviews and sales within its pages. It was, however, rather basic, but it did, like *Yesterday's Memories*, cover many of these early R&B groups.

Of a similar size, but distinctly better, although rather similar in content, was **TIME BARRIER EXPRESS**, which I think surfaced for the first time around 1973-74, as the first issue I have is Volume 2 number 3 from December 1975. Again, I have no idea how, or even why, I have three copies of this publication. All I can guess is that they came along with the two previously mentioned issues as an eBay job lot.

Remaining Stateside and some thirty-odd years later came another of those publications that I would consider as up there with the best – **A TOUCH OF CLASSIC SOUL**. This was published in New York by Aloiv Publishing and edited by Marc Taylor, the first issue appearing in January 2006, with the beautiful features of Phyllis Hyman adorning the cover. What made it different from the others was that it was published in the style of a newspaper, rather than a magazine, measuring 29 x 38cm and consisting of just under three dozen pages. Inside that first issue were articles on not just Phyllis, but Harold Melvin and the Blue Notes, Chairmen of the Board, Honey Cone and Tammi Terrell.

So, was it the first soul newspaper or what? The only way to find out was to ask the editor. *"Lengthy newspaper format,"* came the reply. *"Each issue was the equivalent of 100 book pages."*

With the format settled, why did Marc decide to produce such a publication and what was he aiming for?

"Writing and publishing a book took too long. I felt it was more efficient to profile the artists in a publication that was generated with greater frequency.

"As for my aims, to provide the lengthiest and most in-depth profile of the artists featured."

Due to the page size, these articles could be pretty impressive, with one issue at hand, Vol.4 No.2, having a nine-page feature on The Four Tops. This was followed with a five-page one on the original Vandellas. Great stuff.

Throughout the ten volumes, up to 2015 – *"the last issue was the summer of 2015. I stopped simply because I just did not want to do it anymore,"* said Marc - it is something like a who's who of soul music, with every article well researched, creating an excellent reference library; and believe it or not, back issues of many are still available.

In America, there doesn't seem to be the same wall-to-wall coverage of soul music that we find in the UK, which is perhaps not surprising as it is on this side of the Atlantic that the music was more appreciated. But it is perhaps somewhat strange that the birthplace of 'soul music' was rather barren when it came to the written word, so I can imagine how grateful many would have been upon the appearance of SOUL, again a newspaper more than a magazine.

The magazine, sorry newspaper, is one I did not have in the collection at the time of writing, so I turned to one of the people behind *Soul*, Regina Jones, to tell the story of the publication that would lay the foundations that others would follow. *"'Soul' began in 1966 less than a year after the 1965 Watts Riots in Los Angeles,"* began Regina. *"The idea to create a publication intended for the Black community about Soul, or at that time R&B Music, came directly from being here and watching parts of Los Angeles burn. Also, having been born and grown up in in Los Angeles, both my husband Ken and I were very aware of how Black people were treated and what the protests were all about. 'Soul' literally rose from the fires of lack and poverty with the intention of showcasing the Black entertainers who uplifted through music and later acting."*

Prior to creating 'Soul', Regina's husband Ken was the first black anchor man in Los Angeles, while she was a radio operator for LAPD. Once the publication got underway, Regina was responsible for the advertising, sales and distribution deadlines. *"I was really all about the nuts and the bolts. My motive was never 'Go have fun.' It was a business. I was never a fan of an artist."* Ken was therefore the creative mastermind.

Mastermind should perhaps read masterminds, as

within those first twelve months *Soul* had spread across the States like wildfire, selling 10,000 copies of its first issue and being available in thirty different cities. "*We published 374 issues from April 1966 until early 1982,*" Regina continued. "*It was a newsprint publication every week for the beginning then becoming every two weeks or bi-weekly until the end. It was a tabloid style printing but with a quarter fold for placement on magazine size stands in lots of liquor stores right next to the cash register.*" Every fanzine/magazine editor's dream of free advertising came their way via the numerous R&B radio stations. A mention of the station on the cover would suffice their needs.

There were other magazines at the time, like *Jet* and *Ebony*, which would feature black artists, but as Regina was to say: "*They would feature Sammy Davies Jnr. and Harry Belafonte, but not James Brown, Little Richard or some of the other up-and-coming talents. Those publications didn't do grassroots entertainment or those at the bottom end of the entertainment scale.*"

In an interview with *The Sentinel*, a Los Angeles based newspaper, Regina recalled the early days of *Soul*: "*We produced 'Soul' for several months in our house at the dining room table before we got an office. Who did we think we were in 1966 with office space on 8271 Melrose Ave? There weren't any other black people with office space there except us.*"

"*Ken's idea to publicise it was to build the buzz before it came out. He had a relationship with KGFJ so it was advertised on the radio before it hit the newsstands saying, 'Look for KJFJ SOUL on newsstands now with James Brown on the cover'. Then I made that deal around the country, within the year, we were national and we had radio stations advertising and promoting us in thirty markets.*"

She continued: "*As a woman it was very hard, there were very few women out there in the position I was in. But we had started this publication so I had to make it work, it was as simple as that. The kids have to be fed, the laundry has to be done and the newspaper had to make it to press by the deadline.*

"*My husband and I made a good team; he was the creative, visionary and I was the implementer. If you have a vision, I'm going to take it to the finish line, no matter what's going on, that's just the way I function. That was part of the work of showing up at 'Soul'; no matter what was going on with the children, or the marriage or the finances, I'm still there to do the work and meet the deadlines.*

"*There were feasts and there were famines.*

"*When we started, every black artist was grateful for us to do a story on them. As the white media started to pick them up and write about them, they became less available; you couldn't reach out to them directly as you*

SOUL IN PRINT

had before. Now they had publicists which didn't previously exist. After these artists became a hit in the black market, they wanted white publicity, they now wanted to be a part of pop and mainstream music." But like those UK publications that came to a sudden end, it was the same Stateside. Regina's mother became ill, her marriage fell apart and the publication began to crumble as around them various economic challenges had to be addressed, with bills and wages needing to be paid.

"I basically said it was time to let it go," said Regina. *"But it did feel like pulling the plug on one of my own children when we printed that last issue. I had emotionally reached a point where I didn't care or know what others thought. I know many were disappointed."*

Speaking with Regina and from reading her interviews, it was obvious that she was very proud of her achievement with *Soul*. *"I'm one of those 'What have you done lately?' highly self-critical folk. So, yes, I am proud of what we did with 'Soul',"* she replied, *"and I am very aware that it has a place in history because of the content but still have not figured out what to do to get the word out to as many people as possible today.*

"I like to tell people that I had three very distinct careers. The first was 'Soul'. The second was Solar Records and becoming a publicist for them before branching out on my own and handling thirteen years of the NAACP Image Awards. Then last and not the least in any way was learning how to raise fund, creative events and all kinds of communications aids for a huge childcare development non-profit agency. What I forget to mention is my greatest achievement, raising five wonderful children who became the adults that they

are today and them bringing me thirteen grandchildren and one great-grandchild. That's my most prized achievement. And they all still love me and talk with me. And of course, I totally love each and every one of them."*

Following the publication of its last issue, publisher Regina Jones donated complete sets to University of California Los Angeles and Indiana University.

SOUL ILLUSTRATED was another American publication and covered not only music, but films and social issues of the period during its lifespan of around 1968 to 1972. It came out four times a year, but was only to see some seventeen issues published.

One other American publication I have is **SOUL SOUNDS**, with one solitary copy from September 1972, which was volume five number eleven.

It is a rather strange size, approximately 18.5 x 27.5cm, and consists of thirty-two pages. Although mainly music related, this particular issue carries articles on drug addiction and women's lib, plus a book and film review.

Music wise, there are features on Smokey Robinson's farewell tour with the Miracles, James Brown, Jimmy Castor, B.B. King, Melba Moore and Sammy Davis Jnr, along with other smaller snippets and photos.

Fan clubs were an integral part of the sixties, with countless groups and singers, and not only the 'big' names, having a 'club' set up by individuals who enjoyed the music of these artists. I suppose, in reality, they were simply early off-shoots of the fanzines in a way, with some of those clubs producing their own newsletters.

We have already mentioned the likes of Sharon Davis and The Four Tops fan club, while there was also The James Brown Admiration Society (which was run by Cliff White) amongst others, and since beginning this book, I have stumbled across a few American fan club publications featuring Motown acts – Smokey Robinson, Florence Ballard, Mary Wilson, The Jackson Five and The Ladies of the Supremes. Ok, the latter were not really a Motown act, but they were part of the Supremes family tree.

From the Autumn/Fall of 1994 came the first issue of the JACKSON FIVE FAN CLUB newsletters. A bit late in the day as they obviously had their first recording back in 1969.

Due to the publication coming out in America, it is difficult to say just how many issues appeared, but I know of a couple of issues, the second coming from the Autumn/Fall of 1995.

This second issue comes in with over forty pages, with a complete discography of their Motown releases, plus discographies of Michael, Jackie and Jermaine's solo releases, The Jackson Five on Steeltown plus discography, collecting the Jackson Five and more.

Perhaps not to everyone's taste, but…

June 1998 saw the appearance of THE FORMER LADIES OF THE SUPREMES NEWSLETTER, which featured the line-up of Scherrie Payne, Lynda Laurence and Freddi Poole. This was the work of David Kramlick from San Francisco and was an A4, side-stapled, photocopied publication containing articles and photos over its thirty-two pages.

If you had a liking for the latest incarnation of The Supremes then I think you would have been satisfied with this 'newsletter' as it was quite informative.

No idea how many issues were to follow.

Forget Diana Ross, when it comes to The Supremes it is always, for me anyway, MARY WILSON who

springs to mind and the lady herself had a fan club, which was run from Lake Zurich, Illinois. There was a newsletter published and as would be expected it contained the usual fan club related info.

Florence Ballard
NEWSLETTER OF THE FLORENCE BALLARD FAN CLUB
P. O. BOX 36A02, LOS ANGELES, CALIFORNIA 90036 (213) 658-5260

Photo, courtesy of Kenny "Clifford" Flores

MARCH 1990

Staying with the Supremes, although venturing back to their Motown heyday, in personnel at least, we have THE NEWSLETTER OF THE FLORENCE BALLARD FAN CLUB. Again, I am not sure how many issues were produced, but I do know that the one I have, dated March 1990, isn't the first, as it mentions on page eleven that the newsletter is "*back on schedule after a seven- month delay*". It also mentions "*that improvements will be seen in the quality of the newsletter*", so neither do I have any idea as to what it looked like in its previous life.

The issue that I have here, produced out of Los Angeles, consists of twelve pages, A4 in size, with news, articles and a few photos.

Smokey Robinson & The Miracles
June 1995   The Official Fan Club Newsletter   Volume 1 No. 4

Member of:
NAFC

The First Annual "Serious Collectors"
Issue - - Miracle Memories

Last but by no means least amongst the 'fan club' publications is the SMOKEY ROBINSON AND THE MIRACLES OFFICIAL FAN CLUB NEWSLETTER.

These came my way along with a couple of *Motown Chatbusters* magazines and were bought out of curiosity more than anything else.

Edited by Rhode Island based Marie Leighton, the two issues that I have - Vol.1 No.4 (June 1995) and Vol.2 No.3 (March 1996) - are printed on slightly smaller than A4 card type paper, with the former consisting of sixteen pages and the latter having twelve. Typical fan club fare - articles, adverts and photos - and compared with the previous two publications it is somewhat bland and uninteresting. Thankfully, they were cheap.

News From Motown Records
Volume 3, Number 3
Editor Nancy Leiviska
Monday, March 25, 1974

Let's stay with Motown and look at something completely different, unusual and totally unknown to me until I was edging towards completion of this book. Ok, like one or two other inclusions in this P.S., they are not fanzines or magazines, but can come under the umbrella of 'newsletters'.

The first of the three newsletters is entitled COMOTION and is the smallest. It was issued direct from the Motown publicity department in Los Angeles, California! These in-house 'news brochures' contain information on the latest scheduled released singles and albums from The Grapeview & Motown!

They also include plenty of biographical information on one or more featured artists, typically shown on front covers, and are an absolute "must-have" collector's item for any serious Motown collector or completist!

The closed newsletter measures 23 x 10cm and opens up into a five-fold item. When opened, they measure approx. 46 x 23.5cm.

Issue No.1 appeared on July 10th 1972 and was distributed to 300 company employees in Detroit and Los Angeles. By the time issue No.2 came along, the

issued out of the Motown Publicity Dept. 6255 Sunset Blvd. Hollywood, California.

Let's remain Stateside for a couple more items worth looking at, starting with BLACK STARS, published by the Johnson Publishing Company out of Chicago, Illinois, who were at one time the largest African-

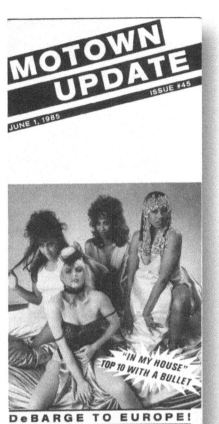

circulation had grown to a 5,000-employee distribution.

There isn't any real regular flow with these newsletters, as Vol.3 No.3 was issued in March 1974, while Vol.3 No.5 appeared in June 1974, but we have Nos. 8 and 9 covering August and September 1974. I unfortunately have no idea as to how many were issued over the course of time, but they were still being sent out in March 1975.

Then there was MOTOWN UPDATE, which was similar to *Comotion*, but contained more in the way of information. The earliest issue I have seen is dated June 1985 and is No.45, while the last I have seen is from April 1986, issue No.54, but once again, how many were actually published remains a mystery.

The third of the trio of newsletters was called WHAT'S GOING ON AT MOTOWN and was a larger 21.5 x 28cm publication when closed. This would open up into three panels and was again

American-owned publishing company in America. They were also responsible for publishing *Ebony* (first issued November 1945, with the last one appearing in July 2016) which did feature African- American artists, but also focused on culture, and *Jet*, a weekly magazine (which later switched to bi- weekly, going digital in July 2014) which first appeared in 2011. Like *Ebony* it featured culture as well as entertainment. *Black Stars*, printed on glossy paper, with colour and black and white photos, was perhaps more musically inclined than the likes of *Jet* and *Ebony*, although you couldn't exactly categorise it as a 'soul magazine'. It was well to the fore in the seventies, with countless articles of interest, but by July 1981 it had ceased publication. The Johnson Publishing Company (formed in 1942) went into liquidation in April 2019, with the photo archive of *Jet* and *Ebony* sold for $30M.

Last from across the pond, unless anything makes an appearance as I bring the book to a close, is SOLID HIT SOULZINE. What a wonderful categorisation for a publication that covers soul music – 'soulzine'. Perfect.

It was produced by Greg Tormo, from New York, and was eight US letter pages in size, folded in half and unstapled. As you can see from the cover, it was given away free and this first issue was dated December 1998.

Content wise, it could be described as a proper soul fanzine, with record reviews, and a feature on the Deep City label, Solid Hit Soul Club, and there's even a venue report on the Blackpool Mecca 30th Anniversary by Kevin Schofield.

How many issues were there? No idea. Another to search for.

From America, it is back across the Atlantic to Finland, and a magazine entitled SOUL EXPRESS. Elsewhere I have sung the praises of David Cole's *In The Basement* and if he was to have a rival in the 'glossy section' of soul publications, then it would be this one.

It was 1989 when *Soul Express* first surfaced, but it was published only in Finnish, with features on Anita Baker, Chapter 8, James Brown and Earth, Wind and Fire. This was its continuing format through to 1993, with the likes of Otis Redding, The Band A.K.A., James Carr and a Philly Special filling the pages. Great if you could speak Finnish, or were simply happy to look at the photographs. Finland, however, is not a country that you would associate with soul music, or even music in general, so I contacted the man at the forefront of *Soul Express*, Ismo Tenkanen, to find out how it had come about. *"When we founded the magazine, we founded also the Soul Society of Finland, where we defined that our aim was to spread the knowledge of soul music in Finland – but also that we want to unite Finnish and international soul fans. The latter became possible when we switched to English. And to fund the society, we declared that we would import soul music records to Finland, to get a greater selection of soul music available in Finland. That's what we have done as well.*

"Many of our contributors were earlier writing to a Finnish fanzine Blues News. However, we got some basic funds to run a real soul magazine in 1989, when we had a weekly soul club (where we played funk, rap and soul, the club was called Black Beat Club) in the very heart of Helsinki, and realised that now we have money to start our own magazine!!! We also got some new contributors when Soul Express started, but it has always been a hobby to everyone."

As Ismo mentioned, the magazine was to switch from Finnish to English and that first English edition in 1993 saw Will Downing and the Whispers as two of the featured artists. But what brought about that change after four years?

"Both for financial reasons – and for the fact that ALL interviews were originally done in English. Why translate them into Finnish when 99% of Finns can fluently read English? Why not write the language our interviewed artist all spoke? I think it was a very simple decision also encouraged heavily by our numerous British soul friends.

174

"We have paid small fees for contributors only for one-two years when we received a subsidiary from Finnish government, aiming to support small fanzines. As soon as we lost it, probably for political reasons (left- wing person as a new cultural minister, maybe she/he hated everything that is American), we started to go international to get more readers and advertisers from abroad – so it was necessary also from a financial point of view, to turn from Finnish to English, to keep the mag alive.

Prior to the switch to English, I wondered if they had many, let's say, European subscribers. *"None, until we switched to English. But we had like thirty music libraries in Finland, which was great, and helped us to spread the knowledge of a soul music magazine nationally. When we switched to English, we started to get readers especially from England. Maybe not as many as we originally wished, but very loyal readers who renewed their subscriptions yearly and kept our mag running."*

I was fortunate to obtain a considerable number of those English editions, and not having seen a copy of this magazine previously, I was somewhat amazed at its excellent content. Its interviews were first class, as were its reviews, and it certainly opened my eyes and ears to a whole host of previously unheard artists, mainly as it could be considered to concentrate more on the modern scene.

There was of course nothing at all wrong with this, but although they included numerous artists who had records that were played on the northern soul scene, I put it to Ismo if they had ever considered a 'northern' section. *"It is not anyone's choice. Our contributors are not suggested to write anything by the editor, they choose themselves, as it is a hobby for anyone. We simply did not have Northern Soul devotees among our*

contributors. Our contributors always choose which CD they review or artist they want to introduce/interview. Northern Soul is not a big thing in Finland. If we received a free sample copy of a Northern Soul CD from a record company, it was surely reviewed, but you could see from the review that maybe it wasn't written by any enthusiast of the genre."

Early issues of *Soul Express* consisted of a couple of dozen pages, but by the time the 2000s were reached it had increased to thirty-two, so there was certainly plenty to read, with some features, such as those on The Spinners and The Dramatics covered in five issues, The Dells in three issues and Al Wilson and The Tymes over two.

It was a far cry from the days of glue and photocopying and due to its high standard, there had to be some difficulties in putting the magazine together, and not simply because of where it materialised from. *"Writing the articles and reviews,"* came Ismo's reply. *"Afterward I am amazed what number of reviews I personally managed to write in our early years for each magazine. Well, I was young and it was my funniest hobby!*

"Layout was fun, everything done by a home computer and by a professional layout software, and the mag LOOKED good compared to many other fanzines, also compared to international fanzines. Also, one of our readers was working at an ad agency and brought our logos at a very professional level. In the 2000s forward when we renewed our Soul Express logo as well."

2006 saw the last of the printed magazines, a double issue dated May 4th – June 6th containing an interview with The Temptations, the OC Smith story and Will Downing album by album. The latter feature was something of a regular one and with reviews of the tracks opened up a number of new sounds.

But *Soul Express* didn't come to an end, as like *In The Basement* it was continued online, and continues to do so as I write, but I can imagine that it would have been sorely missed, not simply in Finland, but elsewhere, so my final question to Ismo was simply why did he stop producing the magazine and concentrate on what is undoubtedly an excellent website? *"The same happened with all soul business – number of quality soul releases was dropping year by year, less CDs to review, less artists to interview due to no new album, less soul artists to visit Finland each year etc.*

"I think we stopped printing at a very good moment, afterwards. I have been running a record shop Soul Town [www.soultown.fi] since 1986, and I even had a street record shop in the centre of Helsinki. You could simply see by our own eyes that the 'soul business' is dying, less clients every week, less new releases every week. It was a good time to switch from street shop and print magazine to Internet/web-shops/eBay /Amazon.

"Thus, everything continued, but even more international and by ten times larger. Who would want less than 1,000 readers for your story/review if you could get 10,000 readers through the Internet? Analytics don't lie – we can see even the top ten countries where our readers are from. And yes, you guessed it right, half of them are from United States."

Not really publication related, but Ismo went on to add: *"My biggest joy in recent years has been when I have been selling my vinyl collection at records fairs in Finland. The younger generation really loves vinyl, and the knowledge they know about soul/funk artists is simply amazing – of course due to YouTube and the Internet.*

"This week [November 2020] I had guy who was younger than my own son visiting my record warehouse (I don't have room for vinyl at my new home!) and he bought gems like Paris: 'I Choose You', Kent Jordan albums (jazz- funk flautist), simply amazing stuff that you couldn't believe someone at that age knows anything about.

"I'm so happy to notice that the word goes on, younger people have found soul and funk and buy soul and funk vinyl all over the various records fairs to get their collection better! All is not lost, even though our generation is getting old with the legendary artists also getting older year by year… The younger generation is also interested in soul music!"

Before drifting back to more familiar shores, I must mention a French produced magazine called **SOUL BAG** which first saw the light of day back in 1968 and must now be around issue 250 or thereabouts.

Like the previously mentioned *Soul Express*, this is a magazine of high quality, A4 in size and professionally produced, plus it also has its own website which can be translated into English if need be.

Although it can appear to be heavily blues linked - early issues had 'Blues and R&B' on the cover - it would appeal to lovers of all areas of soul music. Taking a look through back issues we find names such as Bettye LaVette, Sam Cooke, Otis Redding, Millie Jackson and Denise LaSalle.

With issue 196 (Oct/Nov/Dec 2009) it went full colour, with more pages, and began to appear on the newsstands, continuing to grow from strength to strength. Had it produced copies in English as *Soul Express* had done then there is no telling as to where this magazine could have gone.

It is a highly creditable publication, full of articles, often with accompanying discographies and reviews. All I can say is that it is a pity I cannot read French, or I would be looking at completing a full set of this excellent magazine.

Back in the UK another publication that could be picked up for free at countless venues around the country was **ON THE SCENE**. Again, this began life as a freebie,and I don't have the first issue, but I do have what I think is issue number two and although it is undated and numbered, I think it is from late 2003, as there is an advert for Prestatyn 2004 inside. Although it is A5 in size, it opens out into what is the size of two A4 sheets. Printed in full colour, it is mainly advertisements with snippets of reading here and there.

Published in Blackpool, it was soon to revert to a magazine style publication, while it had the hint of a Scooterist feel about it, as there would often/always be a mod/scooter events listing within the usually eighteen-page A5 publication. There would also be event and record reviews, news, numerous adverts, event listings and the odd article to be found. A couple of years or so down the line it began to carry a price tag of £1, as well as an offer of a yearly subscription.

I have no idea if it is still around as I have not seen a copy for some time.

I was in two minds as to whether or not to include **WHAT'S GOING ON** as it is no more than an advertising publication for Goldsoul; however, as the early issues did contain two or three articles, I decided to give it a mention. Issue one covered November 2011- December 2012 and was sixteen pages, while a year later it had increased to twenty-four pages, but after that it shrunk to A5 size and by issue three it was back to sixteen pages and the only reading was the introduction by Richard Searling and Kev Roberts. It was to disappear altogether after issue seven.

As we near the end of the road, let's drift back to where we came in really, and those black and white, home produced publications. **NORTHERN NEWS**, subtitled 'In and Around Northampton-shire', was a freebie, edited by Len Dopson.

Like many, the date it first saw the light of day and how many issues made an appearance is unknown, but there were at least three, with that particular issue coming out in 1998.

A5 in size, the contents included 'Modern Soul' by Tank, 'Who Needs A Modern Room' by Paul Ambridge, 'Records Under A Tenner' by Carl Fortnum, 'Club Reports' again by Tank and 'Collectors Soul' by Tony Parker. There are also venue reports and adverts to be found within the pages.

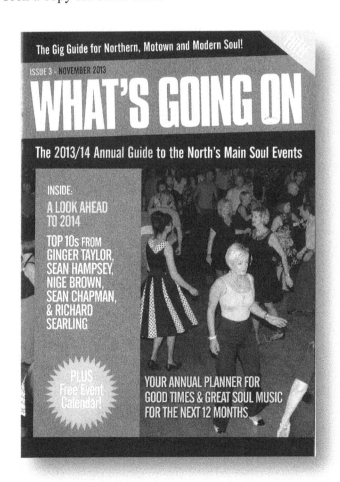

'Volume One – Issue One' was proclaimed on the front page of **THE GRAPEVINE**, which it was, but there was no number two of either volume or number according to the man who put it together – Rod Dearlove. Neither is there a date for this issue to be found, and Rod can't remember, but it comes from some time between April and October 1994 as the content is mainly a look back at the 'Great Yarmouth Soul Essence 3' of April 1994, while there is an advert on the back page for 'Soul Essence 4' at Great Yarmouth in October 1994. All that Rod could say was that it was not available outside of the venue itself.

A4 in size and consisting of eight pages, it looks back at who played what, a question and answer with some of the DJs and a look back at the event in general.

Every collector loves lists, and the soul music lover is certainly no different, be it record sales, a detailed discography of a particular label or whatever. Even those who collect magazines and fanzines can be drawn into the web through publications such as the following.

Firstly, from around the mid-seventies comes Chris Savory's **COLLECTOR'S GUIDE TO RARE BRITISH SOUL RELEASES**. In his introduction, Chris writes: *"Rare and hard to obtain records are always an integral part of record collecting and this booklet attempts to go part of the way to list the ones*

that are collectable on the Soul Music scene. The vast majority of these records belong in the category of 'Northern Soul' but a few others are featured as well. This guide does not list prices as these may fluctuate. It does, however, tend to serve as a basic guide for building up a sizeable and rare British soul collection. Readers may feel that some of the records included here should not be and other more esoteric, and rarer releases have been left out. Suffice to say that no collector's guide is perfect, but I feel this one goes a long way towards it."

I don't really need to say more about this publication as Chris says it all, whilst also mentioning towards the end *"Our own magazine 'Record Sales', the only magazine concerned with the selling of soul-biased material (although it does cater for all music tastes)."* This was A4 in size and priced at 40p.

Along similar lines was a **COMPLETE US & UK ATLANTIC 45's LISTING**. This came out in 1979 and contributors were Wolfgang Weissbrodt, Peter Gibbon, Peter Widdison, Barry McGowan and Brian Finnen, with a cover design by Keith Rylatt. Again, no need to explain more about this publication, as it was simply what it said on the cover.

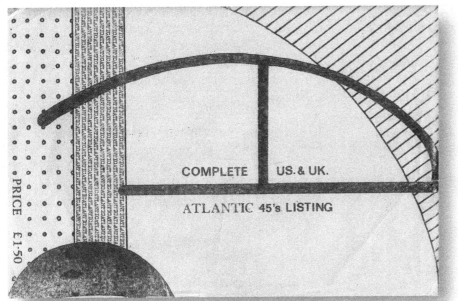

COMPLETE   US. & UK.

ATLANTIC 45's LISTING

PRICE £1·50

A line has to be drawn somewhere, or this book will never reach the publisher on time, so finally we come to the last publication to be featured in this history of soul music magazines and fanzines and, perhaps somewhat fittingly, it is in itself something of a history.

It was issued on April 20th 2001, to celebrate THIRTY YEARS OF NORTHERN SOUL IN TODMORDEN, home of noted soul men Tim Brown and 'Ginger' Taylor, two names that have featured elsewhere within the pages of this book.

This is an interesting little A5 size booklet, consisting of eight pages and printed in black and white on glossy paper, as it recalls all the local venues that played northern soul, along with a mention of some of the tracks that were first spun in the area.

SOUNDS AROUND 2000

From more modern times comes SOUNDS AROUND 2000, produced by 'Martin and Linda' from Clitheroe. As you can see, it has a very plain cover and it was priced at £3.50, which included a collector's tape. This is a publication that I have to hold my hands up and confess to not owning yes, there is the odd one I don't have if you must know, so the following description is not mine, but the owner's, who writes: *"A poor quality publication with a plain cover, with the title on the top left in an awful modern sci fi font. It consists of thirty pages and every page used a different font and different font sizes.*

"One page has colour photos of soul fans without credits, while another has poor black & white photos with names!

"The main contributor seems to be Wayne Hudson, alongside the aforementioned Martin & Linda, while there is a humorous(?) piece from 'Liam Latrine'!!

"Certainly not the best fanzine I've ever seen, but it is aimed at the 'nighter crowd and I don't think there were any further issues but then again, I could be wrong..."

30 Years of Northern Soul In Todmorden.
A commemorative booklet issued at the
Charity Anniversary Evening 20th April 2001, Walsden Cricket Club.

Todmorden is known around the world as an important centre for soul music due to the Goldmine record label. Accolades fall thick and fast on the label and its leading light, Tim Brown. There are in life very few true originators however, and the above label is merely the manifestation and visible pinnacle of a whole youth culture introduced to the Pennine hill town of Todmorden in the late sixties. In **1971** a fiery-headed youth and his affable friend took hold of this culture and gave it a local home. Their names were Raymond 'Ginger' Taylor and Eddie Antemes and the home was the Ukrainian Hall.

Thirty years on it can, quite correctly, be stated that Todmorden is the little town with the big soul reputation, without doubt or argument the most important place of its size within Northern Soul realms.

It is, perhaps, worth taking some time at this juncture to examine the whole Northern Soul phenomenon and it's origins. Certainly these origins were born in far bigger places that 'Tod' (as it is known).

If a place in time could be pinpointed to the birth of Northern Soul then that time could well be **11th September 1965** when the first Twisted Wheel Club in Brazenose St., Manchester closed. All-nighters had run at the club for some two years but were primarily based on genuine R&B such as Bo Diddley, John Lee Hooker and Ray Charles. When the Wheel re-opened at Whitworth Street, it

Written by Tim Brown, with around 200 printed, it was given out at the charity anniversary evening at Walsden Cricket Club.

With Tim's involvement, it wouldn't be anything other than an interesting read.

There are obviously one or two other publications that I might have thrown into the mix, but as they were not on the whole really soul related, I felt that they didn't deserve inclusion earlier.

For example, the *Record Collector* magazine has included lots of soul related features; issue 145 (Sep. 1991) for instance has an eight-page feature on northern soul, while another publication that featured on the high street shelves, *Uncut*, did a soul special in September 2018. There was also *The History of Rock*, which hit the shelves in 1982 and 1984, a weekly publication that covered everything, but had one or two parts that fit into the genre that we enjoy, such as No.17, which covered 'The Roots of Soul', No. 36 – 'Tamla Hits the Top' and No. 47 – 'The Heyday of Soul'; No. 53 featured the likes of The Supremes and The Isley Brothers, while No. 106 – 'Disco Fever' saw the likes of Kool and the Gang, Chic and Donna Summer within the pages.

I had set myself a deadline to get this book finished by the end of February 2021 and as I said a few lines back, a line has to be drawn somewhere.

As I awaited the final two contributions to come in, being reluctant to continually push for the copy to appear, as these guys, like the vast majority of the contributors, were doing it out of the kindness of their hearts as they didn't know me from Adam - or perhaps it was even their love for the music - I contemplated how to bring the curtain down on this journey through time.

That problem was solved as the last day of February drew near, with the arrival of a brand-new soul music fanzine issued only a matter of days previously, bringing the story slap bang up to date. The only unfortunate part was that it did not come from the heartland of northern soul, but from Spain!

KICKS-N-SPINS came to my attention via Howard Earnshaw, editor of the long running *Soul Up North*, who, as deadline day approached, threw one or two other titles into the mix.

Priced at 2€ and consisting of twenty-four black and white pages, the contents were as it said on the cover – Rose Battiste; Joe E. Young; Shena DeMell and Vietnam Goes Soul. Oh, and I suppose I will have to mention that there was also a four-page interview with the esteemed editor of *Soul Up North*. *"A fabulous interview"* was how Howard described it to me, but I will just have to take his word for that. Then again, the editor of *Kicks-N-Spins* must have considered it something, as there was a four page insert with an English translation of the interview!

Not having seen, or even heard about, a Spanish fanzine previously, I was keen to know more, and was fortunate, with the book heading towards the editorial stage, to grab a quick word with *Kicks-N-Spins* editor Jorge Pazos. I asked him for a bit of background behind his publication.

"Since the disappearance of the mythical fanzine Soul Time, a classic on the Spanish scene, at the beginning of 2000, there has not been, until now, a fanzine dedicated to soul. We felt a bit orphaned, so we were almost forced into doing a fanzine about soul music.

The other reason behind it was that in our skinhead club, in addition to having our own official fanzine and also being reggae fans, most of the members are also fans of soul, because this music is part of our culture, so to produce a fanzine about soul was the logical step."

What about circulation numbers and how did he see his fanzine's future? *"It is mainly a fanzine for the members of the club, although there are a few copies for the 'general public', along with promotional issues and exchanges with other fanzines. In the three weeks it has been out, we have sold 116 copies, which isn't bad at all. It is a small fanzine, and I could do one every two months, but everything depends on interviews, collaborators who deliver late etc. It may have a future, part of issue two is done, but it is very much a hobby."*

Had there been many, or indeed any, Spanish soul fanzines in the past? *"There was a good little mod scene in the mid-nineties, but very few soulzines. 'Club42' produced the first, publishing two issues, the first in 1985, the second a year later, and it is very rare. 'PlaySoul' also issued two fanzines. 'Soul Food' issued five very good publications between 1992 and 1994. There were six issues of 'Record Hunter' between 1994 and 1996. 'Backdrop' did three between 2000-2001. My favourite was 'Breakaway', which began as a newsletter, then became a fanzine, and they published thirteen issues between 1994 and 1998. The classic publication, however, was 'Soul Time', published in Barcelona, they did ten issues between 1993 and 2000. One was a 'Detroit Soul Special', the other a 'Euro Issues', the latter being written in English. They were also to publish a couple of issues in 2012. Currently, there is 'Soulville', which first surfaced in 2016."*

With there having been a number of Spanish issues, was Jorge a collector of fanzines himself? *"I have been making and collecting fanzines for thirty years, so let's just say yes. I have a few hundred. Mostly skinzenes, but also a lot of soulzines, which I started buying in mid-1997."*

Jorge was also to mention that there was a good fanzine, *La Pelle Nera*, out of Italy and another, called *Soulful World* (thirteen issues between 2005 and 2001) produced by the Hip City Soul Club in Berlin. More to look for!

So, it has been a long journey from those early sixties days through to the present, but at last, we reach something of an end to the history of soul music magazines and fanzines. It isn't really the end, as there are still one or two publications out there that have still to come my way and so aren't featured here, and more than likely, as the book moves towards publication, one or two previously unknown titles will suddenly appear out of nowhere and find their way into the collection. But they can wait for another day.

Hopefully you have enjoyed turning the pages and looking at the images and I also hope that they have conjured up a few memories along the way.

As I think I said at the start (it was a while back), it is the records that make the soul music scene - without them, there obviously wouldn't be one - but the magazines and fanzines have also played a huge part, documenting the labels, the artists and of course those records. They have also been instrumental in introducing those records and artists to many who, if they hadn't purchased those publications back in the day, would never have known about them.

Thanks for reading.

THE
SOUL IN PRINT
TOP TEN

The majority of publications featured within these pages would often publish readers' Top Tens, DJs' Top Plays or whatever, so why not bring this book to a close with something of the same? So, I spoke with fellow soul publication enthusiast Martin Scragg, who originally got in touch with me after I began writing for *Soul Up North*, but before we look at our joint selection, or get into an argument, I would just like to say that it is perhaps a little unfair to compare those early, cut and paste publications with the desk-top, digital printing publications, so I have created two Top Fives.

Firstly, the 'glossies', or let's say the more professionally produced publications, where Martin and I agreed on three of the five.

For me there was only ever going to be one winner, and that is *There's That Beat*. Quality from the first page to the last; but Martin put that in as fourth in his list. His first, however, was my second - *In The Basement* - one that should really have been available on the High Street. I would probably have put it first, but the scans and layout did it for me, although Martin hit it on the head by saying: *'by far the most perfect of all soul fanzines, superb content of artist choices, news and reviews."*

The third one that we agreed on was *Voices From The Shadows*. I placed it fourth, while Martin had it in third. I felt that it took the fanzines to a different level. *"Does this count as a glossy?"* asked Martin. *"Anyway, not a full-on northern soul publication, but one of the most-quoted sources of all time."*
Of the remaining two, Martin went for *Soul Survivor* as his second choice – *"such a worthy publication,*

and deservedly in a top spot" - and Tim Brown's *Rare Soul Review*, while I opted for *Manifesto* - despite its irregularity of late, it is a first-class publication; and one that I know Martin hasn't seen - *Love Music Review* number nine. It gets fifth place on the back of that one issue. I did have *Soul Survivor* as one of the 'best of the rest', alongside *Soul Express*.

As for the early years publications, our top three were strangely enough identical, although we had them in a different order.

It was difficult to decide on what my first choice would be, but I finally went for *Shades Of Soul*, for its excellent articles on every conceivable subject. A *"statuesque fanzine"* was how Martin described it, but had it in third place behind *Soul Up North* – *"that should go without saying and in any case, Howard would never forgive me. Just brilliant from beginning to end, and still going strong after twenty-eight years"* and *Soulful Kinda Music* –*" one I was sad to see finish".*

I put *Soul Up North* in second place and *Soulful Kinda Music* in third, although I actually made it joint third, as I couldn't decide between it, *Soul Underground* or *Beatin' Rhythm* or *Soul Renaissance*, while Martin threw two others into the mix, with *The Drifter* as his number four - one of the less well-known fanzines, though certainly a goodie, and *Soul Galore* at five – *"the best of all Dave McCadden's five fanzines".*

The best of the rest would be *Whispers Getting' Louder*, *Vintage Soul* and *Collectors' Soul*. But for pure nostalgic value I wouldn't part with *Soul Music Monthly*, *Hitsville*, *R&B Scene* or *Rhythm &Soul USA*.

ACKNOWLEDGEMENTS
IN NO PARTICULAR ORDER

CLIVE RICHARDSON [SHOUT]; ROD DEARLOVE [VOICES FROM THE
SHADOWS/MIDNIGHT EXPRESS]; MIKE RITSON [MANIFESTO]; JOHN E. ABBEY [HOME OF
THE BLUES], DAVE RIMMER [SOULFUL KINDA MUSIC]; DAVE MOORE/JASON THORNTON
[THERE'S THAT BEAT]; HOWARD EARNSHAW [SOUL UP NORTH]; MARTIN SCRAGG
[SOUND OF SOUL]; PAT BRADY [TALK OF THE NORTH]; DAVID COLE [IN THE
BASEMENT]; DAVE HALSALL [BUZZ]; TIM BROWN [RARE SOUL REVIEW]; TONY BERRY
[COLLECTORS SOUL]; STEVE GUARNORI [NORTHERNLINE/BLACKBEAT]; ANDREW LOVE
[LOVE MUSIC REVIEW]; SHARON DAVIS [TCB]; GLYN THORNHILL [OKEH NORTHERN
SOUL]; KEV ROBERTS [TOGETHERNESS/N.SOUL/GOLDSOUL]; MARK BICKNELL [SOUL
UNDERGROUND]; BILL SYKES [SIT DOWN! LISTEN TO THIS!]; TIM ASHEBENDE [TRACKS
TO YOUR MIND]; PETE SMITH [BEATIN 'RHYTHM]; MIKE CRITCHLEY [R&B HEATWAVE];
CHRIS WELLS [ECHOES]; MICK BROWN [SOUL BEAT]; RALPH TEE [GROOVE WEEKLY];
GARY EVANS [THE DRIFTER]; MARC TAYLOR [A TOUCH OF CLASSIC SOUL]; REG
BARTLETTE [MOTOWN INTERNATIONAL COLLECTORS CLUB; VARIOUS MOTOWN
PUBLICATIONS]; FITZROY [THE SOUL SURVIVORS]; REGINA JONES [SOUL]; DAVE
McALEER [FAME/GOLDWAX SURVEY]; JON PHILIBERT [THE ORGANIZATION]; PETER
BURNS [EARSHOT]; PETE HOLLANDER [NORTHERN NIGHTLIFE]; KEITH RYLATT [COME
AND GET THESE MEMORIES]; NORMAN JOPLING [RECORD MIRROR]; TONY CUMMINGS
[SOUL, SOUL MUSIC MONTHLY, SHOUT]; PETE NICKOLS [VINTAGE SOUL]; ISMO
TENKANEN [SOUL EXPRESS]; KEV GRIFFIN [NORTHERN LINE/BLACKBEAT];
DEREK PEARSON [SHADES OF SOUL]; JORGE PAZOS [KICKS-N-SPINS].

THANKS ALSO TO ALL THOSE EDITORS WHO ARE NO LONGER WITH US.
YOUR WORK IS NOT FORGOTTEN.

I WOULD ALSO LIKE TO THANK TEDDIE AND THE STAFF AT NEW HAVEN PUBLISHING
FOR THEIR BELIEF IN THE BOOK AND FOR ALLOWING ME TO ACHIEVE THE AMBITION
OF DOING A MUSIC RELATED BOOK. THANKS ALSO TO MY EDITOR SARAH HEALEY FOR
HER TIME IN WORKING THROUGH THE FINAL DRAFT.

PLUS, AN EXTRA SPECIAL THANKS TO SHARON DAVIS FOR HER FOREWORD AND HER
CONSTANT INSPIRATION.

ABOUT THE AUTHOR

Although the author of more than two dozen books, all football related (mainly on a particular club that he won't name here in case it offends), of which one national journalist wrote: "When it comes to the club's history, it would be fair to describe him as the most prolific author in the business", this is Iain McCartney's first venture into the world of music.

He is a regular contributor to the *Soul Up North* fanzine, whilst also hosting 'Soul Train', a local community radio show. He can also be found DJing locally now and again and was instrumental in bringing the Goldsoul Motown and Soul Weekender to Dumfries where he lives.

Despite having spent all his life in south-west Scotland he did manage to attend the Manchester Twisted Wheel and Blackpool Mecca, but was to miss out on a few years on the scene due to travelling around the country watching football.

But slowly he got back into the music and a couple of magazines made him look out other, older issues, being keen to read up on what he had missed. The pile became bigger, so much so that it fuelled the contributions to *Soul Up North* and kick- started the idea for this book.

Lightning Source UK Ltd.
Milton Keynes UK
UKHW052156070621
385106UK00005B/81